D1470663

ZITA
THE LAST EMPRESS
OF
AUSTRIA

ZITA
THE LAST EMPRESS
OF
AUSTRIA

The story of Her Imperial and Royal Majesty
Zita of Habsburg-Lorraine
and her sojourn in Québec City, 1940-1950

by Leo J. Hammerschmid

CONTENTS

This book is dedicated to
the memory of Her Imperial and Royal Majesty,
Zita von Habsburg-Lorraine,
Empress of Austria,
Queen of Hungary,
Duchess of Bourbon-Parma,
Christian, Roman Catholic, Servant of God,
whose soul left this Earth
on March 14, 1989

ACKNOWLEDGMENT

I am deeply indebted to His Imperial Highness, the Archduke Rudolf of Austria, for his generous assistance in providing me with here to fore unpublished information concerning the Imperial family's sojourn in Canada, to Madame Zoe De Koninck for her invaluable help in opening doors to the Imperial family and for the loan of valuable documentation from her personal files, and to my sister-in-law, Miss Pauline Verville, whose tireless efforts in finding and tracking down former contacts of the Imperial family in Québec City, made the writing of this book possible.

I am also indebted to the religious community in Québec City, particularly to the Sisters of the Collège Jésus-Marie in Sillery, and to the Community of Sisters of Sainte Jeanne d'Arc, for assisting me in my research.

And last but not least, I am indebted to the many people, too numerous to mention, who I have interviewed and who opened their hearts to the memory of the Empress and gave me their impressions and remembrances of Her Majesty who lived among them almost a half century ago.

Leo J. Hammerschmid

"The path of man's civility leads from humanity, to nationality, to bestiality."

Franz Grillparzer
Vienna, 1848

INTRODUCTION

It is not easy for a son to present objectively and impartially his mother. Personal feelings are too strong, particularly towards a Lady belonging to history, who played a major role during the First World War. Nevertheless I will try to convey an objective picture of the Empress, which obviously will be incomplete.

It is known that she had great strength of character. She was always very strict and demanding both toward herself and her children. Thinking back to my childhood I can never remember her taking a holiday or even a day off without us. She had all her meals with us provided we were over the age 5, and during such meals she always encouraged an interesting and educational conversation. She had a particular talent for telling stories or describing events, and was remarkably intelligent and quick-witted in discussion, which she never avoided, whatever the subject. A former Austrian diplomat friend of the family once told me: "In an argument with the Empress one could never defend one's position, but one was limited during the retreat to a difficult rear-guarded action." She had an excellent memory and a solid knowledge about most subjects, particularly her special interests: religion, history and political events. She read a great deal, mostly on these subjects; fast, but still memorizing the interesting and important points.

My Mother was always available to us. Even later on, when we were grown up and had children of our own, she would drop everything if she felt we needed her and come to us for as long as necessary. She hated flying, was never able to drive a car and so always came by train. At the age of 48, I had a bad car accident in Belgium and was unconscious for five hours. When I woke up in the hospital she sat next to my bed, although she had been in the center of France at the time. She was also always willing to look after our children, if both parents had to be away. I must say we felt keenly that she was less severe with her grandchildren than with us.

Until her death at 96, she often discussed with us or our children events of the past with remarkable lucidity, informing us of events that she had never mentioned before. During a recent visit in Zizers, Switzerland, where she lived, we had a long discussion over Archduke Franz Ferdinand and his wife Sophie. They were murdered in Sarajevo, as will be remembered, starting World War One. "He was a difficult man" she told me, and "feared by many", but he liked both my parents and invited them often for dinners and shoots, although they were much younger than he was. At one of their last meetings he told them that he knew he would be assassinated.

What I particularly admired about my Mother was her unflinching courage throughout life, which was based on a deep-rooted faith in Divine Providence.

Only after her death did we fully realize, from the thousands of letters we received from everywhere, how much she was known, respected and admired. Although she seemed like a medieval hermit, living mostly within herself, she had an extensive influence on the outside world.

I was able to assist memorable and stirring Requiem Masses celebrated for her in Switzerland, Belgium, Germany, France and, of course, in Austria. Everywhere all the seats were filled and large crowds where standing inside and outside the churchs. In Vienna, tens of thousands of people, mostly young, lined up for hours to enter the church and to pay their last respects to the Empress. It was for us, but also for our children and our grandchildren, a very impressive and deeply moving experience.

The Empress loved Québec: the unending forest, the majestic St. Lawrence, the peaceful countryside, the numerous churches and convents, the old city of Québec, the immaculate white snow and the deep blue sky. But most of all, she loved "les Québecois", who received our family so well, with a "vieille France" courtesy, hospitality, and last but not least, an excellent sense of humor. There was everywhere in Québec a reflection of European culture and history, a deep religious feeling and a love for the family, indeed for the very large one at that time. Knowing the Empress' background, it was no wonder that she felt happy and quite at home in Québec.

My family and myself are most grateful to Engineer Leo Hammerschmid, for having written a remarkable book on the years my Mother spent in Québec and for augmenting it with an interesting summary of Austria's history and the life and death of the Empress, my Mother.

Brussels, 1989

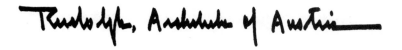

FOREWORD

It is a well known fact that Queen Juliana of the Netherlands found refuge in Canada and lived the war years in Ottawa. It is not so well known, however, that Her Imperial Majesty, Zita of Habsburg-Lorraine, Empress of Austria and Queen of Hungary, also found refuge in Canada and lived in Québec City from 1940 to 1950.

Although there have been a number of books published on the life of the Empress Zita, none of these have dealt with the Empress Zita's Québec sojourn in other than a very cursory way. Furthermore, the few articles that were published in Québec newspapers and journals over the years on this subject, were by their brevity, never intended to treat the life of Austria's Imperial family in Québec as anything more than a sentimental souvenir. It is the purpose of this book therefore, to tell the story of the Empress Zita's ten years in Québec in some detail, since her life here is relatively unknown in Canada, and to a somewhat lesser degree, in Québec.

Although the head of the House of Luxemburg, the Grand Duchess Charlotte, her husband, the Prince Felix of Bourbon-Parma and their six children, also lived for a time in Québec during the war years, their story is not included in this book, other than where it touched the life of the Imperial family.

During interviews with persons involved with the Empress in those years long ago, it became evident to the author that there had been much admiration, affection and reverence for Her Imperial Majesty in Québec. The treatment of the story tries to capture some of the feeling that existed then, and that still can be found in the hearts and minds of many Québecers even to this day.

The spark behind this feeling and the force that still keeps it alive in the hearts of many Québecers today, is the communality of religious culture and language between the people of Québec and the House of Habsburg-Lorraine. The Québecers of the 1940's could identify with this last Catholic Empress of the last Roman Catholic empire in Europe. And because she was a Bourbon, in addition to being an Austrian, the Empress Zita shared a common heritage with the descendents of the sons and daughters of France who had settled in this part of Canada in the 16th and 17th centuries.

This book, which hopefully addresses the historical appetite and curiosity of many Canadians and North Americans, should be of particular interest to the French speaking people of Québec. It should also be attractive to the hundreds of thousands of immigrants who came to America from the lands of the old Danubian monarchy of the Habsburgs, and to the many people her life touched during her sojourn on this continent.

Cognizant of the fact that many North American readers of this book may not be aware of the history of the Habsburg dynasty, the book devotes a portion of its pages to bringing the reader's knowledge "up to speed." To achieve this, the author had to rely on existing works on the history of Austria and the Habsburgs. He obtained such information particularly from the works of the authors Erich Feigl, Tamara Griesser-Pecar, Edward Krankshaw, Richard Reifenscheid, Heinz Rieder and Irmgard Schiel. Appropriate sources for the information used are identified where applicable. It is hoped that, in this way, the reader may obtain a better understanding and appreciation of the greatness and tradition of this devoutly Catholic family whose ancestors ruled "over an empire over which the sun never set." And in order to keep the story interesting and human, the author has taken the liberty to digress from the strictly straight and narrow historical facts, by introducing into the story appropriate anecdotes, spin-offs and developments of human interest, whenever relevant.

One of these developments was the death of Crown Prince Rudolf on January 30, 1889. Because this tragedy brought about the eventual succession of the Empress Zita and her husband to the throne of

Austria-Hungary in 1916, and because this tragedy has so stirred human interest and emotion, it is reviewed briefly in this book.

Many versions of the tragedy at Mayerling have been told over the past 100 years. These have included death through natural causes, death by suicide, duel, murder and political assassination; by poison, saber, revolver and inflicted concussion; and for at least a dozen different motives.

After many years of silence, the Empress recently disclosed her version of what acually happened on that January night in 1889. Her story first appeared in a Viennese newspaper (the Neue Kronen Zeitung) in March 1983 after she had given an interview to a journalist by the name of Dieter Kindermann. Her story also appeared in the book "Kaiser Karl", published in 1984 and written by the well-known Austrian journalist Erich Feigl after he had interviewed the Empress. Both these publications document the view that the death of Crown Prince Rudolf was a political assassination and not a suicide, as was popularly believed. This view of the Crown Prince's death was also the view of the Emperor Charles before he died in exile in 1922, and is the view supported by the Archduke Rudolf of Austria who, as a student, lived with his mother, the Empress Zita, in Québec.

The author is cognizant of the fact that many current historians still believe, in view of certain "evidences" and "sources", that the death at Mayerling was a suicide. However, because this book is all about the Empress Zita, the author has chosen to tell the Mayerling story as seen through her eyes and as revealed in the publications mentioned above.

The reader may note certain inconsistencies in my use of language for names and titles. This is because I have chosen to use names and titles in the original language, where appropriate, and also translations where such names and titles are more familiar in the language of North America. I therefore speak of "Emperor Franz Josef" vs "Kaiser Willhelm" and "Archduke Charles Louis" (the son of the Empress Zita) vs "Archduke Karl Ludwig" (the brother of the Emperor Franz Josef).

And last but not least, the author regrets deeply any omission of characters, names, or references which may have been omitted from the story. Furthermore, some of the information given in this book may contradict references to facts, dates or events in other treatises on the life of the Empress Zita and her family. Where such differences exist, the facts, dates or events described herein are the most accurate, according to the information made available to the author.

Leo J. Hammerschmid
Professional Engineer, retired
Montreal, 1989

PROLOGUE

CHAPTER 1

A PORTRAIT OF THE EMPRESS

Having been named after Saint Zita who lived in the thirteenth century in Lucca, in what is now northern Italy, and whose remains still rest there in the church of San Frediano, Zita of Bourbon-Parma was destined to become not only pious and devout, but also majestic and worldly. She was the seventeenth child of the last Duke of Parma and the fifth child of his second wife, Maria Antonia of Braganza, who was the daughter of King Miguel I and Queen Adelhaid of Portugal. Zita of Bourbon-Parma's upbringing gave her not only a deep conviction of the Catholic faith, but also a great love for all human kind. Her life can be reflected in terms of the three Christian virtues — Faith, Hope and Charity. These virtues were to become the blueprint for her life, and are exemplified in all her deeds and activities. They have led her to become, without doubt, one of the greatest first ladies of all times, rivalling only the Empress Maria-Theresia of Austria who, as the mother of Europe, had lived some 200 years earlier.

The Empress Zita's faith gave her the strength to endure the cross she courageously bore throughout her life. It was a faith not only based on a strong conviction in religious philosophy, and a belief, trust and loyalty to God, but also a faith based on human love which demanded allegiance to her husband, which guided her duty as a mother, and which instilled in her heart her deep love for her country, Austria-Hungary. She was guided first and foremost by her devotion to duty and her deep concerns for the welfare of all her peoples. She was a woman of peace and tranquility, and yet she was destined to suffer two world wars, severe upheavals in the social order of things, and great personal misfortunes including the early loss of her husband, the tragic loss of her country, and the cruel loss of most of her worldly possessions. Had she not possessed great faith, she might have succumbed long ago, and the lives of literally thousands upon thousands of peoples her life has touched in her 97 years on this Earth, would have been poorer for it.

Her faith gave her the strength for survival that she needed to bring up and guide her eight children after the premature death of their father, Emperor Charles I of Austria. The fact that each of her eight children succeeded not only in his/her spiritual, but also temporal life, can be attributed to the love, perseverance, guidance and faith of their mother. Each and every one of her children reflects her piety and strong Christian beliefs, and each and every one of them has demonstrated the perseverance needed to succeed in life, in times other than the social prominence to which they were born. Their will of purpose, their drive for recognition, their devotion to spiritual values, and their complete confidence in God's providence, all stem from Faith, that first of all Christian virtues implanted in their spiritual genes by their mother, the Empress Zita of Austria.

The second Christian virtue — Hope — equally directed the life of this most imperial of women. Her trust in God and in the basic goodness of man was unshakeable. Even the horrors of the first world war, to which she was a witness, did not weaken her spirit nor her faith in God. If anything, it resolved her not only to pray for peace, but to actively work for its achievement.

When her husband became Emperor of Austria in November of 1916 upon the death of the 86 year old Emperor Franz Josef I, she immediately undertook, together with her husband, steps towards the reinstitution of peace. Their aim was two-fold: first, to end the pain, the fighting and the suffering of their peoples; and second, to restore the thousand year old Danubian Monarchy to its former glory. In short, Zita strove to end the war that she and her husband had inherited, and to uphold the God-given, as she believed, Christian Empire on the Danube. She had immense hope in the goodness and desire of all people involved in this unholy conflict, to end hostilities. But, alas, it was not to be. A formal attempt to end hostilities which she and her husband made on December 16th of that same year, the first of many, fell on deaf ears. Peace with a return to the old order of things was neither acceptable to the German High Command, nor in tune with the war aims of the Entente powers.

However, their hopes for peace prevailed. While the young Emperor (he was then 29 and the Empress 24), explored and planned new initiatives, his wife prayed, hoped and believed in "Gott Erhalte", the belief that God was on their side and hoped that He would support them. After all, together, they had made plans for peace even before they became Emperor and Empress. As far back as 1911, when they were not even in line for the throne, they jointly discussed and developed plans for the sustenance and good of the empire. The Emperor Charles had many ideas which he tried out on his wife. The Empress Zita would criticize, support and help develop his plans until they appeared complete and viable. Since many of their plans were thought out and developed long before they would replace Crown Prince Franz Ferdinand as Austria-Hungary's heir to the throne, the Imperial couple were well prepared to assume the responsibilities that became theirs in November 1916. These plans included not only tactical deeds such as the replacement of stodgy advisers and persons of long-standing influence at court, but strategic plans to change the monarchy from a two-legged power structure consisting of Austria and Hungary, to a multi-legged federation with politically independent parts, all under the Habsburg crown — a sort of Austrian commonwealth. Those in the old Emperor's court, who expected things to go along as they were, were quickly awakened to find new vigor driving the wheels of the empire. This new vigor provided hope, not only for peace, but also for the solution to many internal problems that had in the past proven difficult to eradicate. At any rate, the couple's new programs came too late, and did little to improve things. Nevertheless, the Empress still hoped for and undertook other initiatives to gain peace. One of these was the famous "Sixtus Affair", where the Empress and the President of France, a Mr. Raymond Poincaré, prevailed upon the two brothers of the Empress, the Princes Sixtus and Xavier of Bourbon-Parma who were fighting with the Belgium army on the side of the Entente powers, to act as intermediaries in attempts to win a separate peace between Austria-Hungary and the Entente. Unfortunately, a change in government in France gave power to one Alexander Ribot, who together with Prime Minister Lloyd George of Britain, vetoed any attempts to make such a peace. However, even this did not dash Zita's hopes. She continued until the end of the war to strive for peace — a peace at almost any cost, so long as it ended the suffering of her peoples and would conserve the empire.

As the course of history has shown, the Central Powers lost the war, and the Austrian-Hungarian empire was dismembered by the Treaty of St. Germain-en-Laye. Nevertheless, and even when confined to exile in Switzerland, the Emperor Charles and the Empress Zita never gave up their hope and continued their struggle for a restoration of their monarchy — if not in Austria, then at least in Hungary.

Although Austria was declared a Republic in 1918, Hungary had remained a Constitutional Monarchy, and Charles of Habsburg-Lorraine and Zita of Bourbon-Parma had, after all, been crowned King and Queen of Hungary in Budapest on December 30, 1916. These facts nurtured their hopes and drove the Imperial couple to make two attempts at regaining power in Hungary from its regent, Admiral Nikolaus Horty. Unfortunately for them, these two attempts failed and their place of exile was subsequently changed by the Entente Powers to Madeira. When the Emperor later died there in 1922, the future of the Imperial family was totally dependent on the hope and determination that existed within the Empress Zita. Fortunately, she was endowed with an abundance of this virtue, and it carried her through, from Madeira, through Spain and France, to Belgium, and from there, during the Second World War, to America and Québec City.

The Empress' hopes for her family were continually nurtured by her complete trust and loyalty to God. Thus, her love for her family and devotion to duty and responsibility allowed her, with the help of her many admirers and spiritual advisers, to sustain herself, and to succeed, not only in surviving in the face of unparalleled adversity, but also to educate and bring up her eight children in a manner not often achieved by others under much more favourable circumstances. This driving force sustained the hope which accompanied the

Empress throughout her entire life, and which finally found its culmination in her children — all of whom achieved successful careers, have the respect of their peers throughout the world, and have become themselves models of Christian virtues in a world where such values are no longer common.

The third Christian virtue — Charity — perhaps personifies the Empress Zita the most. As a very small child, and in days long before medicare and social services as we know them today, she was taught by her father that giving aid to the poor and helping the unfortunate was not only a Christian virtue, but a Christian duty.

In those days, back at the Palace Schwarzau, the Duke of Parma made it a policy that 10% of one's income should be devoted to the poor and underprivileged. The children put this lesson into practice by saving 10% of their allowances and using this money to help the poor of Schwarzau and also of Pianore. They combined their individual 10% contributions so as to have sufficient money to buy materials from which they then made clothing for the needy. Each year, the Parma clan would go to a textile factory in nearby Neunkirchen and there buy, at very reduced prices, all the remnants they could afford. These would then be turned into clothing for the poor children of their villages. In addition, they had to learn to sew, mend and darn, not only their own clothes, but also those of the sick and aged. They also each had to assume a sort of patronage over some poorer or otherwise unfortunate child in the village and help that child in whatever material way they could. In addition, the children used their own funds to provide new clothing every Christmas for 12 boys and 12 girls.(9)

These acts of charity were intended to instill in each child, a sense of Christian duty. In the young Zita, the lessons learnt were imbedded deeply, and she was to draw on them again and again to help her fellow countrymen. Many years later, as an exile in Québec, she would again put these lessons into practice by organizing and sending CARE packages to her needy and unfortunate countrymen still living in the lands of her old Danubian monarchy. She had remembered from personal experiences after the First World War, the extent of suffering and deprivation that existed following the end of hostilities. Her

9/ p. 21-22

later charitable works in Canada and in the United States were to her not only necessary acts of charity, but also her Christian duty.

The Empress Zita was also to be a recipient of the charity of others. After the fall of the monarchy in November 1918, and their expulsion and dispossession by Austria's First Republic in April 1919, the family found itself almost penniless. The Emperor Charles was one of the few monarchs in history who did not stash away a fortune in some foreign land. Hence, when his empire crumbled, he had no money to fall back on which could be used to support his family. When he was exiled he was totally dependent on the Entente Powers and on the charity of friends for support and sustenance. Even after the death of the Emperor on April 1, 1922 in Madeira, the Empress had to depend on the charity of others until many years later, when her sons and daughters were able to finally earn money on their own.

The foundation supporting her Christian virtues was a deeply rooted Christian faith directed at deeds. Her religiousness was not a superficial one. It was not just a matter of going to church and performing churchly customs. It was a real, profound, almost un- believable faith in the goodness of man and in the overwhelming power of God. Unbelievable, because her deeds have gone so far beyond human expectations, and have achieved such remarkable results that no matter what personal misfortunes befell her, she was always able to respond with great dignity and forgiveness towards her transgressors. The Empress was always a very great Lady. She was very majestic, yet simple; very commanding yet obedient, and above all loyal to God, to her husband, to her children and to her country, and yet magnanimous to the world that showed her so much pain, misfortune and suffering.

So who was this saint, this great lady, this Empress and Queen, and where did she come from? She was born on May 9, 1892 in Pianore in what is now northern Italy, to a French father, the Duke Robert of Bourbon-Parma and a Portugese-German mother, Princess Maria Antonia of Braganza. She was their fifth child, although the Duke had 12 other children from a previous marriage with Princess Maria Pia of Naples-Sicily. His first wife had died on September 29,

1882, and he married Princess Maria Antonia on October 15, 1884.(9)

Zita's father, Duke Robert of Bourbon-Parma, was a French nobleman whose ancestry went directly back to the Sun King Louis XIV of France. His father, Duke Charles III of Bourbon-Parma, was the last reigning duke in Parma. He was murdered by Italian anarchists in 1854, when young Robert was 11 years old. His wife, Princess Louise of Bourbon, granddaughter of the last legitimate King of France[1], Charles X, fled with the young Robert to Frohsdorf in Austria, where her brother, the Count of Chambord, lived in exile in the Château at Frohsdorf, some 55 km south of Vienna. He became the boy's protector, and undertook the guidance and education of the young Robert of Bourbon-Parma.(9)

Frohsdorf was a sort of "Versailles in exile" and capital of the French legitimists who had fled the French Revolution. It was also here that Robert's father, Duke Charles III and his mother, Louise of Bourbon, were married in 1845. Frohsdorf was a Bourbon retreat. It was here that Marie Thérèse, Duchess of Angoulême and daughter of Marie Antoinette and King Louis XVI of France, sought refuge and lived for many years. She was also the tutor of the Count of Chambord, whom she had brought to Frohsdorf, and who would have become King Henry V of France under a legitimistic inheritance.

Upon their death, these Bourbons were laid to rest at Gorizia, in what is now northern Yugoslavia. Gorizia became a sort of "St. Denis-in-exile." The last king of France, Charles X, lived and died there, and was buried in the chapel of the Franciscan Convent of Castagnavizza. At the time of Charles X's death, Gorizia was part of greater Austria, and had been recommended to Charles X, who was in failing health, for its beneficial climate, by the Austrian Emperor Ferdinand I. Other Bourbons buried at Gorizia included, the Duchess of Angoulême and her husband, and the Count and Countess of Chambord.

---

1. see note page A-5.

9/ p. 27, 31-36

Duke Robert of Bourbon-Parma and his wife the Duchess Maria Antonia settled in the Palace at Schwarzau in the province of Lower Austria, which the Duke acquired in 1889. It was a spacious, artistic structure on which construction had started in 1697 and which was completed by Austria's eminent Baroque architect, Fischer von Erlach. In earlier, times it had sheltered such prominent guests as the Empress Maria Theresia, the Holy Roman Emperor Franz II, and Napoleon I Bonaparte. Tastefully displayed on the gable of the château, are the crests of the Ducal family of Parma, and the crest of the Bourbons — three golden lillies on a field of blue — as well as other crests of previous occupants. Above all these crests, there is the Royal Crown of France framed with the chain of the Spanish Order of the Golden Fleece.(10)

The palace at Schwarzau, with its beautifully surrounding grounds, was the home of the Bourbon-Parmas from July through December of each year. February to June was usually spent in their Villa della Pianore, their "country home" in northern Italy. It was situated near the little village of Pietrasanta, north of Viareggio in the Tuscany, overlooking the Ligurian Sea. Across the water lay Corsica, and not far off the coast was the Island of Elba where Napoleon spent his first exile.

As a result of these yearly migrations to the sea, four of Maria Antonia's children, including Zita, were born in Italy. All the rest were born either in Switzerland at the Bourbon Château of Wartegg on Lake Constance, or in Schwarzau. For this reason Zita has sometimes been called an Italian — although her upbringing was French and her mother tongue was German.

Two days after her birth, this fifth child of Maria Antonia was christened. As was the tradition, she was named after her parents, her godparents, and a number of saints and relatives. She was given the surnames of Marie des Neiges, Adelgunde, Michelle, Gabrielle, Josephine, Antonia, Luise, Agnes, and of course, Zita. It is said that the name Zita was suggested by her godmother, the Countess Adelgunde Bardi, who was the sister of Maria Antonia, and also that Pope Pius X, had suggested this name to Duke Robert with the hope that it would guard the child, a servant of God, throughout her life. His

---

10/ p. 27

rationale was that St. Zita, who lived in Lucca in the thirteenth century, was considered in Italy to be the protectress of servants. It was also Pope Pius X who, some years later when Zita came to him for his Papal blessing on the occasion of her betrothal to the Archduke Charles, predicted that Zita and her future husband would one day inherit the throne of Austria-Hungary, and this prediction was made long before the Archduke Franz Ferdinand was assassinated at Sarajevo.(10)

Even as a child, Zita showed many characteristics inherited from her mother. Among these were her mother's grace and charm, her somewhat firm facial features, her large communicative eyes, her unbending will, and her readiness to overcome adversity and meet a challenge.(10)

The foundation for little Zita's education began at home. It consisted of total devotion to God and dedication to duty and responsibility. These attributes were instilled in her through an early and fundamental religious training by her mother, herself a devout Roman Catholic, and later, by a resident priest, the Abbé Travers, who was the spiritual adviser to the Duke of Parma and his family. The day to day language in the Parma home was French, as was the language of instruction. In addition, the Duke spoke with his children in Italian, and his wife, Maria Antonia, spoke with them in German. From a very early age, the children had a trilingual upbringing, not to mention Latin which they had to learn for the religious services held daily in their in-house chapel.(10)

From the very beginning, it was emphasized to little Zita, as well as to her brothers and sisters, that religion was not only a matter of Christian customs and catechism, but, more importantly, the living of a life according to the teachings of Christ. Help for the needy and downtrodden was put high on her order of religious priorities.

Little Zita's religious training was further enhanced, when at the age of eleven, she was sent off to the Convent of St. Joseph in Zangberg, near Munich. The convent was staffed by Salesian nuns whose mission in life was to educate the daughters of Europe's elite, and to instill in them a strong Catholic orientation without bigotry. There Zita learnt that overcoming hardships and carrying out one's

---

10/ p. 23, 26

duties and responsibilities were part of God's mandate. She also acquired a deep inner reverence for the Blessed Virgin, and to accept a femininity modelled after the mother of God, but without softness of character. In addition to the normal academic curriculum, and because the bottom line of the educational process at St. Joseph's was to produce young ladies able to move about in the highest social circles, young Zita was also taught the social graces, including etiquette, behaviour, manners, music and dancing. The language of instruction at Zangberg was German, which gave Zita the opportunity to formalize her training in her mother tongue.(10)

At the tender age of 17, the young princess was sent to finishing school. The place chosen by her mother (her father had died while she attended St. Joseph's) was the Benedictine convent of St. Cecile at Ryde on the Isle of Wight, off the south coast of Great Britain. The prioress of this Benedictine convent happened to be Zita's maternal grandmother, Mother Adelhaid, who, after the death of her husband Dom Miguel, King of Portugal, entered this convent. In addition, other relatives of Zita were also nuns at St. Cecile at the time she entered the convent school in February 1909.

One was Mother Adelhaid's niece, Agnes von Löwenstein-Wertheim-Rosenberg, and another was Zita's older sister, Adelhaid who, incidently, was also a very beautiful woman. Two of Zita's other sisters were later to also join this convent as nuns — namely Franziska and Maria Antonia.(9)

St. Cecile was an elite convent and catered to very select young ladies of the aristocracy. Here, Zita studied theology, philosophy, history, literature, music, and above all, perfected her English.(10)

The end result of her upbringing and Catholic education was a beautiful, intelligent, vivacious young woman, versed in four languages, at ease among the aristocracy of the times, and sparkling with vigour and self confidence, yet politely withdrawn and always behaving with the utmost dignity and reverence.

Now, educated in the highest tradition of Europe's Catholic elite, Zita was ready for marriage. Not only was she a young woman possessing a natural physical beauty, she also radiated much charm

10/ p. 29-30, 33, 35-36
9/ p. 84

and great dignity. The majority of her contemporaries at the time were impressed with her outward appearance and by her deep brown eyes. She was a young lady with a faultless figure, thin though not skinny, and her long dark brown hair was usually worn in turbanlike form, surrounded with soft wavy curls. She liked to wear dresses having light, radiant colours and contemporary styles, very unlike the dark, somber dresses which were to mark her appearance during her premature and long, everlasting widowhood.(10)

As a very eligible Roman Catholic princess from a highly respectable Bourbon family, with a pedigree that was second to none (she could after all trace her family back not only to the Bourbon Sun King of France, Louis XIV (1638-1715) but also back through the House of Farnese, to Alexander Farnese who later became Pope Paul III (1549).

This very eligible young lady was soon in demand on the European royal family circuit. A proposal from Don Jaime, Duke of Madrid, was formally received by Zita's mother, Maria Antonia, but did not result in any commitment on the part of Zita. It did however, upon getting to the ears of the young Archduke Charles Franz Josef, result in his quickly formalizing the relationship that had developed between himself and Zita of Bourbon-Parma.(10)

The relationship between Archduke Charles Franz Josef and Princess Zita started when they were both still children. Young Zita lived in the palace at Schwarzau, the family home of her father, Duke Robert of Bourbon-Parma and her mother, the Duchess Maria Antonia of Bourbon-Parma. Young Charles Franz Josef lived with his father, the Archduke Otto and his mother Princess Maria Josefa of Saxony, in the Villa Wartholz in Reichenau only a few kilometers distant from Schwarzau. Also, Charles Franz Josef's grandfather, the Archduke Karl Ludwig, who also lived at Reichenau, married his third wife (the previous two having died), the Infanta Maria Theresia, daughter of King Miguel I of Portugal and sister of Zita's mother, Maria Antonia. A family relationship therefore existed between the two families living at Schwarzau and at Reichenau, and visits between them were often made.

10/ p. 41-42

On one of these visits, when Princess Zita was one year old, the young Charles Franz Josef, who was then five years old, was brought to Schwarzau by his aunts Maria Annunciata and Elisabeth Amalia (daughters of the Archduchess Maria Theresia and the Archduke Karl Ludwig) to visit his "Uncle and Auntie Parma." Needless to say, neither of the children were at that time (1893) cognizant of their future destiny. Over the years, such inter-family visits continued, and as the children became older, they often played together and with the other children in the family, and became good friends. The friendship was interrupted, of course, when Princess Zita was sent off to the Salesian Convent of St. Joseph in Zangberg in Upper Bavaria. It was not until some years later, when Zita was almost eighteen years old, that the relationship was to continue.(10)

While attending the Benedictine Convent of St. Cecile on the Isle of Wight in 1909, Princess Zita gradually found herself suffering more and more from the effects of the damp maritime climate prevalent on the island. She often felt ill, lost her rosy cheeks, developed a pale appearance, and had little appetite. Later that summer, when she was visited by her cousin Maria Annunciata, she returned with her to Austria-Hungary, and later went with her to Franzensbad in Bohemia to undertake a cure at the local health spa.(10)

It was in the late summer of 1909 that the paths of Princess Zita and the Archduke Charles Franz Josef crossed again, but not by chance. Many things had changed in Austria-Hungary just prior to and during the young life of Princess Zita.

First of all, Crown Prince Rudolf, the Emperor Franz Josef's only son and heir to the Imperial throne, was murdered at Mayerling on January 30, 1889. He was the victim of a plot by the ultra-socialist and anti-monarchist, Georges Clemenceau of France, who wanted to disassociate Austria-Hungary from its alliance with Germany and Italy. The mission, instigated by Georges Clemenceau and organized by one Cornelius Herz, was to be accomplished by getting Crown Prince Rudolf to overthrow his aged father, Emperor Franz Josef, take control of Austria-Hungary, and join France and Russia in an

---

10/ p. 28, 36

alliance of revenge against Germany. The revenge was to atone for France's humiliating defeat by the Prussians at Sedan in 1870.(8)

Cornelius Herz, who was born of German parents in Besançon, France in 1845, had emigrated with his family to the United States in 1848. He grew up in Chicago, became an American citizen, returned to Europe where he studied medicine in Vienna, and then returned to New York. It was there that he became very active in left-wing socialist politics, and met Georges Clemenceau who, as a refugee from the France of Napoleon III, was studying medicine in New York. Both men shared extreme left-wing socialist beliefs, and both men were extremely anti-monarchistic. They not only swore eternal war against all Bonaparte and Bourbon royalists in Europe, but also became politically implicated in the assassination of the Emperor Maximilian I of Mexico in 1867. When in 1870, Napoleon III declared war against Prussia, the resulting defeat of the French army at Sedan brought about circumstances for severe social change within France. Both Clemenceau and Herz returned to France and profited from these circumstances.(8)

On September 2, 1870 when the French Republic was re-established, Clemenceau was the mayor of Montmartre. His active political career had started, and he eventually rose to become President of the Council of Ministers of the Republic. Cornelius Herz, never far behind, became, among other things, head of an electrification program and then Minister for Post and Telegraph. He also headed an Institute for fundamental scientific research, and made extensive business trips throughout Europe, Russia, South and Central America, the Middle East, China and Japan, and to the U.S. and Canada. Cornelius Herz was a very extraordinary man, possessing much knowledge in all things scientific, economic and in medicine. However, the one thing he did not possess was a respect for order and morality. The only things of value to him were Georges Clemenceau and money.(8)

When Clemenceau had decided to break apart the German-Austro Hungarian-Italian accord, he needed an efficient, trusted, and ruthless organizer — and this man was Cornelius Herz. He sent Cornelius Herz off to Vienna to undertake the delicate task of winning Austria-

8/ p. 26-65

Hungary away from Germany and towards France. The old Emperor, Franz Josef I, was too wounded by past French military activities against his empire to be receptive to such a proposition. However, Crown Prince Rudolf, a much more modern man, influenced to some degree by the socialistic trends of the times, might be amenable to Clemenceau's plan. After all, he had always been interested in the activities of Leon Gambetta, the founder of the third French Republic; had been friends with Moriz Szeps in Vienna, who had both political and family connections with Georges Clemenceau (his daughter Sophie had married Georges Clemenceau's brother Paul) and spent many intellectual evenings at the home of Emil Zuckerkandl who was married to Sophie's sister, Bertha. In addition to the social and intellectual exchanges with the Szeps-Zuckerkandl-Clemenceau clique in Vienna, Crown Prince Rudolf was also greatly impressed by the scientific activities of Cornelius Herz, whom he had met on numerous previous occasions.(8)

When Cornelius Herz approached Crown Prince Rudolf with Georges Clemenceau's proposition, he did not at all expect the vehement reaction of the young Habsburg. The Crown Prince flew into an almost uncontrolled rage against Georges Clemenceau, and supported his father. Cornelius Herz had gone too far. He knew immediately that the knowledge he had thus imparted on the Crown Prince could backfire and become a threat to Clemenceau and to France. If the attempt to dismember the Central Powers accord became known to the German Government, the consequences to both France and Austria-Hungary could become very serious. It could have meant an immediate declaration of war on the part of Germany against France, and the possible occupation of all of Austria-Hungary by German troops. It therefore became immediately evident to Cornelius Herz that Crown Prince Rudolf must be silenced. The danger to his person was also quickly recognized by the young Rudolf.(8)

It was in the Fall of 1888 that Cornelius Herz had imparted to Crown Prince Rudolf the suggestion to participate in a plot against his father. And it was in the ensuing months that the Crown Prince lived in constant fear of his life, and during which he committed his fears to paper in a letter to his wife, Princess Stephanie of Belgium. For internal political reasons, Rudolf could not go to his father with

8/ p. 26-65

this dangerous revelation. He went instead to his uncle, the Archduke Karl Ludwig, with whom he discussed the whole dastardly affair and worked out precautionary measures to be taken. Unfortunately these were not enough, and Crown Prince Rudolf was murdered in Mayerling shortly afterwards.(8)

It was January 30, 1889. The Crown Prince had organized a hunting party at Mayerling for some of his old friends. Among the invited guests were his uncle Dom Miguel of Braganza, and the Countess Maria Vetsera. His uncle and some others declined the invitation for various reasons, but a few, including the Countess Vetsera, attended.(8)

It appears that on the way to Mayerling, Crown Prince Rudolf was warned of an impending danger, and while at Mayerling, he ordered all the windows to be shuttered. He also gave strict instructions to the staff that the telegraph machine was not to be used. It seems he did not want any contact, physical or otherwise, with any possible assassin. As an additional precaution, the Countess Vetsera was assigned a room at the farthest end of the lodge, so that if there would be trouble, she would not be involved.(8)

Late that night however, two hired assassins did gain entrance by means of ladders to the sleeping quarters of the lodge, and attacked the Crown Prince with knives and sabers. Rudolf tried to defend himself, and in the ensuing struggle, had his fingers cut off while holding a table as a shield. He was subsequently subdued and shot. The assassins then repeated their murderous task on the young Maria Vetsera, and carried her dead body to that of the dead Prince in order to implicate him in a scandal. The assassins then escaped into the night and were never identified, nor brought to justice.(8)

Following the murder of the Crown Prince at Mayerling, the whole sordid affair was committed to secrecy on the orders of the Emperor Franz Josef. He did not want, for both internal or external political reasons, to publicize the truth, and chose instead to release a love-suicide motive for the Crown Prince's death. All those who knew the truth were sworn to secrecy for 50 years. Pope Leo XIII was advised of the true circumstances of Rudolf's death and the Pope's blessing

---

8/ p. 26-65

for a Christian burial under the circumstances of a supposed suicide death, was received.(8)

The death of Crown Prince Rudolf changed the succession of the Habsburg throne to Emperor Franz Josef's oldest brother, the Archduke Karl Ludwig. The Archduke who lived at Villa Wartholz in Reichenau had two sons: the Archduke Franz Ferdinand who was later assassinated at Sarajevo; and the Archduke Otto who was the father of the Archduke Charles Franz Josef, the future Emperor Charles I. Unfortunately, however, the Archduke Karl Ludwig predeceased Emperor Franz Josef. He died in 1896, and the succession thus went to his oldest son — the Archduke Franz Ferdinand.(8)

But, as history has shown, things were not to be as expected. Georges Clemenceau had not given up his vendetta against Germany, or against the now even more hated Habsburgs. He actively supported the socialistic uprisings in the Balkans against the Austrians, and struck another blow at Emperor Franz Josef at Sarajevo. It was June 28, 1914. The new Crown Prince and his wife, the Countess Sophie Chotek, were visiting this capital of the Austro-Hungarian province of Bosnia-Herzegovina, when members of the "Black Hand" left-wing socialist organization, with the support and encouragement of Clemenceau, carried out their successful assassination of Crown Prince Franz Ferdinand and his wife. Europe was never to be the same again. This date was to become symbolic for Clemenceau's revenge, because five years later on this same day, Georges Clemenceau dictated the terms and conditions of Germany's surrender at Versailles. He followed this up in September of 1919 at Saint Germain-en-Laye with a similarly devastating treaty with Austria. Georges Clemenceau's revenge was now complete — Germany had been brought to its knees, and the Hohenzollerns in Germany as well as the Habsburgs in Austria, had been effectively eliminated.(8)

With the death of Franz Ferdinand at Sarajevo in 1914, the young Archduke Charles Franz Josef became heir to the throne, and with him, Archduchess Zita was to become his Empress. However, this possibility had been foreseen many years before by her mother, the Duchess Maria Antonia, and also by the Emperor Franz Josef. In fact, it had, as already mentioned, also been prophesied by Pope Pius X.

_____

8/ p. 26-65

When planning the educational options for her daughter, the Duchess Maria Antonia directed young Zita to the best of convent schools, with the intention that if she did not marry, she would enter the convent. After all, three of Zita's sisters had already followed religious vocations.

But Maria Antonia also had other intentions for her daughter Zita, for she had already picked out a suitable bridegroom for the young princess. He was a young man of high standing, so high that there was no eligible young man higher. He was the Archduke Charles Franz Josef, second in line to the throne in 1909 when Zita came back from her finishing year at St. Cecile. It remained only to bring them together at an appropriate time and place. The time was to be mid-summer 1909, and the place was Franzensbad in Bohemia, where Princess Zita had been taken by her cousin Maria Annunciata to recuperate from the effects of the harsh climate at St. Cecile. Neither Princess Zita nor the Archduke Charles Franz Josef were aware of the manipulations that were being carried out to bring them together.(10)

The Archduchess Maria Annunciata, daughter of the Archduchess Maria Theresia (sister of Maria Antonia and therefore Zita's aunt) and the Archduke Karl Ludwig (who was young Charles Franz Josef's grandfather) choreographed the meeting. Maria Annunciata, who was therefore Zita's cousin and Charles Franz Josef's aunt, had become the First Lady at court following the assassination of Emperor Franz Josef's wife, the Empress Elisabeth, known affectionately as "Sissi." She therefore was privy to the Emperor's innermost thoughts, including those concerning his succession.(10)

With the pretext of visiting his aunt Maria Annunciata, the Archduke Charles Franz Josef was invited to Franzensbad. There he again met Princess Zita whom he had not seen for over 10 years. She had changed in the intervening years into an attractive, vibrant, charming young woman, and the Archduke was obviously very much impressed. He was stationed at the time in Brandeis on the river Elbe, some 100 miles distant. Nevertheless, he found himself making the trip to Franzensbad more and more often. His attraction to Princess Zita deepened, and she in return was attracted more and more to this handsome young officer of Regiment No. 7 (The "Duke of Lorraine and Bar"). Their mutual attraction flourished from encounter to encounter, and grew to profound love in the ensuing two years.(7)

Meanwhile, back at the Hofburg, Emperor Franz Josef was pondering the future of the Habsburg dynasty. Since the Crown Prince Franz Ferdinand had chosen to enter into a morganatic marriage, any children he would have with his wife, the Countess Sophie Chotek, could not ascend the throne, and he therefore became concerned that the next in line to his throne should make an appropriate marriage to ensure the continuation of his dynasty. He therefore requested young Charles Franz Josef to come to the Hofburg. The ensuing discussion centered around the need for young Charles to find himself an appropriate wife. When the Archduke started to reply, the Emperor interrupted him and said that this was an order and that he would give him six months time to select a wife from the established Gotha. The Archduke replied that this would not be necessary as he had already made his choice — Princess Zita of Bourbon-Parma. The Emperor was very pleased and gave the Archduke his blessing. The rest is history, and the engagement of the Imperial couple was announced at Villa delle Pianore near Lucca on the occasion of the name day of Zita's mother. It was June 13, 1911.(9)

As it was the expressed wish of the Archduke Charles Franz Josef that his fiancée should visit the Holy Father in Rome to seek his benediction and blessing, the Princess Zita journeyed to Rome on June 24, 1911. Accompanied by her brother, Prince Sixtus, and her sister, Princess Isabelle, Princess Zita had an audience with Pope Pius X.(9)

Following receipt of the Blessed Sacrement from the hands of the Holy Father, Pope Pius X remarked to the Bourbons of his pleasure that Princess Zita was going to marry the heir to the Habsburg throne. To this the Princess remarked that it was the Archduke Charles that she was going to marry — not the heir to the throne. Pope Pius X repeated his prediction that the Archduke Charles will become heir to Emperor Franz Josef, and that he was happy over this since in his judgement, Charles Franz Josef was the reward that God had given to Austria in return for all that Austria had done for the Church of Rome.(9)

Following her audience with the Pope, Princess Zita remarked that it was good that His Holiness did not speak ex-cathedra on political matters. It was not until after the assassination of the Crown Prince Franz Ferdinand at Sarajevo some three years later, that Princess Zita suddenly realized the truth of the pontiff's prediction.

The wedding between Princess Zita and the Archduke Charles Franz Josef took place in the Bourbon palace in Schwarzau on October 21, 1911. Among the many invited guests were the Emperor Franz Josef of Austria-Hungary, King Frederick August of Saxony, Crown Prince Franz Ferdinand, Don Jaime, Duke of Madrid, who was the Head of the House of Bourbon, and numerous archdukes and archduchesses.(9)

Just before noon, the guests entered the chapel of the villa, which had been especially decorated for the occasion. The walls were covered with red damask, the niches were decorated with laurel trees in large ornamental pottery, and the statue of the Madonna was embellished with flowers and branches of evergreens. In prominence before the altar were two prayerstools for the bride and groom, covered with red damask and decorated with gold fringe. To the left of the altar, slightly raised, was a fauteuil in yellow damask for the Emperor, and to the right, a red fauteuil for King Frederick August.(9)

When the bride and groom entered the chapel, the court orchestra played the Hymn of the Duchy of Parma, especially composed for the occasion by Christian Eder, the director of the court orchestra, and the Austrian national anthem composed by Josef Haydn.(9)

The procession up the aisle of the chapel saw the groom flanked on one side by Emperor Franz Josef, and on the other by his mother, the Archduchess Maria Josefa. The bride was escorted by Don Jaime, the Duke of Madrid, and by the Duchess of Bourbon-Parma, Maria Antonia, the bride's mother. They, in, turn were followed by King Frederick August of Saxony, the Crown Prince Franz Ferdinand, and the remaining members of the Imperial family, princes and

---

9/ p. 122

princesses, archdukes and archduchesses. The solemn religious service was performed by Monsignor Bisletti, the majordomo of His Holiness, Pope Pius X, whom the Pope had personally sent for the occasion. The ceremony was carried out in the French language, and the resounding "Oui" from the bride and groom signalled to all the happiness in the hearts of the two principals of the occasion.(9)

After the religious ceremony, the principals and guests returned to the dining room on the second floor of the palace. Prominently displayed in the Stucco ceiling above the guests were the Bourbon lillies on fields of blue, and looking down from life-size portraits on the walls were Kings Louis XIV, Louis XV and Charles X of France. Tables decorated with fresh flowers, were arranged in order of prominence, with the newlyweds in the center, together with the highest ranking guests. A nine course wedding déjeûner, served on family silver, included a cream of lettuce soup, moussettes of hare, roast rack of lamb, lobster à la parisienne, roast turkey, salads, asparagus spears, pineapple and raspberry ice, cheeses, fruits, and desserts.(9)

When the déjeûner was finished, Emperor Franz Josef addressed the newlyweds and their guests. He welcomed the Archduchess Zita as a member of his House, the House of Habsburg, and thanked Her Royal Highness, the Duchess of Parma for her assistance in bringing together the joining of the hearts of Zita and Charles Franz Josef. He also thanked her for the gracious and warm reception extended to his person and to all the guests. In addressing the newlyweds, he wished them the best of luck in the hope that they would both find joy and happiness in their life-long endeavours. He closed his remarks by saying that God should protect and guard the Archduke Charles and the Archduchess Zita, and that both should live long and happy lives.(9)

During and after the déjeuner, the band of the Imperial and Royal Infantry Regiment No. 67 played for the entertainment of the invited guests. Their selections included the "wedding march" by Mendelssohn, the waltz from the Student Prince by Lehar, and various compositions by Leoncavallo, Ziehrer, and Johann Strauss.(9)

9/ p. 122

After refreshments, the guests were invited to view the many presents that the Archduchess Zita had received. These included a pearl necklace from her husband, and a diadem of diamonds from the Emperor. The many gifts displayed on viewing tables appropriately laid out in the Maria Theresian hall of the palace, transformed the hall into a veritable treasure room.(10)

However, the bride herself outshone all the radiance and glitter that was apparent in the hall. She wore an oyster coloured bridal gown of satin duchesse embroidered with silver threads in delicate designs. The train of the dress, three meters long, was adorned with Bourbon lillies framed in garlands of myrtle. Its front was decorated with genuine valenciennes in high flounces, and its sides were also embroidered with myrtle branches.(9)

On her neck, the bride wore an antique broach in the shape of a myrtel garland, and on her breast she carried a corsage of fresh orange blossoms and myrtle. In her hair lay a crown of myrtel, covered with a long veil which was held in place with a magnificent diadem of diamonds. The wedding ring, a simple band of gold, which she had received from her husband, bore the inscription "Zita of Bourbon-Parma", and a similar one that she gave to her husband was inscribed "Charles of Austria."(10)

Before the wedding festivities came to an end, Monsignor Bisletti extended his blessing and best wishes to the newlyweds, and gave them a hand-written letter from Pope Pius X. The letter expressed the hope that God would guard the virtuous couple, and that they in turn should trust in God. It also added, that in those bitter hours from which even this couple would not be spared, their firm belief in God would be their crutch. Were these words by the Holy Father, another premonition in the life of this couple, a warning of the hardships that lay ahead, and of the suffering they would endure? Only history would tell.(10)

10/ p. 56
9/ p. 123, 125

BOOK 1
THE HABSBURGS

CHAPTER 2

AN OVERVIEW (950-1916)

The Habsburgs are a European dynasty that traces its origin with certainty back for more than 1000 years to Guntram the Rich, who died in the year 950. One of his descendents, Bishop Werner of Strassburg, built a fortified castle, the remains of which still stand impressively at the confluence of the Aar and the Reuss rivers in the Aargau of present-day Switzerland. Because of hawks that inhabited the castle tower, the castle became known as the Habichtsburg — habicht being the German word for hawk.(1)

The descendents of Guntram, and their descendents, became known as the Habsburgs, a phonetic derivative of Habichtsburg, and this family developed into the European dynasty that now bears this name.

But who are they and where did they come from originally? This question has kept scholars busy for many centuries, and its solutions are still not provable. A number of theories have however evolved overtime.

One legend, initiated by the followers of Rudolf I (1218-1291) was that the dynasty arose from Roman stock, and particularly from the Colonna family, which in turn traces its predecessors through the Counts of Tuskulan to the genera Iula, and hence Julius Caesar. This legend was very popular with the Habsburgs of the 13th and 14th century.(1)

However, in 1476 another theory arose. This theory proposed that the Habsburgs developed not from the Colonna family, but from the Pierleoni family, another old Roman dynasty. The Pierleonis evolved through the Count of Aventin from the old roman Anicierns. The

Aniciern family produced a number of very prominent religious figures, namely Pope Felix III (492-496) and Pope Gregory I, the Great (590-604). In addition, it also produced St. Benedict, the founder of the religious order that bears his name. This theory gave credence to the Holiness of the Habsburgs at a time in history when the Counter-Reformation was in full swing.(1)

In addition to the two Roman theories described above, a Franken theory also evolved around the end of the 15th century. Emperor Maximilian I (1459-1519), who was deeply interested in his genealogical past for reasons of state and political reassurances, strongly believed in this theory. He carried out extensive genealogical research to support this theory which purports the descendency of the Habsburgs from the Franks, quite possibly from the Carolingians, but most probably from the Merovingians. This theory was particulary useful to the Emperor Maximilian because through his marriage with Maria of Burgundy, he initiated the westward influence of the House of Austria over the Dukes of Burgundy, and through them, inherited Franco-Burgundian lands, the rights to which, this theory bolstered.(1)

A fourth, and probably the most plausible theory for the ancestry of the Habsburgs, is that the Habsburgs evolved from the Etichons, the allemanic dukes of Swabia and Alsace, who were also forefathers of the Dukes of Lorraine. This theory was first put forward by the French historian Jérôme Vignier, who concluded in 1649 that both the House of Habsburg and the House of Lorraine evolved from the same source — the House of Alsace. Support for this theory was also given by a 17th century genealogist named Hausmeier Chlodevechs II, and later in 1721 by the Hanoverian scholar and bibliophile Johann Georg Eccard von Eticho. The Emperor Charles VI of Austria (1685-1740), also a scholar of Habsburg genealogy, commissioned a study by Pater Marquard Herrgott (1694-1762) which also supported the Etichon family as the common ancestor for both the House of Habsburg and the House of Lorraine. This relationship between the House of Habsburg and the House of Lorraine was firmly consummated in 1736 when the Empress Maria Theresia(1717-1780) married Francis Duke of Lorraine (1708-1765), creating the modern House of Habsburg-Lorraine.(1)

1/ p. 31-32

The European Habsburgs, from the time of Guntram the Rich until the middle of the thirteenth century, were all faithful servants of the early German-Roman kings and emperors, and as such were staunch defenders of the Roman Church. They are mentioned in the 1135 annals of the Benedictine Abbey of Muri in Switzerland which was founded by Count Radbot of Habsburg in 1027, and which, since 1971, contains the burial crypt of the modern Habsburgs. Habsburg ownership of lands and estates in Oberrhein and in the middle Schweiz go back to 1009. Further acquisitions extended the Habsburg estates by the year 1250, from the Jura, eastward along the valley of the Rhine, to the Black Forest, and westward from the central Alps to Burgundy.(1)

It must be remembered that during the dark ages after the fall of the Roman Empire of the Caesars, civilization and Christianity existed mainly in secluded monasteries, and Slavic hordes of nomads overran and populated most of middle Europe. It was not until 800 AD that order was restored and Christianity could again come out from hiding. Mainly responsible for this resurrection was the German king, Charles the Great, or Charlemagne as he came to be known. He set himself up as protector of the Church of Rome, and established a Christian empire throughout central Europe. He swore to uphold the Roman Catholic faith within his realm, and to protect the Church of Rome and its head, the Pope, against all enemies. He was subsequently crowned Emperor of the Holy Roman Empire in Aix-La-Chapelle in 800 AD, and as such was ruler of a conglomeration of Christian lands headed by counts, dukes, princes and kings, all of whom were subservient to the Emperor.(1)

From Charlemagne until the middle of the thirteenth century, various German kings were elected Holy Roman emperors, and their subservient rulers maintained order in the realm and ensured the support and extension of the Christian faith. During all this time, some ten generations of Habsburgs — counts, dukes and princes — served the German kings of the Church of Rome.(1)

In 1245, when the incumbent Roman-German king died without an apparent successor, the empire was thrown into confusion and discord. It was not until 1273, when a Council of Electors established

---

1/ p. 33, 40

by Pope Gregory X elected a new Roman-German king, that order was re-established. He was Rudolf of Habsburg (1218-1291) and he was the first Habsburg to be elected German king. He was crowned at Aix-La-Chapelle on October 24, 1273.(1)

Rudolf I, and his Habsburg descendents, were to remain sovereign rulers in Europe for the next 645 years. During this period, Habsburgs would directly influence the destiny not only of Europe, but also of Africa and America.(2)

Rudolf's victory over King Ottokar Przemysl II of Bohemia in a battle at Duernkrut on August 26, 1278 was a watershed in Europe's destiny. King Ottokar had opposed Rudolf I's election, having himself amassed a small empire including Austria and Hungary, which extended from the Adriatic to the Baltic. His defeat by Rudolf of Habsburg ensured German instead of Slavic dominance over central Europe, and was to mean for Europe what the Battle of the Plains of Abraham almost 500 years later through Montcalm's defeat by General Wolfe, was to mean for North America.(4)

King Rudolf died in 1291 and was followed by a succession of Habsburg dukes, princes and kings, who often quarrelled among themselves, building up their individual centers of power at Graz in Steiermark and Innsbruck in the Tyrol. They also battled the ever self-conscious Swiss, a long drawn out struggle that gave rise, among other things, to the legend of William Tell.

It was the Habsburg Duke Rudolf IV (1339-1365) of Austria who founded the University of Vienna in 1365 and laid the foundation stone for the building of the tower for Vienna's magnificent St. Stephen's Cathedral. He also, in the same church, built a tomb under the high altar, in which countless members of the House of Habsburg found, from 1362 to 1576, their last resting place. From then on, the crypt under the Capuchin Church in Vienna was used as a burial crypt for the Habsburgs.(4)

The next two centuries saw Habsburg power greatly increase in Europe, largely at the expense of France whose kings saw in the Habsburgs, formidable rivals for their own claims to leadership of the empire. This animosity between France and the House of Austria

---

1/ p. 40, 45-47
2/ p. 109
4/ p. 15-16

was to appear again and again for hundreds of years and severely affected Europe's political destiny.

Although Habsburg expansion in eastern Europe was largely achieved by the sword, expansion in western Europe was achieved mainly through the use of the marriage bed. King Matthias Corvinus of Hungary once remarked, "Bela gerant fortes, tu, felix Austria nube. Nam quae Mars aliis, dat tibi regna Venus." Translated from the Latin, this means, "The mighty wage war, but you, lucky Austria, marries. What Mars grants others, Venus gives to you."(4)

This marriage-bed diplomacy of the Habsburgs was first implemented in 1473 when the Emperor Frederick III arranged for the marriage of his son Maximilian to Maria, daughter of Duke Charles of Burgundy. Through this union (1477), the Habsburgs acquired the Dukedom of Burgundy which stretched from the Netherlands, over Luxemburg, Lorraine and Alsace, to the Alps. This acquisition greatly enhanced the House of Austria, and forestalled a similar plan by King Louis XI of France who had hoped to marry the Dauphin (the later King Charles VIII) to this same bride.(2)

The Emperor Frederick III believed in the high and inescapable destiny of the Habsburgs, and invented the acronym A.E.I.O.U. This became a sort of signature for the Emperor, a formalized "we", since he always addressed himself in the plural. It was also a symbol of mysticism with which the Emperor always associated himself.(2)

The Austrian historian Alphons Lhotsky, in a 1971 study, identified some 86 meanings for the symbol: 72 in Latin, one in Greek, and 13 in German. The most well known of these are "Austria erit in Orbo Ultima"(Austria will exist eternally) and "Alles Erdliche ist Oesterreich Untertan" (Everything on earth is subordinate to Austria). And then there was another version which appeared at the time on the wall of a military academy in the city of Wiener Neustadt, south of Vienna. It read "Aerarisches Essen ist Oft Ungeniessbar" (Military Food is Often Unpalatable).(24)

Through his subsequent marriage to Maria of Burgundy, the Emperor Maximilian I laid the foundation for the House of Habsburg as a world power.

4/ p. 19, 31
2/ p. 76
24/ p. 87

Maximilian's betrothal in 1494 of his own two children to those of their Catholic majesties of Spain, King Ferdinand and Queen Isabella (who had financed Christopher Columbus' epic voyage of discovery two years earlier) had not only far-reaching territorial consequences for the House of Habsburg, but served as a tactical manoeuver of great significance against the King of France, who at the time was stirring up the Osmanian Empire of the Turks against Hungary and Austria. The union that Maximilian forged with Spain, and consumated through the marriage of his children with those of the King and Queen of Spain, laid the foundation for a Spanish Habsburg dynasty which was to parallel the existing Austrian branch for 200 years.(4)

Maximilian I was a very cultivated man; merry, humorous and cultured. When he was not engaged in fighting wars or jousting with his knights, he encouraged the arts. He cultivated scholars and philosophers, and made his court famous for poetry and music. He even established a choir of young boys, to sing for the court and in Church. This choir, which has become known as "the Vienna Choir Boys" was later to nourish Joseph Haydn and Franz Schubert, and even today, still thrills audiences in Vienna, and through its periodic tours, the world.(4)

It was however, not until two generations after Maximilian that the full impact of the inter-marriages of the Habsburg and Spanish thrones would bear great fruit. Two grandsons of the Emperor Maximilian I were to inherit the Habsburg thrones in Europe. The eldest of the two, Charles V (1500-1558) became King of Spain, and the younger Ferdinand I (1503-1564) became King of Bohemia and Hungary.

Charles was born in Gent, Belgium, and since his father died when he was only six years old, the young prince was brought up under the protection and influence of his aunt, Margarete of Austria, in the Court at Brussels. She was a very shrewd woman and was able to enlist the best of the Wallonian aristocracy as governors and teachers for the young Charles. Among these was a professor Adrien Florszoon from the University of Louvain, who later appeared in history as Pope Hadrien VI. He was not the only prominent teacher from this

---

4/ p. 29, 35-36

university to influence a Habsburg prince.(2) Some 400 years later, a Professor Charles De Koninck from the same university would greatly influence two more Habsburg princes, the Archdukes Rudolf and Charles Louis, in Québec City, 3000 miles away.

Upon the death of Maximilian I in 1519, Charles V was that same year elected Roman German Emperor at Frankfurt, and crowned the following year at Aix-la-Chapelle. Ten years later he was confirmed in his exalted position by Pope Clemens VII himself, who again crowned the Emperor at Bologna, Italy. After 250 years, the House of Habsburg had now become an unchallenged world power. Its realm extended from Rumania in the east to the Netherlands in the west, and from Poland in the north to Sardinia, Sicily and the north coast of Africa in the south. Through its domain over Spain and Portugal, Habsburg power and influence also reached out over the Atlantic to most of South America. The Habsburg Emperor Charles V truly had dominion over an empire on which the sun never set.(2)

Charles was in his 21st year when he was vested with the responsibility of Emperor. He had entered this exalted vocation with a high sense of religious seriousness, and a zeal that embodied a revival of Charlemagne's dream of a united Christendom. Charles was to sacrifice his life to this dream which unfortunately he was unable to bring to fruition.(4)

Firstly, in 1517, Martin Luther had posted his ninety-five point thesis to the door of the church at Wittenberg. It was the beginning of the Reformation and its aims were diametrically opposite to the intent of the Holy Roman Empire.(4)

Secondly, the young Emperor's dream was further shattered, when King Henry VIII of England himself defied the Pope in order to divorce Catherine, the daughter of King Ferdinand and Queen Isabella of Spain, and therefore the Emperor's aunt. This action by the King of England, removed England from the Catholic community of nations.(4)

Last, but not least, the continued attempts by the Catholic King Francis I of France to undermine the power of the Emperor through four wars on the continent and by allying himself with the Muslim

---

2/ p. 107
4/ p. 45

potentate, Suleiman the Magnificent, whom he urged to attack the Habsburgs from the rear, further diluted the Emperor's dream of a unified and peaceful Christendom. The reign of Charles V, therefore, saw the first Turkish invasions of Europe. Three successive waves of Muslim invaders threw themselves at the defences of the empire — in 1526, 1529, and again in1632. Although beaten back from Vienna, the invaders remained in the western part of Hungary for 150 years. It was not until the end of the seventeenth century that the Muslim's were driven out of Europe for good.(4)

The seventeenth century was a difficult one for the House of Habsburg. Continued incursions by the Muslims on their eastern flanks, and the ever continuing spread of Protestantism throughout Germany, Bohemia and Hungary, occupied the resources of this most Catholic dynasty. In Spain, the Inquisition supported by the Habsburg King Philip II, ruthlessly attacked all nonadherents to the Catholic faith. At the same time, the Austrian Habsburgs were attempting to deal with the Reformation through agreements, prohibition, and finally armed conflict. The struggle centered in Bohemia, and it was there, in 1618, that events occurred which eventually triggered off that most bloody religious struggle known as the Thirty Years War.

With the death of the Habsburg Emperor Matthias in 1618, King Ferdinand II was elected head of the House of Habsburg. As emperor he introduced his own counter reforms which alienated his Protestant subjects and which disrupted the fabric of society. These counter reforms eventually resulted in an open rebellion in Bohemia and, in 1618, two Imperial armies moved into Bohemia to seize Prague and put an end to the rebellion. Ferdinand II, who was then 42, had embarked on his crusade to return Catholicism to Europe.(4)

But, alas, it was not to be. The Hungarians revolted and joined the Bohemians. The Catholics rallied around the Habsburgs, and the Imperial forces, now under the veteran Wallonian General de Tilly, closed on Prague and, on November 8, 1620, defeated the rebels at the Battle of the White Hill. From Austria's point of view, the war should have been over. The Protestant movement in Bohemia and

---

Hungary had been defeated. However, even though they had won the battle, they had not won the war.

In the shadow of the Bohemian revolt, two large political camps emerged in Europe, divided mainly on religious lines. The Emperor Ferdinand II, as the champion of Roman Catholicism, was supported by Pope Paul V, by his distant cousin King Philip III of Spain, by the Grand Duke Cosimo of Tuscany, and by the Catholic League headed by Duke Maximilian of Bavaria. The Protestant Union, composed mainly of German and Bohemian Protestant nobles was supported by King Christian IV of Denmark, by King Gustav Adolf II of Sweden, by Prince Carl Emmanuel of Savoy, by King Charles I of England, and by the Catholic King Louis XIII of France. The French Foreign Minister, Cardinal Richelieu, had seized this opportunity to further harass his Habsburg opposition who now circumvented France through Spain in the south, the Netherlands in the north, and Austria in the east.(2)

The ensuing bloody conflicts that consumed Europe for the next 30 years devastated the continent. The Swedes, under their warrior King Gustav Adolf I, literally laid waste all the Catholic lands in their path of violence, and swept south and west in a great half-circle across the Rhineland provinces, down and around to the east, deep into Bavaria, and into Austria itself. They destroyed everything that was Catholic, burning churches and monasteries, destroying schools and cemetaries, and even occupied Prague. These wars also saw the deaths in 1632 of the Imperial General de Tilly, and of the Swedish King Gustav Adolf, both in battle.(4)

After 24 years of war, the cause of the war was forgotten. Mercenary armies fought for loot. German princes, both Catholic and Protestant alike, fought for territorial aggrandizement. The Emperor Ferdinand II died in 1637 — an old man at 59. And France, under Cardinal Richelieu, moved to destroy Spanish power and instilled a crushing defeat on the Spanish army in 1643.(4)

When peace was finally declared in 1648, the Treaty of Westphalia saw profound changes on the continent of Europe. Sweden gained parts of Prussia, the Dutch Netherlands were torn from Spain and became Holland, Switzerland achieved independence, France gained

2/ p. 158-159
4/ p. 81-84

the northern fortress towns of Metz and Verdun, and most of Alsace. Spain still held parts of the Netherlands which would later become Belgium. France, now under the Sun King Louis XIV became a world class military power, and the Holy Roman Empire was fragmented into hundreds of independent states headed by an Emperor who had very little power over them. The Emperor, however, still was supreme over all his many subordinate dukedoms, principalities and kingdoms that made up the now unified Austria. The unification of what previously were separate and distinct Habsburg lands into one, made possible for the first time the term "House of Austria" as an idea to describe the unified states in their entirety.(2)

In the remaining part of the Empire, in those lands that were not part of the House of Austria, Protestants were free to openly practice their religious convictions, and were allowed access to all offices of state of the Empire, the offices of which were moved from Vienna to Mainz. The freedom granted to Protestants by the Treaty of Westphalia was a severe blow to the Papacy. As it turned out, the big losers in the Thirty Years War were Rome and the Catholic Church, and the winners were Protestantism and the Catholic King of France, the Sun King Louis XIV, whose glory was to outshine even that of the Emperor.(2)

The Habsburg prince that inherited the empire at the end of the Thirty Years War must have felt like the captain of the Titanic. The empire was devastated. The Swedes had ransacked and destroyed everything in their path. Towns and villages had been overrun and burned to the ground. Castles and fortifications were left in ruins, some of which can still be seen to this day as vivid reminders of this unholy of holy wars. The new Emperor had a lot of rebuilding to do. Nevertheless, the Habsburgs had a legacy of greatness, and it did not take them long to bounce back. Perhaps it was because of necessity brought on by resurrected opposition from their Hungarian lands, and by renewed French support not only for the Hungarians, but also for the Muslims of Turkey who had boasted they would not rest until the Sultan's horses could be stabled in St. Peter's at Rome. The Habsburg who took up this challenge was the Emperor Leopold I (1640-1705).(4)

2/ p. 271-272
4/ p. 39

In 1683, a Turkish army of 200,000 men, led by the Grand Vizier Kara Mustafa, swept up the Danubian plains from the east on its way to Vienna. The Emperor Leopold, however, was already at Passau drumming up support to fight the Turks, when the Turks laid siege to Vienna. With the full support of Pope Innocent XI, who granted indulgences far and wide, the Emperor Leopold was able to conjure into being an imposing command of fighting men under the leadership of the Duke Charles of Lorraine. It was at Passau also, that the Emperor Leopold first came into contact with Prince Eugene of Savoy, whose presence was to have a most important influence on the destiny of Austria. The Prince, having been snubbed by King Louis XIV of France, had volunteered his services to the Habsburg Emperor, and served on the staff of Duke Charles of Lorraine in the international contingent that was heading towards Vienna to fight the Muslims.(2)

At the same time that Duke Charles of Lorraine was marching on Vienna from the west, King Jan Sobieski of Poland was leading an expeditionary army that was marching towards Vienna from Cracow. They met on the Kahlenberg, a mountain north-west of Vienna, and combined their forces. On September 12, 1683, King Sobieski, the Duke of Lorraine, and their generals heard a mass read by the Papal Legate, Marco d'Aviano, after which the Catholic forces opened a three-pronged attack on the Turks. The battle raged all day and, in the afternoon, Count Starhemberg , who with 16,000 men had defended the siege from July to October, came out from behind the city walls and joined the Catholic armies in their defeat of the Muslim hordes. By nightfall, the siege on Vienna had been broken, and the Turks were routed and put to flight. They did not stop until they were deep inside Hungary.(24)

The following year, 1684, the Turks were pursued by an allied force headed by the Emperor Leopold I, King Jan Sobieski of Poland, and the Republic of Venice, and driven out of Hungary. In all, the pursuit was to last sixteen years, and it was not until 1697 at the Battle of Zenta that an Imperial force of 40,000 men led by Prince Eugene of Savoy, defeated a horde of 120,000 Turks. Through skillful tactics and great military leadership, the Prince devastated the Turks, and

---

24/ p. 154
2/ p. 185

the subsequent Peace of Karlowitz on January 26, 1699 ended forever the Turkish threat against Europe.(2)

Eastern Europe having been secured, the Emperor Leopold still had to contend himself with problems arising out of the Spanish succession in the west. The death of the Habsburg King Charles II of Spain in 1700, brought to an end the Spanish Line of the Habsburg dynasty which had started with the Emperor Charles V exactly 200 years earlier.(2)

Three European dynasties were to immerse themselves in a struggle for the crown of Spain, primarily on grounds of kinship. King Louis XIV led the French demand on the basis of his marriage with the Infanta Maria Theresia, daughter of King Philip IV of Spain. The Emperor Leopold I based his claim on the long established relationship between the Spanish and the Austrian dynasty of the Habsburgs. After all, his mother was a daughter of King Philip III of Spain. A third, and somewhat more distant claim was made by the Prince Elector of Bavaria, who claimed succession on the ground that his mother was the daughter of the Emperor's first wife, the Infanta Margaretha Theresia.(2)

First to take action was King Louis XIV of France. While the Spanish Habsburg lay dying on his death bed in Madrid, a French lobby at his Court got him to sign a testament nominating King Louis XIV's grandson, Philip of Anjou, as his successor. King Louis XIV then immediately sent his grandson off to Madrid as king apparent.

In the meantime, the Emperor Leopold had fully expected his younger son, Charles, to ascend the throne in Spain and thus establish a new Habsburg dynasty.

The underlying moves and counter moves, and the self interests of England and Holland, resulted in a Grand Alliance being set up in The Hague between Austria, England, Holland, Prussia, Savoy and Portugal against France, whose only ally was Bavaria. With the Bourbon pretender sitting in Madrid, and the Grand Alliance in his back pocket, the Emperor Leopold I declared war on France, and sent his own son Charles on his way to take over the Crown of Spain.(2)

2/ p. 188-190

The ensuing struggle saw wars fought in Spain, in the Spanish Netherlands, in southern Germany, and in northern Italy. The Emperor invested command of his southern armies to Prince Eugene of Savoy who, with his great victory at Zenta only recently behind him, beat the French armies in northern Italy and caused them to retreat.

Shortly thereafter, British forces under the command of General John Churchill, Duke of Marlborough, joined with Prince Eugene, and together they beat back the Bavarians and the French in the north. The war against France continued for four more years, and it was not until Prince Eugene's devastating defeat of the French at Malplaquet in 1709, that France's military and economic power came to a standstill. At the same time, there were unresolved skirmishes taking place in Spain itself between the Bourbon Philip in Madrid and the young Archduke Charles of Habsburg, whom the Emperor had proclaimed King of Spain.(4)

Unfortunately however, both the Emperor Leopold I and his successor, the Emperor Josef I, died before the succession in Spain could be resolved, and the Archduke Charles suddenly found himself successor to the Emperor's throne in Vienna. On his return trip to Vienna, he passed through Frankfurt/Main where he was crowned Emperor Charles VI. It was the first time since 1500 that a Habsburg Emperor also claimed the crown of Spain.

However a change in policy within the Grand Alliance, especially by England, no longer supported the continuance of a dual Habsburg dynasty in Spain and Austria. The French immediately took this occasion to again pick up arms, and it was not until Queen Ann of England suggested that peace negotiations be undertaken to end the fighting, that peace was restored. By the Treaty of Utrecht in 1713, recognition was given to the Bourbon Philip as King of Spain, and the Spanish Netherlands, northern Italy and the kingdom of Naples were accorded to the House of Habsburg. The biggest winner, however, was England which received Gibraltar and Majorca, as well as Newfoundland and Nova Scotia in North America.(4)

A problem of succession however, was still to plague the Emperor Charles VI. As his only son Leopold died at birth, he was left with

4/ p. 94-95

only girl children to carry on his destiny. He therefore immediately, after Utrecht, convened a conference in Vienna at which he proposed and received acceptance for a proposal called the "Pragmatic Sanction." This law nullified the heretofore Law of Primogenitur which until then had always ensured that Habsburg succession would always be carried out in the male line. By ensuring the throne for his eldest daughter Maria Theresia, the Emperor Charles became the first Habsburg "feminist."

However, the ensuring of this policy in the eyes of his allies as well as those of his European enemies, caused him to strike bargains with the many rulers of Europe that he might not otherwise have made, had he had the consolidation and strengthening of his empire as his first priority. His course of convincing rulers to pledge themselves to recognize the integrity of the Habsburg inheritance in his, Charles VI's designated successor, led him to alienate himself from England and Holland, and led him into a damaging war with France which caused him to lose lands and influence in Italy. His pursuit of recognition for his Pragmatic Sanction by Saxony, resulted in his unhappy participation in the War of the Polish Succession.(4)

Charles VI's obsession with the need to secure the hereditary lands beyond challenge for his daughter, were motivated by the consideration that his various and scattered lands could be up for grabs by anyone with a plausible claim in the event that he himself should suddenly die, and by the knowledge that if either of the two daughters of his deceased emperor brother Joseph I were to survive him, she and her husband whoever he may be, would be senior to any daughter of Charles VI.(4)

Nevertheless, Charles VI succeeded in his great endeavour, and when his daughter Maria Theresia married Duke Francis III, Stephen of Lorraine in 1736, he gave her a wedding full of Imperial splendor, the likes of which had not been seen in the Empire before. It took place in the Church of Saint Augustin, next to the Hofburg palace, and was officiated by the Apostolic Nuntiate Passionei who proclaimed the bride and groom as the most beautiful couple he had ever seen.(4)

Under the Emperor Charles VI, Vienna was blossoming into a splendid capital. Many noble families of the time built splendid

4/ p. 98-99

palaces within the city walls, and the still standing magnificent National Library and Spanish Riding School with its Lipizzaner stallions, were conceived and built. At the same time, Prince Eugene of Savoy built his monumental Belvedere Palace which was to rival the Sun King's Palace at Versailles. In addition, the Emperor commissioned Fischer von Erlach to build his masterpiece, the Charles Church, as a thanksgiving for deliverance from the plague and, at the same time, as a monument to himself, Charles VI.(4)

The Emperor Charles VI was also to leave a mark on history in his struggle against the Turks. In the summer of 1716, the Grand Vizier, Damad Ali, attacked Venice and threatened Rome. When the Emperor came to the rescue, the Grand Vizier declared war on him, and when a Muslim horde of 70,000 was decimated by Prince Eugene of Savoy at Peterwardein, Pope Clemens XI celebrated the Austrian victory by raising the Catholic Feast of the Holy Rosary, initiated 150 years earlier by Pope Gregory XIII to commemorate the victory of Don Juan of Austria over the Turks at Lepanto, to the Roman Catholic Feast of Thanksgiving. This feast has come down to us to this day and we still celebrate it every year in early October.(2)

Charles VI also saw the death of Prince Eugene. This great man, who passed away in his sleep at the age of 73 on April 21, 1736 lived to serve three emperors — Charles VI, his brother Josef I, and their father Leopold I. He had served them all faithfully, and always in a way that enhanced the power of the Emperor and the glory of the Empire. As the saviour of Christianity, he guarded Austria and the Holy Roman Empire of German Nations from Turkish invasion, and the Christian Churches of Europe from Islam.

The Emperor Charles VI had married only once. His consort, who was selected for him by the Court in Vienna, was Elisabeth Christine of Braunschweig-Wolfenbuettel, a name not unfamiliar in Québec.

It was this family which, related to the Hanoverian Kings of England, would many years later send German troops to Québec to fight against the Americans during their War of Independence in 1776. Many of these mercenaries later inter-married with young ladies of New France and settled in and around Québec City.(21)

4/ p. 99
2/ p. 109
21/ p. 48

Upon the death of the Emperor Charles VI on October 20, 1840, the House of Habsburg was without a male heir. The heir to the throne was the Archduchess Maria Theresia. She was then 23 and, by all standards, a beautiful young woman. Educated by the Jesuits, the Archduchess had, in addition to Catholic doctrine, been taught history, art, music and languages. She spoke a flawless French and was quite at home in Latin, which was the language of administration used in Hungary. At the age of eleven, her education was taken over by the Countess Charlotte Fuchs, who instilled in her young charge the etiquette of the court, and prepared her as best she could, for the responsibilities of Head of State, which at the time was not a certainty but a strong probability since the Emperor had still not conceived a son.(2)

She also met for the first time, when she was only 12, the young Franz III Stephen of Lorraine, whose father was a cousin of her father, Charles VI and of her uncle Josef I, and whose mother was Charlotte of Orleans. Young Franz of Lorraine spent much time at the Court in Vienna, and by the time the Archduchess Maria Theresia was 17, she was madly in love. Although his advisers had suggested other more politically appropriate candidates as suitors for the Archduchess, the Emperor Charles VI let Maria Theresia choose the man she loved.(2)

The imperial marriage took place in the Augustin Church in Vienna on February 12, 1736, only four years before the Emperor died. The 23 year old Archduchess thus became Queen, but as a woman, could not become Emperor. This task befell the Elector-Prince Karl Albrecht of Bavaria, who was crowned Emperor Charles VII of the Roman-German Nations in Frankurt/Main on January 24, 1742.(2)

Immediately following her assumption of power in Vienna, the predators surrounding the young Queen started to salivate at the prospect of tearing Austria apart and claiming as big a piece as they could for themselves. Among them were the Elector Prince Albrecht of Bavaria, King Frederick II of Prussia, and the Habsburg's long time enemy, France.(4)

2/ p. 221-223
4/ p.101

The foreign minister of King Louis XV, André Hercule Cardinal de Fleury, said openly "There are not longer any Habsburgs." The thought that the young ruler could resist the mighty of Europe was so foreign to him, that her resistance never even entered his thoughts. But resist them, she did.(2)

First she entered into an agreement with the Hungarians to whom she granted long sought privileges and rights. Then she met the flower of the Hungarian nobility which had been convened at Pressburg by Count Emmerich Esterhazy, and received on her head the Holy Crown of St. Stephen in a coronation ceremony in the Church of St. Martin. Maria Theresia, Archduchess of Austria, was now Her Apostolic Majesty, Queen of Hungary. After the ceremony, she mounted her horse and rode up the ceremonial Crowning Hill, drew the Sword of St. Stephen from its hilt, and pointing it in the four corners of the empire, swore that she would defend Hungary against all enemies.(2)

However, things were not going too well for the young Queen on the battlefields. The Prussian King had defeated her Austrian forces at Mollwitz in the north, and had entered into an alliance with France, Spain and Bavaria against her. Maria Theresia turned to her Hungarians for help. Wearing the Holy Crown of St. Stephen on her head, she met the Hungarian parliament and appealed for their help in the name of the Kingdom of Hungary, in her own name, and in the name of all their children. What followed was described by Count Johann Palffy, who wrote: "The Hungarian magnates fell to their knees, drew their swords,and exclaimed — Vitam et sanguinem pro majestate vostra." (Our life and blood for Your Majesty). The Hungarian parliament immediatley ordered mobilization, and placed an army of 100,000 men at Her Majesty's disposal.(2)

When the Bavarian Elector-Prince Karl Albrecht marched on Bohemia and had himself proclaimed King of Bohemia, the young Maria Theresia called on her Hungarian troops and marched against Bavaria and France.(2)

However, in order to have a free hand in the west, she decided on a diplomatic attack in the north. She entered into a peace agreement with the King of Prussia in which she gave over to Prussia, her

2/ p. 222-225

Silesian lands. With their Prussian allies no longer involved in the war, the French and Bavarians found themselves at a disadvantage in Bohemia, and retreated back to Bavaria. Maria Theresia entered Prague, and was subsequently crowned Queen of Bohemia in the Church of St. Veits-Dom. As the crown of St. Wenzel was being placed on her head by the Archbishop of Olmutz, Count Jakob Liechtenstein, news arrived of a resounding victory over the Bavarians at Blaunau. At the same time, King George II of England, who had come to the aid of Austria, defeated the French army at Dettingen. Thus within two years of assuming office, and at the tender age of 25, Maria Theresia once again had domain over the lands she had inherited. However, there were still problems to be solved.(2)

Upon the death of the Bavarian Elector-Prince Karl Albrecht who had become Emperor Karl VII at Frankfurt some years earlier, the opportunity to return the Emperor's crown to Austria arose. Maria Theresia arranged a truce with his successor, the Elector-Prince Maximilian III Josef, and got him to endorse the Pragmatic Sanction. And in return for turning over some lands which her Austrian armies had gained from Bavaria, the young Queen succeeded in obtaining the Elector's support for the election of her husband, the Grand Duke Franz Stephen as Emperor Franz I. Not only had she achieved the return of all her inherited lands to the House of Habsburg, but she was able to obtain for her beloved husband the highest and most exalted position in the realm. At the end of September 1745, Maria Theresia accompanied her husband to Frankfurt where the coronation took place. Having herself being crowned Queen of Hungary and of Bohemia, Maria Theresia could now, through the crowning of her husband as Emperor, call herself Empress.(2)

After further attempts by the Prussian King Frederick II, and interference by France, Maria Theresia, with the aid of England's King George II, was able to maintain her position intact, and even got the Prussian King's acceptance of Emperor Franz I as German Roman Emperor. All opposition to the Empress Queen ceased in 1748 by the Treaty of Aix-La-Chapelle, when the Pragmatic Sanction was fully endorsed on an international basis.(2)

2/ p. 226, 227-229

Maria Theresia now had time to undertake some internal reforms, which continued until 1762 and which remained in force until 1848. She effectively organized the administration of her realm into eight departments or commissions, and revamped the taxation system. She also embarked on a series of foreign diplomatic initiatives which were intended to secure the empire. This included, amongst other things, an alliance with France and Russia, against an alliance that the Prussian King Frederick II had engineered with England's King George II. The result was the Seven Years War which broke out in 1756 and which, for the first time since 1477, saw cooperation between the Habsburgs and the Bourbons. The winners of this struggle were neither Prussia nor Austria. Both countries had suffered huge military losses. In the end, which came in 1763, Austria did not achieve the goal of recapturing the Silesian provinces from the Prussians, and Frederick II, greatly weakened and economically brought to his knees, agreed to support Maria Theresia's son, the Archduke Josef, as successor to the Roman Emperor Franz I. France also did not gain much from her participation in this war. Forced to sue for peace by the British, France had to forgo her claims in the Indian Ocean and lost her dominion over New France, the consequences of which changed the face of North America forever.(2)

After the death of her husband in 1765, the Empress-Queen nominated her son Josef as co-regent, and a few months later, had him crowned Roman Emperor.

Her personal life with Franz of Lorraine was an exceedingly happy one. It was a marriage made in Heaven, and it gave the Empress-Queen 16 children. These not only greatly enhanced the happiness the family found together, but also conveniently provided the "Mother of Europe" with the opportunity to further enhance the power and influence of the House of Habsburg through the marriage bed.

The high point of her achievement as a marriage broker was the betrothal of her youngest daughter, Maria Antonia (Marie Antoinette), with the Dauphin of France, later known as King Louis XVI. This union was intended to bind the House of Habsburg with that of the Bourbons, and became the corner-stone for a grand alliance between Austria and France. Unfortunately, as we know

---

2/ p. 227-229, 230

today, both lost their heads on the guillotine during the French revolution, and the Empress-Queen's grandiose plan never did materialize.(2)

On the death of his mother, Josef II became the absolute ruler of the Empire. From the very beginning, he showed that he was more interested in the social well-being of the masses, than in enlarging the power of the nobility or the state. He became known as the "Farmer Emperor", mainly because of his policies which led to the freeing of the farmers from their dependence on the landowners. He also reconfirmed the freedom of all to practice the religion of their choice, and he ended the forced resettlement of Protestants from their homelands as colonizers to far-off lands within the Empire. But the most significant act he initiated, was the abolishment of some 200 monasteries and convents which did not have a functional purpose. Those that were directly involved with the saving of souls, the caring of the sick, or whose main purpose was teaching, were not affected. With the proceeds from the sale of the abolished monasteries and their lands, he established a fund which was used to pay the salaries of priests and chaplains, and the establishment of seminaries for the training of new priests.(2)

These reforms did not please Pope Pius VI, who, in 1781, journeyed to Vienna to intercede with the Emperor. But all this did not change the Emperor's actions. He continued his social reforms by building the first General Hospital in Vienna, and freeing the Jews from their ghettos. It was also the first time that Jews were to receive family names. The reforms brought on a new meaning to citizenship. Freed from their destiny from birth, individuals of all religious persuasions could, for the first time, strive to any position in the realm, strictly on the basis of merit.(2)

However well meant, these many social changes were not always welcomed by the people, particularly in the distant lands and provinces. The changes were sometimes seen as too radical, and the resulting resistances caused Emperor Josef II to unduly react with police force. He eventually became somewhat unpopular and died from severe bronchitis in February 1790.

His brother, Leopold II, who until Josef's death had been Grand Duke of Tuscany, assumed the inheritance and was crowned Emperor

---

2/ p. 239, 250

in Frankfurt/Main on October 9, 1790. He inherited a troubled empire, still not completely healed from the wounds of the social reforms initiated by his brother. Although his reign was to last only two years, he strove, through his interior policies, to stabilize the monarchy. He ensured the continuation of agreements with Hungary, and allowed himself to be crowned King of Hungary in Pressburg and King of Bohemia in Prague, which his brother, for political reasons, did not do. When Leopold II died suddenly in 1792 from chronic appendicitis, he was succeeded by his eldest son, Franz.(4)

At this point, in order to better understand the pressures on the monarchy, we must look at what was happening in France. Socialist movements had been gaining momentum for some time and, in 1789, resulted in the storming of the Bastille. It was the beginning of the French Revolution, which was to last for five years.

King Louis XVI had tried to stop the socialists and failed. His wife, Marie Antoinette, wrote in 1790 to her brother, the Emperor Leopold II, for help for the restoration of the rights and privileges of the Bourbon King. In his answer, Leopold II advised his sister that in his opinion, it was not possible to turn back the developments taking place in France. "I have", he wrote to Marie Antoinette, "a sister, the Queen of France. But the Holy Roman Empire does not have a sister, and Austria does not have a sister. I can only operate in accordance with the wishes of my people, and not in the interest of my family." When France was declared a constitutional monarchy in 1791, its king had no more power and came under the control of the National Assembly. A shadow had fallen over the royal houses of Europe, and Austria, together with Prussia and England, entered into a coalition aimed at revolutionary France.(25)

The reaction in the French National Assembly was to challenge the Emperor Leopold II to reconfirm the Austro-French defence agreement of May 1, 1756 against England and Prussia. The Austrian refusal prompted the National Assembly to force King Louis XVI to declare war on Austria. Only Prussia joined the Austrians, and the war, which the German forces expected to be easy and over in a short time, was to last 21 years.

4/ p. 129
25/ p. 191

It was 1792, and the Emperor Leopold II had just died. His son, the Archduke Francis, born and raised in Florence where his father Leopold II had reigned for 24 years as the Grand Duke of Tuscany before becoming Emperor, came to Vienna. He was 16, and he inherited not only the empire, but a war with France. Unfortunately, the ideas of the revolution were also spreading eastward, and his first efforts to reverse this trend led him into conflict with his Hungarian subjects. He put down their uprisings with severe force, and established a strong police force to ensure their control.

In the meantime, back in France, a young general by the name of Napoleon Bonaparte had seized power, and began to re-establish order out of chaos. He also led most successfully a series of military actions against Austria and her allies, and caused the Emperor Franz II the loss of his outlying possessions — first those along the Rhine, and then those in northern Italy, including Venice. In 1805, as Emperor of France, he let himself be crowned King of Lombardy, defeated the Emperor Franz II, and forced him to renounce his position as Roman Emperor. The Holy Roman Empire created by Charlemagne 1000 years earlier, had come to an end. Franz assumed the title of Franz I, Emperor of Austria, and in an attempt to buy peace, he married his eldest daughter Marie Louise to Napoleon.(25)

Following Napoleon's defeats in Russia, Austria joined Russia and Prussia, and together they defeated Napoleon at Leipzig in 1814. Napoleon was forced to abdicate, and was exiled to Elba. His son by Marie Louise, whom Napoleon had made King of Rome, was recalled to Vienna and became the Duke of Reichstadt. Ostensibly, he was Napoleon II, but he was never to leave Austria.

The reconstruction of Europe was undertaken by the Congress of Vienna which started on September 18, 1814 and was to last until June 9, 1815. For nine months, Vienna bustled with emperors, kings, princes, dukes and diplomats, representing 200 states, cities, dukedoms and principalities. Organized by Austria's illustrious German Foreign Minister Klemens Wenzel Nepomuk Lothar Count von Metternich, and hosted by the Emperor Franz I of Austria, work on Europe's reconstruction began. Lead players were Austria, Prussia, Russia and Great Britian. Charles Maurice Talleyrand represented

25/ p. 196

the defeated France. Among the results achieved at the Congress: Austria received the Tirol, Vorarlberg and Salzburg from Bavaria; Great Britain received Malta, the Cape lands and Ceylon; Switzerland was forever guaranteed her neutrality; and the deposed Empress of France, Marie Louise, was granted the Dukedom of Parma.(24)

The Congress had not yet completed its work when in February 1815, Napoleon escaped from Elba and started his march on Paris, the consequence of which was Waterloo. After the final defeat of Napoleon and his internment at St. Helena, from which he was never to return, Austria, Russia and Prussia entered into a defensive union known as the Holy Alliance. It was a treaty of mutual assistance, aimed at establishing a defensive barrier against revolution and subversion, and it was to provide the Emperor Franz with some 20 years of relative peace.(4)

The period immediately after the Congress was a period of very swift economic expansion and prosperity. The Austrian industrial revolution had started. Foreign industrialists, including Englishmen, Frenchmen, Swiss, Belgians and Germans, came and opened factories, and peasants from the mountains and plains came to work in them. Life in Vienna under the rule of Franz II/I, saw times of defeat and times of glory. All in all, it was a time of prospering, a time of elegance, and a time for weeping and rejoicing. But above all, it was also a time for music.(4)

Haydn who lived from 1732 to 1809, celebrated the defeat of Napoleon at Trafalgar by the British with his "Mass in Time of War", which he performed personally for the Duke of Wellington at Esterhaza. He also wrote the Austrian national anthem "Gott Erhalte", which was to remain the Austrian national anthem for 100 years, and the melody of which, even today, serves as the melody for West Germany's national anthem. Haydn died in Vienna, during Napoleon's occupation in 1809, with a French guard of honour at his door.(4)

Mozart, though he died one year before Franz became Emperor, composed much of his mature work during the time of the Emperor's internship as Grand Duke of Tuscany. His famous opera "The Magic Flute" and his great "Requiem Mass" were composed in 1791.(4)

24/ p. 228-229
4/ p. 137, 139

Beethoven came to Vienna in 1792, the year Franz II was crowned Emperor, and dedicated his Third Symphony to Napoleon. He later withdrew this dedication and the symphony became known as the "Eroica." At the time of the Congress of Vienna, Beethoven performed his one and only opera, "Fidelio", for the congress delegates.(4)

Schubert, although not too financially successful, nor in the best of health, was inspired by the aura of the times to compose his beautiful music, and leave his tantalizing Symphonies and Lieders to humankind forever.(4)

The Emperor Franz I of Austria died on March 2, 1835 at the age of 67, after 43 years as head of Empire. He had married three times and fathered in all 13 children. Of these, his eldest son, Ferdinand, succeeded him as Emperor of Austria, his daughter, Marie Louise, married Napoleon Bonaparte and became Empress of France, and a daughter, Leopoldine, married Dom Pedro I in Rio de Janeiro and became Empress of Brazil. The Emperor Franz I's second oldest surviving son, the Archduke Franz Karl was to become the father of the future Emperor Franz Josef I and great grandfather of the future Emperor Charles I, husband of the Empress Zita.

The Emperor Franz I's oldest son, Ferdinand, who was feeble, epileptic and somewhat mentally arrested, succeeded his father at the insistence of Metternich who believed that with a handicapped emperor on the throne, he, Metternich, would in effect control the Empire.(4)

However, within a few years of Ferdinand's accession, the underground currents of revolutionary activity began to gain strength, and in 1848 broke into open revolt against the House of Habsburg. At the same time the very existence of a multinational state was being threatened by the spirit of nationalism — Lombardy and Venetia for the Italians, Hungary for the Magyars, Bohemia for the Czechs. The resulting unrest and chaos could not be controlled until some time later when Metternich was thrown out, Ferdinand was forced to abdicate, and a new Emperor was proclaimed. The new Emperor was Franz Josef, the son of the Archduke Franz Karl and the Archduchess Sophie of Bavaria. Franz Josef, although only 18, was a youth of great

4/ p. 137, 139, 140, 141

promise with a clear, cool head and a fine appearance. He became Emperor Franz Josef I on December 2, 1848.(4)

Young Franz Josef was a pleasant, happy, warm-hearted boy. He was handsome, well-built, and presentable in every way. He was also intelligent, and saw himself, a Habsburg, chosen Emperor by the Grace of God, as the coming together of all nationalities within his Realm. He was the state within a multinational state, to whom all peoples of the Empire should be loyal. He was Austria, and he strove to maintain the Empire as he had inherited it. He had unfortunately two disadvantages that were to keep him from achieving his goal. Firstly, he lacked the quality of political and military advisers, the incompetence of whom he would soon discover, and secondly, he underestimated the strength of the nationalistic feelings of his multinational subjects.(4)

Franz Josef had the misfortune to live in an age of change notable for the rise of nationalism on the part of the weak, and of empire-building on the part of the strong. He also lived in an age that saw two of the most gifted statesmen that the world has ever seen — Bismarck and Cavour.(4)

Although Franz Josef did not want change, others in Europe did. The Hungarians, prodded by Napoleon III, and led by Lajos Kossuth, were again developing their revolution. When this revolution became a full-scale war of liberation, the Emperor called on his partners in the Holy Alliance for help, and with the help of Czar Nicholas I of Russia, he subdued the insurgents and restored peace.(4)

South of Vienna in northern Italy, strong feelings of nationalism also gnawed at the Empire. Count Cavour, first minister to the Sardinian King Victor Emmanuel, was scheming to turn this nationalism to his master's advantage by uniting all Italy under the Sardinian crown. However, he needed an ally, whom he found in Napoleon III, and then provoked Austria into declaring war. Incompetent military strategy on the part of Austria allowed the Sardinians and the French to join forces. The resulting battle at Solferino in 1859 was a disaster for Austria, and caused Franz Josef to lose Lombardy forever.(4)

4/ p. 141-142, 147, 150-151

In the meantime, the Prussian Foreign Minister, Prince Otto von Bismarck, schemed to drive Austria out of Germany and to unite all the German states and principalities into one unified German Empire. With this goal in mind, Bismarck built up the Prussian military machine into the world's then most modern fighting force, equipping it with a new breech-loading, quick-firing rifle. By 1866, Bismarck was ready to take on Austria which he then skillfully manoeuvered into war. Their two armies met at Koeniggraetz, and when the battle was over, Austria was again defeated. Four years later, Bismarck consolidated his Prussian supremacy in Europe by defeating the French at Sedan in 1870 and bringing down Napoleon III.(4) This humiliation of France was not to be forgotten by the French, and would, in due course, be the motivating factor behind the murder of Crown Prince Rudolf of Habsburg in 1889, making him the "first victim of World War I".

The Habsburg Emperor, having first lost Lombardy and Venetia, and now his German provinces, took his supreme humiliation with outward calm. He immediately started to reorganize his realm. The Hungarians emerged from their acceptance of submission, came forth again with new demands, and Franz Josef could no longer ignore them. Together with Ferenc Deak, Hungary's elder statesman, the Emperor set out to restructure the whole monarchy. By the Hungarian Compromise Agreement of 1867, Franz Josef established the dual monarchy of Austria-Hungary. The Hungarians, as well as the Austrians, now had their own parliament, sharing the person of the Emperor, the army, and a joint foreign ministry for foreign affairs. The arrangement was to last until his death, and was to see Vienna emerge as the most brilliant city in Europe.(4)

Starting in 1857, Vienna's old fortifications were demolished, providing a route for a vast, tree-lined, circular boulevard. It was the Ringstrasse, and it became the setting for a host of imposing build-ings fitting for an Imperial capital. It saw completion of the Vienna Opera House, and the addition of the new Burgtheater, the new University, the Parliament Building, the City Hall, the Palace of Justice, and various imposing museums, hotels, parks and gardens. The Imperial winter palace, the Hofburg, was given a new wing and a huge parade ground called the Heldenplatz (hero's square). Here,

4/ p. 154-158

statues of the Archduke Karl, brother of the Emperor Franz II/I, who had beaten Napoleon at Aspern in 1809, and of Prince Eugene of Savoy who had conquered the Turks in 1716, were erected. And not too far away, across the Ringstrasse, a magnificent statue of the Empress Maria Theresia, completed in 1888, looked down on them both.(4)

However, in the midst of all this glory, undercurrents of tragedy were building up which were soon to engulf all of Europe in a horrendous world war which would spell the end of the Habsburgs as a ruling dynasty.

The turning point in the international process, which was to culminate in the breakout of hostilities in 1914, was the ascendance of German power in Western Europe, and the ascendance of Russian influence in the Balkans. Both these thrusts had profound effects on Austria-Hungary.

The defeat of Austria by Prussia at Koeniggraetz (Sadowa) in 1866, and the defeat of France at Sedan in 1870, consolidated Germanic power and unified Germany into one powerful force on the continent of Europe. It also brought into being in France, a revitalization of socialism which was to spread eastward to Russia and down throughout the Balkans. The unrest caused by this eastern thrust of socialism, set in motion events at Austria-Hungary's back door which culminated in the assassination at Sarajevo, and the declaration of war by Austria-Hungary against Serbia. The fuse lit by these acts, quickly exploded into the pandemic theater of war that was to occupy all of Europe and the world from 1914-1918.

Poorly guided by his advisers, and suffering from old age, the Emperor of Austria, had again let himself be manipulated into acts and actions over which he was to have little control. He was 84 years old when the war broke out, and two years later he was dead. No harder working monarch had ever lived. No one had ever wanted so much to ensure peace for his peoples, yet no one suffered more than did this old man whose entire life saw nothing but the slow disintegration of his Empire, tragedy for his family, and humiliation for his person. It was this state of affairs that the Archduke Charles and the Archduchess Zita inherited when they assumed the throne of Austria-

4/ p. 156, 158

Hungary upon the death of Emperor Franz Josef on November 21, 1916.

CHAPTER 3

ON THE THRONE (1916-1918)

Following the death of the Emperor Franz Josef I, his grand nephew, Charles Franz Josef automatically inherited the throne and became Emperor Charles I. Nevertheless, he was crowned Apostolic King of Hungary in Budapest on December 30, 1916, and the Empress Zita was crowned Queen of Hungary at the same time. Although the young couple would soon be forced to give up their Imperial throne, they never renounced or were forced to give up their Hungarian throne. The Empress Zita, to the day of her death, was still legitimately, Queen of Hungary.(9, 10)

Immediately upon assuming power, the Emperor Charles set about to change the old order and to work for peace. He replaced the old advisers to the Emperor as well as the Chief of the General Staff and the Field Marshall of the Army. He also appointed a new President of Ministers, thereby shaking up the old order and placing himself firmly in command. His goal was to end the unholy war that he had inherited, and to bring peace to all the suffering peoples of his Empire, as well as to those other millions of innocent people who were suffering throughout Europe, the Middle East, and in Africa.(9, 10)

In this endeavour, the Empress Zita not only gave him her whole-hearted support, but played a very major role in the peace initiatives that they launched almost immediately following their assumption of power. It must be noted that the Empress Zita had two brothers, the Princes Sixtus and Xavier of Bourbon-Parma, who were fighting on the side of the Entente, and it was through these men that the Imperial family decided to launch its peace offensive. Furthermore, the time seemed ripe for such a move, for at the same time across the

9/ p. 266-278
10/ p. 120-127

ocean in the United States of America, President Woodrow Wilson had also sent out peace feelers to both the Entente and to the Middle Powers in an attempt to end hostilities in Europe.(9, 10)

Consequently, almost immediately upon the death of the old Emperor, the Empress Zita sent a letter to her brother, Prince Sixtus of Bourbon-Parma, who was serving in the 13th Artillery Regiment of the Belgian Army. The Empress requested him to intercede in Paris on Austria-Hungary's behalf, and to assist her and her husband to work towards the cessation of hostilities and for an honourable peace.(9, 10)

The initiative was further pursued on December 5, 1916, when the Empress's mother, the Duchess Maria Antonia also wrote a letter to her son, Prince Sixtus, telling him she urgently wanted to meet with him for the purpose of discussing the peace initiative.(9, 10)

In preparation for the meeting with his mother, Prince Sixtus, together with his brother Prince Xavier, went to see President Raymond Poincaré in Paris. It was January 23, 1917. The French president was very sympathetic, but nevertheless made it clear to the two Bourbons that in order to achieve peace, certain conditions must first be agreed to by Austria-Hungary and by its German ally. He informed the two princes of these conditions, and then sent them on their way.(9, 10)

On January 29, 1917 the two brothers arrived in Neuchâtel, Switzerland, where they met with their mother. In the course of the meeting, the Duchess Maria Antonia passed on to her two sons, her daughter's concerns and hopes for peace, and delivered to them a letter from her Imperial son-in-law, the Emperor Charles. This letter implored the two princes to assist Austria-Hungary in its quest for peace.(10)

Before parting, the Duchess also expressed her hope that her two sons would soon come to Vienna to discuss steps towards a solution to the war. Prince Sixtus passed on to his mother the terms and conditions for peace which the French President had given to him. They were:

1) The return of Alsace-Lorraine to France.

9/ p. 266-278
10/ p. 120-127

2) The recreation of the Kingdom of Belgium.

3) The recreation of a larger Serbia which would include Albania, and

4) The cessation of Constantinople to Russia.(10)

On February 1, 1917, the two princes returned to Paris via Pianore, where they rested briefly at their old summer home and birthplace of the Empress Zita.(10)

In early February 1917, the Emperor Charles arranged for a second meeting with the Princes Sixtus and Xavier in Neuchâtel. This time it was for the purpose of passing on to them a reply to the President of France, and also to invite them to come to Vienna. The two Princes arrived in Neuchâtel on February 11, 1917, and immediately went to No. 7, rue du Pommier, the home of Monsieur Boy de la Tour.(44) He had been informed of their visit and was to be their host for the next few days. It was to this house that Count Tamas Erdoedy, friend and confidant of the Emperor Charles, secretly made his way from Vienna. He arrived in Neuchâtel on February 21, and following a marked up street map which had been prepared for him in Vienna so as not to have to ask for directions, found his way to the house at No. 7 rue du Pommier where he met with the two Bourbon princes. He passed over to them four documents and immediately returned to Vienna. These were:

1) An unsigned secret memorandum written in French by the Emperor's foreign minister Count Czernin, and manually modified by Emperor Charles. It reaffirmed the solidarity of Austria-Hungary with its allies, that a separate peace with any one member of its allies would be impossible, and that the Emperor would, with all his influence, try to persuade Germany to accept peace,

2) A personal letter from the Empress to her sister Maria Antonia, a nun at the Benedictine convent at Solesmes in France, and

3,4) Two personal letters from the Empress — one to each of her two brothers, Sixtus and Xavier, inviting them to come to Vienna. A half hour's discussion face-to-face, she told them, would be better than a dozen voyages to Switzerland.(9)

10/ p. 126
9/ p. 270-271

The two princes returned to Paris on March 5 and met with President Poincaré. They apprised him of their discussion at Neuchâtel, and showed him the Emperor's secret memorandum. Although the President of France did not read much substance into Count Czernin's memorandum, he did see a glimmer of hope in the Emperor Charles' annotations, and he agreed that the two Bourbon princes should go to Vienna.

The Princes Sixtus and Xavier left France for Vienna on March 19th. Already, circumstances on the Eastern Front were creating conditions favourable to Austria-Hungary. The Russians had asked for peace, and Czar Nicholas II had abdicated on March 15. The fourth condition for peace that had been stipulated by the French president, had now been eliminated.(9)

The journey to Vienna was not an easy one. After all, the war was in its third year, and neutral countries like Switzerland literally crawled with spies, agents, and counter-spies. In order to throw off any pursuers and to minimize the possibility of being identified, the brothers laid false trails wherever they went, and used their many language skills to help blend their identities into those of the local population through which they travelled. They travelled by train and by car, and even on foot, through Switzerland, the valley of the Rhine,and through Liechtenstein. Accompanied by Count Erdoedy, who had joined them in Switzerland, they meandered their way across the border into Austria, and reached Vienna on March 23. It was in the dark of evening that they arrived at Palace Laxenburg, the residence of the Imperial couple in Vienna. They crossed the courtyard, passed numerous guards to whom they offered the appropriate passwords, and entered the palace by a small side door which led directly to the Emperor's apartments. One more door, and they found themselves in the salon of their Imperial sister, the Empress Zita.

Their reunion was very emotional, for they had not seen each other for a long time. They reminisced joyfully, but then quickly came to the purpose of their visit — how to bring about a peaceful and honourable solution to this murderous war. The mission of the two Bourbons was to end the war as quickly as possible and to obtain for France, the lost provinces of Alsace and Lorraine. The mission of the

---

9/ p. 274

1. The Empress Zita.

2. The Habichtsburg in Switzerland.

3. Duke Robert and Duchess Maria Antonia of Bourbon-Parma.

4. The Villa Pianore in Italy.

5. The Palace at Schwarzau.

6. Official wedding portrait.

7. King Charles IV and Queen Zita of Hungary with Crown Prince Otto.

8. The Laxenburg near Vienna.

9. The hunting palace at Eckartsau.

10. The Villa Prangins in Switzerland.

11. The Quinta del Monte on Madeira.

12. The deceased Emperor Charles I.

13. The widowed Empress Zita in 1923.

14. The Château de Ham in Steenockerzeel.

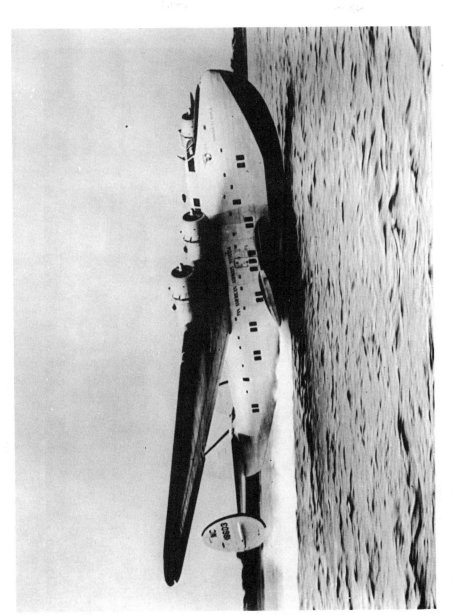

15. Flying the Atlantic.

16. Inside the Boeing clipper.

Imperial couple was not only to end the war, but also to end the terrible suffering being imposed on the people on both sides. They also hoped to make an honourable peace for Austria-Hungary and save as much of the monarchy as they could.(9)

The main thrust of the discussion centered on how pressure could be applied on Austria-Hungary's German ally to return the provinces of Alsace and Lorraine, and to make peace before the two warring sides would not only destroy each other, but all of Europe as well.(9)

The Emperor expressed his belief in a stable, European balance of power, in agreements that would permit all nations and peoples to live together in peace, and added that he was prepared to do everything in his power to achieve these goals.(9)

As head of the House of Lorraine, he was prepared to recommend the return of Alsace-Lorraine to France. In so far as the demands from Russia were concerned, he had no comments, but the demands from Italy were not acceptable to him. And before the discussions were completed, the Emperor sat down at his writing desk and penned in his own handwriting, the first of two "Sixtus letters."

"My dear Sixtus" it began. It made reference to the continuing endurance of the monarchy, with the full cooperation of all its nationalities, and of its military successes in the Balkans. France, he continued, had also shown remarkable evidence of endurance, and he admired, he said, the traditional bravery of its armies, as well as the spirit of sacrifice of its people. It is therefore, he added, even though France and Austria are currently enemies, satisfying to see that France is not separated from Austria by severe animosity. Likewise, he continued, there is much sympathy in the Austrian-Hungarian monarchy for France, and he hoped for the end of a war for which he personally bore no responsibility. Therefore, and in order to establish the sincerity of his precise feelings, he begged Prince Sixtus to advise the President of France, Mr. Poincaré, secretly and unofficially, that he would do his utmost to convince his ally to support the just return of Alsace-Lorraine to France.(24)

He also affirmed his belief that Belgium, together with its African colonies, must again be re-established as a sovereign country, and

9/ p. 276
24/ p. 307

that the sovereignty of Serbia would also be guaranteed. In addition, he guaranteed that Serbia would be given free access to the Adriatic. The current developments in Russia greatly concerned him, he added, but until these are resolved, he hesitated to make any commitments. He closed by requesting to hear the views of France and England in response to the views that he had delivered in this letter, so that, hopefully, a basis for official discussion could be arrived at.(24)

The letter to Prince Sixtus was intended as a generous offering to the Entente, and particularly as the basis for further discussion. Its weakness, however, was that it totally ignored the demands of Italy, which were aimed at Italian territorial expansion at the expense of Austria. Re the discussions themselves, both parties felt that they were very positive, and they jointly believed that they had achieved the real basis for an honourable peace. But who was going to convince the Germans? The two Bourbon princes left Vienna on March 25 and immediatly returned to Paris where they reported their discussions to President Poincaré.

In the meantime, and while discussions were going on in Switzerland, winds of change were sweeping across Europe. The Bolsheviks were taking control of Russia, and the Czar had abdicated. The Russian Revolution was in full swing, and its repercussions were influencing political thought in the Balkans. The Empress Zita and her husband would soon learn that the ideas of socialism born in France and now maturing in Russia, would soon offer to their monarchy a greater threat than they had ever known. Communism, the antithesis to Christianity, had been born.

In France, the government of Aristide Briand fell on March 19, and was replaced by one, ideologically much more to the left of centre. It included Georges Clemenceau, known as "the Tiger", and Alexandre Ribot, who now became President of the Council of Ministers. Whereas Briand and his cabinet had been generally sympathetic to the continuation of the Austro-Hungarian monarchy, the duo Clemenceau-Ribot was against anything that was monarchistic or Catholic. They were left-wing socialists first and foremost, and they hated the Habsburgs even more than they hated the Pope. These were the conditions to which the brothers Sixtus and Xavier returned

---

24/ p. 307

when they left Vienna on March 25 with the highly confidential "Sixtus letter" from the Emperor.

On March 31, Prince Sixtus met again with Raymond Poincaré, and showed him his letter from the Emperor Charles. The President of France viewed the letter as a positive step, and immediately arranged that it be transmitted to King George V. Alexandre Ribot, as head of the French Cabinet of Ministers, was entrusted with this mission. He immediately left for England, and there showed the "Sixtus letter" to David Lloyd George, the British Prime Minister. Although Lloyd George saw in it a way to peace, peace was not Ribot's aim. Together with Clemenceau, he wanted revenge for Sedan through the total destruction of Germany. Furthermore, he saw in the destruction of the Habsburg monarchy, the elimination from power of the last great Catholic dynasty remaining in Europe, — a dynasty which stood as a buffer against the spread and influence of French socialism, to which he and Clemenceau had dedicated their lives. Besides, had not the Habsburgs harboured the French Bourbons at Frohsdorf and the Portuguese Braganzas at Seebenstein in Austria?(9)

Ribot, determined to quell any hopes for peace now played his Ace of Spades. He had recognized the one weakness in the "Sixtus letter" — the fact that no mention was made of Italy's claims — and insisted that the Italians be brought into any peace considerations. As it turned out, David Lloyd George had entered into a secret agreement, dated April 26, 1915, linking England, France and Italy, by which Italy had agreed to switch its support from the Middle Powers to the Entente in return for the promise of territorial gains at the expense of Austria-Hungary.(9)

It must be remembered that on December 5, 1912, Italy had entered into an alliance with Austria-Hungary and Germany, and since the outbreak of hostilities in 1914, had been actively at war with France and England. The price for Italy's betrayal of its allies had been the promise by the Entente to give to Italy the Austrian province of South Tirol up to the Brenner Pass, as well as Austria-Hungary's Adriatic harbour of Trieste and half the Dalmatian coast. These conditions were of course unknown to Austria-Hungary when Italy suddenly

9/ p. 276-277

declared war against its ally on May 23, 1915. It was therefore no wonder that Austria-Hungary was shocked when Italy about-faced and became its enemy.

It must also be remembered that Habsburgs had been Emperors over Italy for many years, and although some of their former Italian possessions had already been lost through wars and social revolution, Italian cultural influence had been strongly felt in Austria's development. Italy's architectural, musical, gastronomical and religious influence had greatly contributed to Austrian culture, and many Italian families of stature had established roots in Vienna, and had participated in the Habsburg Court, in its government, and in its armed forces — especially in the Austro-Hungarian navy which had become the third largest in the world.

Also in religious matters, Austria had much in common with her southern neighbour. His Holiness, Pope Pius X, like many of his predecessors over the past millenium, was a strong supporter of the House of Habsburg. After all, as Emperors of the Holy Roman Empire, Habsburgs had always staunchly defended the See of Rome and the Holy Roman Catholic Faith. And after all, it was Pope Pius X who had blessed this Austrian Habsburg who now was the Emperor Charles I and Italy's enemy, in return "for all that the House of Habsburg had done for the Church of Rome." Furthermore, Pope Pius X had found in the House of Habsburg, champions for his cause — the cause of Roman Catholicism — against the socialist ills of France, which he believed stemmed from the abandonment of Catholic religious practice and from the destruction of the monarchy in France.

It is a fact, too, that the church in those days prior to and during the First World War, was very much against the new wave of socialism that was spreading ever eastward. The Church saw in the Habsburgs champions ready to do battle against their un-Christian foe. Even Angelo Giuseppe Roncalli (1881-1963), Cardinal Patriarch of Venice who later became Pope John XXIII, had served the House of Habsburg. Born near Bergamo in Lombardy, just a few kilometers north-east of Milan, he grew up in an area that had been part of the Habsburg Monarchy for many years. When Angelino Giuseppe

Roncalli joined the priesthood, he served first as a sergeant in the medical corps and later as a lieutenant in the corps of chaplains, on the side of Austria-Hungary.

Meanwhile, back at the Hofburg in Vienna, the Emperor Charles wondered how he might meet with and influence the German Kaiser to accept France's conditions and make peace. However, it was the Empress Zita who hit upon the pretext for such a meeting. She had never met the German Kaiser's wife, Auguste Viktoria, and this would be the excuse for a meeting with the Hohenzollerns, at which they could also bring up the matter of their peace offensive. The Emperor Charles sent a telegram to Kaiser Wilhelm II, suggesting a meeting for the above purpose, and also, "to discuss certain pending matters of state." The meeting took place on April 3, 1917 at Bad Homburg in southern Germany, and was attended not only by the rulers of Germany and Austria-Hungary and their wives, but also by a host of top Government and military leaders from both countries.(10)

While her husband and his generals and advisers were attending to matters of state with the German Kaiser and his entourage of military advisers, generals and other prominent members of the German Court, the Empress Zita took it upon herself to break the ice with the rather distant, unfamiliar, Auguste Viktoria, who stemmed from the House Schleswig-Holstein-Sonderburg-Augustenburg.

From the very beginning, they got along marvelously. The charm of the Empress Zita quickly melted the cold exterior of the German Empress, and the two soon found they had much common ground — particularly the suffering of their peoples and the deep concerns for the terrible slaughters of the young men fighting in this terrible war.

During dinner, the Empress Zita approached the formidable Count von Hindenburg, and challenged him over a recent German air raid on the villa of King Albert I of Belgium, whose wife, the Queen Elizabeth was the Empress Zita's first cousin. "You could have killed her", she told the Count, "but fortunately no one was hurt." "Just imagine", she said to him, "what damage the French could now do to us if they knew of this meeting in Bad Homburg and decided to bomb us." "What damage they could do to our war effort", she added

10/ p. 128

— but then she quickly assured him that the French would never bomb a meeting where two women were in attendance. "After all", she added, "the two German pilots who had bombed the villa of the Belgium King would not have done so had they known that there were ladies inside". The Empress Auguste Viktoria laughed at Count Hindenburg's embarassment, and the two ladies suggested he might have more important things to do than to pass the time with them. To this, the Prussian Field Marshall replied that he had lots of time — after all it was wartime and fighting the war was the job of his generals.(10)

As the meetings progressed, it was evident to the Empress that although Auguste Viktoria and her husband seemed sympathetic to ending the war, their generals would have none of it. After all, they were having considerable successes with their newly launched U-boat offensive, the eastern front was crumbling in their favour, and the Americans had not yet entered the war. Furthermore, Germany had allowed Wladimir Iljitsch Uljanow (later known as Lenin) who was in exile in Switzerland, to pass through Germany to pursue his revolution against the Czar. They reasoned that once Imperial Russia was overthrown, the Bolsheviks would make peace, and the German troops fighting on the eastern front would be freed to fight France and England. The consequences of this assumption were eventually to be regretted not only by Germany, but by most of the western world. And the Empress Zita, and her husband, quickly realized that the German generals were so busy thinking of war that they had no time to think of peace.(10)

When the Empress Zita and her husband left Bad Homburg, they were despondent. They had found their German ally totally unreasonable, and realized only too well that the German generals were not in the mood to end their war — how could they then be expected to make peace and return Alsace-Lorraine back to France? It was then that the Empress Zita and her husband realized that the road to peace, if it existed at all, ran squarely through their own hearts, and they would have to look for it alone. They still hoped that their initiatives through Prince Sixtus would somehow allow reason to triumph over hatred and bring peace back to Europe.

10/ p. 129-130, 133

However, at about this same time, the Italians let it be known through an intentional leak to the German Embassy in Switzerland, that Italy would be prepared to make a separate peace with Austria-Hungary, provided that the Trentino region of the South Tirol were ceded to Italy. This demand, which was considerably less than the demands the Entente had made known through Prince Sixtus, was received with considerable caution by the Austrian Emperor, and he would take no action pending the outcome of Prince Sixtus' mission to Paris.

The Ace of Spades that had been dealt by Alexandre Ribot to David Lloyd George, turned out to be Stanley Sonnino, Italy's very anti-Habsburg Foreign Minister. It was he who had engineered his country's betrayal of Austria-Hungary in 1915, and he was in no mood in 1917 to change his views, or to withdraw his demands.(9)

As it happened, the prime ministers of France, England and Italy then met in the small, French, resort town of Saint-Jean-de-Maurienne in the Savoy to discuss the Austrian peace initiative brought to France by Prince Sixtus. It was April 19, 1917. Since the proposals transmitted by Prince Sixtus affected only France and England, and did not touch upon Italy, their acceptance would have meant that Italy would have to withdraw from its London Accord of 1915. The Italian Prime Minister, however, would have none of this, and in addition to the original promises made to him by France and England, he now enlarged his demands for territorial gains. He now wanted near east and African colonies as well, and this, Ribot and Lloyd George were not prepared to accept. Consequently, Sonnino's stand killed the peace proposals that had been placed on the table. The flicker of light that Prince Sixtus had brought to President Poincaré, had been extinguished by Ribot and Sonnino.(9)

The task of advising Prince Sixtus that the peace mission had failed, was given to David Lloyd George. He, among the three Entente prime ministers was the only one who still had some consideration for Emperor Charles and for Austria-Hungary. He realized full well that the Emperor's peace initiative had been directed at France and England, and that Austria-Hungary could not make peace with Italy on the terms demanded by Sonnino. When Prince Sixtus was advised of the failure of his mission, he realized that his only remaining option was to go back and inform his Imperial brother-in-law of the circumstances leading to the breakdown of the peace discussions. This was done through Count Erdoedy whom he again met in Neuchâtel in late April.

Though exceedingly disappointed on hearing the bad news from Count Erdoedy, the Empress Zita and her husband now saw in Italy's Swiss peace initiative, a remaining faint glimmer of hope. They called upon Count Erdoedy to return one more time to Neuchâtel in order to meet with and again bring back to Vienna, Prince Sixtus of Bourbon-Parma.

Count Erdoedy arrived in Neuchâtel on May 5, and handed to Prince Sixtus two more letters. One was from the Emperor, officially requesting a personal meeting in Vienna, and the second was from the Empress to her brother. "Conditions are changing", she told him. "The Italians are demanding more from you (the Entente) than from us", she said, "Please come."(10)

On May 9, Prince Sixtus together with Count Erdoedy once again arrived in Vienna. It was the 25th birthday of the Empress. The prince spent the night at Count Erdoedy's home in the Landskrongasse, and on the following day the two men again made their way to the Laxenburg Palace.(10)

It was a beautiful spring morning when the Austrian Empress and her husband received her sibling. She welcomed him with open arms, and confessed to him her desires for ending this horrible war. Then, together with the Emperor, they discussed developments in their peace offensive which now appeared to have stalled in its tracks. The demands made by Italy through the Entente were not acceptable to Austria-Hungary. Perhaps, the Imperial couple suggested, France and England could be prevailed upon to make a separate peace with Austria-Hungary, which then hopefully could come to an honourable agreement with Italy. But this also was not to be.(10)

When the Prince left Vienna, he carried with him another letter — the so called "Second Sixtus Letter" — in which the Emperor thanked the Prince for his considerable efforts and assistance. In it, the

---

10/ p. 135

Emperor expressed his great satisfaction that France and England shared with him the basic considerations for peace in Europe, and acknowledged his understanding that France and England did not believe peace was possible without the participation of Italy. However, Italy had now made a separate peace proposal of its own, in which it now apparently renounced its former claims over the Slavic lands along the Adriatic, and demanded only the Italian speaking Tirol. "I have asked for confirmation of this proposal", he added, "and will do nothing until you can determine France's and England's answer to my peace proposal." "The good agreement that the monarchy has been able to reach on so many issues with France and England, he said, convinced him that agreement on the remaining considerations must be possible."(9)

The ball was now in the court of the Entente. Prince Sixtus returned to France and, on May 20, 1917, delivered the Emperor's latest peace proposal to President Poincaré and to Alexandre Ribot. Whereas the President of France was sympathetic, the President of the Council of Ministers was not. The Americans had now entered the war, and whereas the chief of the revolutionary government in Russia, Anatole Kerenski, had asked for peace in February 1917, he now suddenly declared his government in favour of the continuation of the war. Alexandre Ribot, a strong supporter of the socialist movement in Eastern Europe, and a die-hard anti-monarchist, would not go along with the Emperor's peace offensive and chose instead to continue the war. In England, on the other hand, both King George V and David Lloyd George were ready to make peace with Austria-Hungary, and could see the many advantages to the Entente of a separate peace between the Danubian Monarchy and Italy — millions of Austrian-Hungarian soldiers would no longer be enemies of the Entente, Turkey and Bulgaria would be physically cut off from their remaining German ally, the considerable Austrian-Hungarian naval forces in the Adriatic and Mediterranean would be neutralized, and the Russian and Danubian wheat baskets would once again be available to feed the hungry mouths of the French and English people. And what was most evident to the British, was that the combined war machines of France, England and the United States, could be focused directly on the Prussians. Unfortunately, all these advantages could

9/ p. 289-290

not be seen by the duo Ribot-Clemenceau, and the horrible bloodletting that had already taken millions of human lives, was to be inflicted on millions more before the senseless slaughter could be stopped.

In June 1917, Prince Sixtus put aside his diplomatic task, and returned to his regiment in the Belgium army. The fight for peace was lost by the Austrian Emperor. However, the fight for the continuation of the war was won by the German generals. The German Admiral Holtzendorff had unleashed 120 brand new U-boats against England, and forced the Austrian Emperor to allow the German navy to use the Austrian-Hungarian, Adriatic harbours of Triest, Pola and Cattaro. "England will fall within four months", he boasted to the Empress Zita while on a visit to Vienna in early 1917. He accused her at dinner, of being against the U-boat war, as well as against the war itself. The Empress did not deny this, nor did she chastise him for his tactlessness. Instead she told him that she was against war, as was any woman who preferred to see humanity in happiness rather than in pain and hunger. The Admiral shrugged off the Empress Zita's remark, and added that he himself worked best on an empty stomach. The Empress, remarking that he was sitting before an empty dinner plate that had shortly before been filled with food, admonished him by noting that it was easy to make such remarks on a full stomach.(9)

The war continued. And although the Russian front soon saw peace negotiations with the advent of Lenin as leader of the revolutionary armies, and the war in the Balkans and in Italy continued to favour Austria-Hungary, the price at home in sacrifice, suffering and hunger was forever mounting. The inflation of pain was not only being felt by the nations of the Danubian Monarchy, but also by Germans, Frenchmen, Englishmen and Italians, not to mention the numerous nations in the Balkans, the Near East, and in Africa.

In the late summer of 1917, this situation brought about an attempt by the Vatican to reach an agreement of understanding between the warring nations to make peace. Pope Benedikt XV called for an immediate cease-fire from all belligerents, for the freedom of all peoples, and for the renunciation of all claims for war damages and

---

9/ p. 296

costs. He proposed that Germany should withdraw completely from Belgium and from the lands and territories it occupied in France, and that the disagreement between Austria-Hungary and Italy should be left to a plebiscite by the people living in the disputed territories. In addition, Pope Benedikt XV called for an independent Poland.(11)

Although the Middle Powers reacted favourably to the Pope's recommendation, the Entente showed some reservations. The United States of America, whose troops and war materials were now streaming across the Atlantic and whose entrance into the war had now shifted the balance of power in favour of the Entente, vetoed the Pope's proposals. As a result, hopes for peace were again extinguished.

It was not in America's interest to make peace. Her prime objective was to totally destroy German dominance in Europe, and although Austria-Hungary was not its main enemy, she wanted to dissolve the Austrian-Hungarian monarchy so that its many nations could become independent and act as buffer states against any German resurgence in the north, and against the spread of communism from Russia into Eastern Europe. The price for America's foreign policy was to be the end of the Habsburg monarchy.

The last year of the war found the Empress Zita and her husband fighting to keep up morale and preparing for the inevitability of a forced peace, the handwriting for which they could read on the wall. The Emperor sent a memorandum to the German Kaiser in which he outlined in some detail his views of the hopelessness of their situation and the folly of continuing the war. Not only were their military options declining, but the possibility of revolution within the Empire was increasing. Five monarchies had fallen so far in this war — and one of them, Russia's, had been among the strongest in the world. He stressed that the discontent of the people was very evident, especially among his Slavic peoples, and the degree of tension throughout the land had risen to unbearable proportions. He continued to point out the hopelessness of the situation by noting that the U-boat offensive had not achieved its aims and was now greatly counterbalanced by the entrance of the Americans into the war. He cautioned that he expected renewed land offensives by the Entente

11/ p. 178

against which their limited and ever diminishing military power could not win. If the monarchs of the Central Powers are not capable of bringing about peace in the next few months, then our people will do so over our heads, he added. He closed by warning that the inevitable revolutionary wave that is bound to follow, will totally negate all that for which the Kaiser's and his own forces had fought and died for.(9)

In his reply to the Emperor Charles, the German Kaiser let it be known that Germany not only had full confidence in the success of its U-boat offensive, but that they not only hoped for victory, but expected to achieve it. The die was cast. The blind, unrealistic attitude of the Germans, led more by the Prussian military mentality than by the wishes of their Kaiser, condemmed the Central Powers to an inglorious end.(9)

In the Spring and Summer of 1918, German offensives launched against the allied forces in France appeared to be successful. The German Kaiser even had a tall wooden observation tower built on the west front behind the German lines, some 50 kilometers from Paris, so that he could personally watch the German breakthrough which his Generals Ludendorff and Hindenburg had assured him would split the French and English, and force the English back into the sea. Hundreds of thousands of German and allied soldiers were sacrificed at Arras and LaFère, at the Somme and Amiens, and at Armentières and Reims, and on the Marne. However, the continuous arrivals from America, steaming across the Atlantic at the rate of 250,000 men per month, together with guns, tanks, planes and, above all, high morale, were used by Marshall Foch to the greatest advantage. On August 8, 1918, the "black day of the German army", as Ludendorff was later to call it, the allied forces broke through the German lines and forced the German army into a retreat from which it was never to recover.

At the same time that the German war machine was being defeated by Marshall Foch, Germany's allies in the Middle East were also capitulating. In late September, British armies forced the surrender of Turkey, and allied armies operating out of Macedonia forced Bulgaria to a cease-fire.

9/ p. 300-301, 303

In Vienna, the Emperor was still striving to save his monarchy, but the epidemic brushfire of nationalism that had surged through his Empire, fanned by President Wilson's 14 point conditions for a cease-fire, and London's support of national governments in exile, made continuation of the status quo impossible. The rise of nationalism nullified any and all hopes of the Emperor's dream of an Austrian commonwealth of independent nations under the Habsburg crown, similar to what Great Britain was to achieve many years later. The rallying cry of the nationalists, "Im eigenen Haus und unter eigener Oberherschaft (In our own house and under our own rule)", which was to be heard again in the Province of Québec in the 1960's as "Maîtres chez nous", was to become the death knoll of Austrian imperialism.(11)

By the end of the summer, Austria-Hungary's military capacity had bled to death, and its peoples were starving. In Vienna, bread rations were again cut in half, and no matter how hard the Empress and her valiant husband tried, the end had arrived. A cease-fire was arranged and went into effect at 3 p.m. on November 4, 1918. It was the feast day of the Emperor, and a High Mass was celebrated for His Majesty in St. Stephen's Cathedral in Vienna. From the choir, the National Anthem, "Gott Erhalte", composed by Josef Haydn in 1798, was heard for the last time for a Habsburg Emperor in a public place. Many of those attending the mass, and who understood the full significance of what was happening, prayed with tears in their eyes.(10)

The Imperial couple held on for seven more days. They had been deserted by all but a few faithful supporters and servants. In his last function as the Foreign Minister of Austria-Hungary, Count Andrassy advised the victorious Entente that His Majesty is first and foremost concerned, not for his crown and dynasty, but for the means by which the old Empire's various nationalities could best be transformed from their liquidated past to their new independence. The Entente's reply coldly stated that since the member nations of the former Austrian-Hungarian monarchy had decided on self determination, the governments of France, Great Britain and the United States, could not deal on their behalf in such matters with his Imperial and Royal Majesty. In addition, President Wilson congratulated Karl

11/ p. 219
10/ p. 160

Seitz, the president of Austria's National Assembly, on having been freed from the yoke of oppression of the Austrian-Hungarian monarchy.(11)

There now appeared to be no purpose for their Majesties. Furthermore, pressures were being brought to bear on them to abdicate. The Emperor withdrew, with the Empress Zita and his secretary to an anteroom in the Schoenbrunn Palace in Vienna, to consider a document prepared for the Emperor's signature by the provisional government of the new republic.(11)

At first, the Imperial couple hesitated, for they were not sure that the document did not translate into an abdication. This they would never do. Like her husband, the Empress deeply believed that a sovereign ruler could not abdicate. He may be deposed, she said, or his reign may be declared no longer in force; a sovereign may be murdered, but a sovereign could never abdicate. After all, there was still the family. If the Emperor was deposed, there is still his son Otto to consider, and if he too should cease to exist, there were other Habsburgs. No! Abdication was out of the question for the Imperial family, and if because of their stand, the Imperial family would be forced to endure the same fate that had befallen the Czar and his family, and then that would be the will of God.

After much consideration, both the Emperor and the Empress Zita concluded that the document prepared by the Austrian National Assembly, was a renunciation of the business of government, and not an abdication. With this, the Emperor signed the document. It read:

> *Since my ascension to the throne, I have tried incessantly to lead my peoples out of this terrible war, the start for which I have no responsibility.*
>
> *I have never hesitated to maintain constitutional order, and I have opened the way for my peoples to develop their stately independence.*
>
> *I accept in advance whatever decision German Austria will take for its future form of government.*
>
> *The people have, through their representatives, taken over government. I renounce all participation in the business of government.*

11/ p. 269

At the same time I am relieving my government from office.

*May the people of German Austria carry out and strengthen their new
order in harmony and reconciliation. The well being of my
peoples was from the very beginning the aim of my warmest
desires.*

Only inner peace can heal the wounds of war.

Vienna, November 11, 1918
(signed) Charles   (11)

In the days that followed the collapse of their empire, thousands
upon thousands of socialists and disgruntled Viennese blamed the
Emperor, and especially the Empress Zita, for losing the war. They
accused her of being Italian and a traitor, and of selling out Austria-
Hungary to France through her Bourbon brothers and the Sixtus
Affaire. They had forgotten that the Empress also had three brothers
who served on the Austrian side.

Furthermore, as soon as the cease-fire had been signed, the
Hungarian Infantry Regiment No. 69 which had served as the
Emperor's personal guard at Schoenbrunn Palace in Vienna, was
recalled to Budapest. With the Emperor looking on, they marched
off, leaving him and his family virtually unguarded. Anyone of the
many disgruntled Viennese could have walked into Schoenbrunn and
assassinated the Imperial family.

Fortunately, however, when the news of the Emperor's predica-
ment became known at the Military Academy at Wiener-Neustadt, a
group of 20 cadettes, loyal to the crown, immediately came to Vienna
and served the family as personal body guards. The Empress was very
much moved by this expression of loyalty during the harsh times that
had overtaken her family. There were of course a few other close
family associates who remained loyal and stayed with them at
Schoenbrunn. They consisted of a number of ladies in waiting,
adjutants, personal servants, and other employees whose love and
loyalty could not be denied.(10)

However, the political scene in Austria did not allow the Emperor
to remain in Vienna. The Entente Powers neither wanted the
Emperor's participation in any post-war, Austrian government, or

11/ p. 270-271
10/ p. 162-163

even more, his personal presence in the Capital. The Emperor, no longer in power, but certainly still the Emperor, believed that some day he could return to power. He requested a plebiscite of the people as to their preferred form of government. However, even though the Entente Powers insisted on the rights of self-determination for the nations of Europe, they did not accord this democratic right to German Austria. The plebiscite never took place.

Not wishing to leave their homeland, the Imperial family chose instead to withdraw from Vienna and take up residence at the family castle at Eckartsau in the Marchfeld, some 40 kilometers east of Vienna, and not far from today's Czechoslovakian border. It was high time for them to leave, for unrest was growing steadily, and the presence of communist "red guards" everywhere was threatening the life of the Imperial family.(10)

Before leaving Schoenbrunn, the Emperor and his family gathered for the last time in the palace chapel. There they prayed for those who would be left behind, and expressed their hope that God someday would bring them back to Schoenbrunn. They then made their way to the large ceremonial hall of the palace, where all those who would be left behind had gathered. Personal thanks and handshakes were accorded each person in attendance, and although most of those gathered were deeply moved, the Imperial couple impressed their well-wishers with their composure.

They then left the palace, walked down the large outside staircase, and made their way to the automobiles that had gathered in the courtyard to transport them out of Vienna. As they embarked on their journey — it was almost 6 P.M. on the evening of November 12, 1918 — the Empress looked around for the last time and recalled the many happy moments of her youth. She could not help but wonder what hardships would lay ahead.

It had become dark when the Imperial exodus finally left the palace grounds, not through the main gate where a curious crowed had by then gathered, but by a small, unobtrusive, west gate. The entourage then left the city through a series of side streets which lead to the main road to Eckartsau. Accompanying the entourage were 24 infantry bodyguards in military transport carriers. (11)

10/ p. 162-163
11/ p. 272

The Emperor Charles and the Empress Zita, together with four of their children, were in one car. Count Josef Hunyady, adjutant to the Emperor, sat up front with the chauffeur. The one year old Archduke Charles Louis travelled in the arms of his governess, the Countess Therese von Korff Schmising-Kerssenbrock in the second car, together with the Emperor's mother, the Duchess Maria Josefa of Saxony, and Count Ledochowski, who acted as their bodyguard. The remainder of the entourage, consisting of adjutant Emmerich von Schonta, Bishop Seydl (the family's personal chaplain), and the Countesses Bellegarde and Schoenborn, together with a few personal servants, were dispersed among the remaining vehicles.(11)

As they left for Eckartsau, the sound of machine guns firing in the air could be heard over the gardens of Schoenbrunn. The provisional government had that day voted against the monarchy, and German Austria had been declared a republic. After 640 years, two months and 16 days, the House of Habsburg no longer ruled Austria.

11/ p. 272

CHAPTER 4

IN EXILE (1918-1922)

It was late evening on November 12, 1918 when the Emperor Charles, the Empress Zita, and their children arrived at Castle Eckartsau. It was an imposing structure, built and rebuilt over the centuries by its various owners since it was first erected by a nobleman named "Ekkehart", on the banks of the river Au in the year of our Lord 1180. The name "Eckartsau" stems from this humble beginning, and Eckartsau saw over its 738 year existence much history and many masters. In its last 200 years, it had served as a barock hunting lodge for Count Kinsky (1732), was used as a retreat by the Empress Maria Theresia (1760), and again as a hunting lodge by Crown Prince Rudolf (1889) and later by the Archduke Franz Ferdinand before his assassination at Sarajevo (1914). Owned by the family of the Archduke Karl Ludwig, father of Franz Ferdinand and grandfather of the Emperor Charles, it became the property of the Emperor after the death of Franz Ferdinand.(23)

Eckartsau had suffered destruction in many wars, and had each time been re-built and enlarged. It was accessible by drawbridge over a medieval moat. Although a more recent reconstruction under renowned Austrian architect and builder, Lucas von Hildebrandt, and redecoration by some of Austria's greatest Fresco artists (Franz von Roettiers and Daniel Grans) gave it an air of magnificent elegance, it was a cold, almost impossible to heat structure. This, together with the fact that the winter of 1918-1919 was extremely cold in Central Europe, made the Imperial family's stay there very arduous. In addition to subtracting from the creature comforts of the Imperial family by subjecting the castle to constant dampness, the nearby water of the river March must have occasionally reminded the Emperor of Napoleon's sojourn on Elba.(23)

No sooner had the Imperial family settled themselves into their new home, when a delegation arrived from Budapest. It brought to the King of Hungary a document for his signature, similar to the one he had already signed in Vienna, officially renouncing his participation in the business of government in Hungary. Again he signed the document. However, again he did not abdicate. As King of Hungary, he told the delegation, he had made an oath to Almighty God, and only God could deliver him from this oath through death.(10)

Life in Eckartsau soon took on the characteristics of a small court. The Emperor held audiences, kept pace with political developments throughout his old Empire, and took up considerable correspondence with his former contacts in the Entente. But first and foremost, he occupied himself with lobbying for the continued independence of German Austria through contacts in Paris and in London. After all, the government of the newly established republic in Vienna was already planning for the annexation of German Austria with the Republic of Germany.

It soon became very evident to Dr. Karl Renner, the socialist President of Ministers in Vienna, that although the monarchy had been liquidated, Austria still had a sovereign on its soil. Austria was a Republic, he wrote, without republicans. He was afraid that many people, if given the opportunity, might support the return of the monarchy. There was only one solution — the Emperor must leave. Banishment from Austria would be best for the Republic, he thought. The Dynasty must depart.(10)

There were other factors that made such a course of action imperative to the President of Ministers. The "red guard" had become very powerful, and the safety of the Emperor and his family was a state responsibility. The new government had turned the Emperor into a normal citizen, and as such they had the responsibility to protect him.(10)

The possibility of moving his family to a foreign country had also crossed the mind of the Emperor. Not only would it be better for the

---

23/ p. 33-34
10/ p. 172

children, thought the Empress, but her husband would have more freedom of action in his mission to keep Austria independent, and perhaps someday return as its monarch. So, when the President of Ministers came to Eckartsau on January 19, 1919 to sound out the Imperial family on leaving Austria, he found sympathetic ears and general agreement to such a plan. The Emperor, on pretext of a bad cold, however, did not personally see Dr. Renner. He had subordinated this courtesy to his adjutant, Count Ledochowski.

While arrangements were being made with the Government of Switzerland to receive the Imperial family, a British Colonel named Edward Lisle Strutt came to Eckartsau. He was sent by the British Government who had learnt of a plot to assassinate the Emperor, to aid and protect the Imperial family. Colonel Strutt came to Austria from a British regiment in the Balkans, and was an officer and a gentleman in true British fashion. He came from an aristocratic family, was very well educated, and spoke a fluent German. He was greeted by the Emperor at Eckartsau on February 22, 1919.(10)

The Emperor had been advised of the Colonel's coming. He wore for the occasion, his Field Marshall uniform decorated with the Order of the Golden Fleece, the Iron Cross, and the Grand Cross of the Victorian Order of Great Britain. The Empress, dressed in black, wore magnificent pearls, and although looking pale and tired, impressed the British Colonel with her strong sense of character softened by evident charm.

The physical danger to the Imperial family was quickly evident to the Colonel, and he immediately took steps to improve their security. With the help of Colonel Thomas Cunningham of the British military mission in Vienna, he established a bodyguard of British soldiers at Eckartsau. Intelligence reports had placed some 300 "red guards" in the area surrounding Eckartsau, and Colonel Strutt wanted to make sure that the fate that befell the Czar at Ekaterinburg would not be repeated at Eckartsau. It was imperative therefore to move the Imperial family to Switzerland as soon as possible.(10)

By March 23, 1919, all the necessary arrangements for the transfer to Switzerland had been completed, and the Empress Zita had informed her mother, the Duchess Maria Antonia of Bourbon-Parma

10/ p. 174-175, 177

who was living in Wartegg, Switzerland, of her family's impending visit.(10)

There was however, one problem. Dr. Karl Renner, now Chancellor of the Republic, let it be known that he had two reservations: One, that the Emperor was leaving Austria without having abdicated; and two, that he was leaving on his own (without Austrian participation) with a small party of family and followers. The Chancellor therefore insisted that the Imperial train would have to undergo a strict inspection of all baggage and that its Imperial passengers would have to undergo body searches before being allowed to leave. With cool determination, the Colonel advised the Chancellor that if this were the case, the Emperor would not leave Austria, and that the British Intelligence Service in London would be advised that the Austrian government was impeding the departure of the Emperor. Colonel Strutt then drafted a telegram to London conveying this message. On it, he also requested the British Government to immediately resume its blockade of Austria and to secede all aid to the new Austrian republic. He showed the telegram to the Austrian Chancellor and warned him that should the train be held up en route for any reason by Austrian authorities, he would respond with military force. Colonel Strutt added that if anyone threatened to harm, or even so much as touched any one of his Imperial charges, he would personally shoot that person to death on the spot. All this was a bluff by the British Colonel, as revealed later is his memoirs — but it worked. The Austrian Chancellor immediately rescinded his threat and allowed the train and its passengers to proceed unmolested on its journey.(9)

The exodus from Eckartsau took place on Sunday, March 23, 1919. A special train had been assembled at Kopfstetten, the railway point nearest to Eckartsau. It consisted of three passenger cars, two baggage cars, and one open freight car for automobiles. A British escort of one non-commissioned officer and six military police, in addition to Colonel Strutt, were to accompany the family into exile.

In the afternoon of March 23, 1919, two British military transport trucks, each with four British soldiers as guards, transported the Imperial baggage from the castle to Kopfstetten. Among the baggage were two steamer trunks: one contained the personal jewelry of the

10/ p. 177
9/ p. 418

family; the other, the Emperor's private documents. For security, both trunks were identified as the property of one Colonel Edward Lisle Strutt, British Officer of His Majesty's Infantry Regiment. The Colonel also carried on his person for safekeeping, the Empress's six strand pearl necklace that she had received from the Emperor as her wedding present, and a diamond tiara that had once belonged to the Empress Maria Theresia.(10)

At exactly 7:00 p.m., after the Imperial family and its entourage had heard Mass in the Palace chapel, and after which the entourage sang for the last time in Austria to a Habsburg Emperor Josef Haydn's national anthem "Gott Erhalte (God Preserve)", the Imperial party left Eckartsau. In addition to the Emperor Charles, the Empress Zita, and their five children, the party included the Emperor's mother, the Count Ledochowski and Baron Schonta, the family's personal chaplain — Bishop Seydl, the Countesses Bellegarde, Kerssenbrock, and Agnes Schoenborn, and a small number of personal servants, including the Emperor's secretary, a Baron Werkmann. Many tears were shed as the Imperial entourage, protected by a force of British soldiers commanded by Colonel Strutt, left in four automobiles for the railway station at nearby Kopfstetten.(10)

About 2,000 persons had gathered at the railway station to say goodbye to their sovereign. Among these was a group of ex-Austrian soldiers, whose salute the Emperor acknowledged, wearing his Austrian Field Marshall uniform. There was no jubilation among the crowd that watched, only sadness. It was as if they had come to a funeral, for it was the end of an era. Some 700 years had passed since the first Habsburg King was born, and it was only six dozen kilometers north of Eckartsau, at Duernkrut in the Marchfeld, that on August 26, 1278, King Rudolf of Habsburg had defeated King Ottokar of Bohemia and established the dynasty that was to last for over 640 years.(10)

All through the night of March 23-24, 1919 the Imperial train travelled across Austria. By morning it had reached the Swiss border where it stopped at Feldkirch in Austria. There, the Emperor released his Departing Manifesto in which he again stressed his refusal to abdicate. It read:

10/ p. 179

"Whatsoever the German Austrian government, the provisional and constitutional National Assembly has decided, or may at some future time decide over my refusal to abdicate, is for me and my House null and void."(10)

The Empress Zita, longingly looked back over the mountains to her beloved Austria, and wondered how long it would be before she would again return. It was not until 63 years later, in 1982, when the Empress had reached 90 years of age, that her homecoming would again be allowed. Appropriately enough, she then chose to enter Austria again at Feldkirch from where she had left in 1919.(10)

Upon arriving in Switzerland, the train made its way to Staad on Lake Constance, where the Imperial family disembarked. They were met there by the Empress' mother, the Duchess Maria Antonia of Bourbon-Parma, and the family then travelled by motorcade to Castle Wartegg. This castle belonged to the Empress's grandmother on her father's side, the Duchess Louise of Bourbon-Parma, whose father was the last Duke de Berry, who, in turn, had been the son of the last legitimate King of France. Wartegg was a refuge point for many of France's deposed Bourbons. Here lived, since June 1914, the four half-sisters of the Empress Zita. The Empress' mother sought refuge there in December 1918, together with her own children — Isabelle, René, Felix, Louis and Gaetano. The Archduchess Maria Theresia and the Princess Elisabeth of Braganza had also found refuge at Wartegg, and in November 1918 were joined by the Duchess Maria Antonia's brother, Dom Miguel.(10)

Wartegg was an almost unbelievable happening for the Empress Zita. Here, after many years and much pain and hardship, she was once again with her childhood friends. Here, she could relax, and once again enjoy the tenderness and security of family.(10)

The Emperor passed his time following developments in his old monarchy.He did not see himself as an ex-Emperor or ex-King, and viewed himself as a sovereign ruler, still wearing the Crown, but prevented by forces beyond his control, to exercise his Imperial and Royal responsibilities.

The children, too, were not allowed to forget their station, nor their God-given role — especially the Archduke Otto; their education had

10/ p. 177-180, 181-182

been, and was continuing to be, directed towards long-term, future responsibility.(10)

Meanwhile, back in Vienna, on April 3, 1919, the Austrian parliament passed the so-called Habsburg Laws which, lifted the right to rule Austria from all members of the House of Habsburg-Lorraine, banished them from Austria, and confiscated their properties; and made their return contingent on renouncing their membership (in this House) and declaring themselves faithful citizens of the Republic. This law, which the Emperor considered to be most unjust, suddenly plunged the Imperial family into great financial difficulty. Although they did manage to take with them into exile their private jewels and some 7,000 Swiss Francs in cash, a stipend of funds, generated through their properties back home, was suddenly cut off. In order to finance his family's daily needs, the Emperor Charles now had to periodically sell off some of the family jewelry for cash.(10)

While at Wartegg, the Emperor was given an opportunity to greatly improve his finances. A group of former associates visited him there and offered to purchase his shares and interests in various large undertakings that were formerly under Habsburg control. They offered him enormous sums of money for the rights to such actions and interests. There were however to be two conditions: one, that the Emperor would not return to old Austria for at least 25 years; and two, that he would abdicate. The Emperor thanked them for their kind intentions, and informed them that his abdication could not be bought. His principles were not for sale.(10)

On April 18, the British Colonel Strutt was recalled to his Regiment, and took leave of the Emperor and his family. One month later, on May 20, 1919, the Imperial family also took leave from Wartegg, and continued their journey into exile. They moved to Prangins, some 25 kilometers north of Geneva, on Lac Leman. There they were given the use of a villa which, together with a number of smaller associated buildings, provided the family with sufficient space for its own personal needs and also for its associates and servants.(10)

The Villa Prangins was situated on a small hill overlooking the Savoy Alps and Mont-Blanc. It was surrounded by a small park and garden, from which it was accessible by a wide external staircase.

10/ p. 181-183, 184-186

The family rooms were located in the Parterre and the grand living room was used as a reception hall. The most beautiful room was turned into a chapel in which the Imperial family could attend daily mass and receive Holy Communion. The second floor provided living quarters for Bishop Seydl, the family's chaplain, for Colonel Count Ledochowski, and for the Countesses Kerssenbrock and Bellegarde. The Emperor's mother was installed in a comfortable, adjoining building, and the family staff was distributed among the buildings of the small complex.(10)

It was the end of May 1919, and having suffered through the intense cold of the winter at Castle Eckartsau, the Spring air in the mountainsof Switzerland seemed warm by comparison. Life in Switzerland could prove to be endurable.

The family now numbered seven — in addition to the Emperor and the Empress, there were 5 children: the Archduke Otto, age 6; the Archduke Robert, age 4; the Archduke Felix, age 3; and the Archduke Charles Louis, age 1. A sixth child, yet unborn, made the fateful journey from Austria to Switzerland in the womb of the Empress Zita.

The Empress, now heavy with child, prepared for its birth. This took place on September 5, 1919, on which day the Empress presented her husband and the world, with her sixth child, a son — the Archduke Rudolf. When the Emperor advised the Swiss president of his son's birth, he noted that his youngest son had seen his first light of day in the land of origin of the House of Habsburg.(9)

As the year went by, the family quickly settled into its new surroundings. The Emperor held court, received guests, and worked feverishly on his determined project to ensure the independence of German Austria at the coming peace conference at St. Germain-en-Laye. The freedom that the Emperor enjoyed at Prangins allowed him to pursue with greater intensity than what would have been possible at Eckartsau, his various interests and activities. These included not only working for an independent Austria, but also throwing himself into the task of helping the hundreds of thousands of Austrian-Hungarian prisoners of war, who had to be freed and rehabilitated. And he did not only limit his activities for the benefit of German Austrians, but for all Austrians. To him, the idea of nationalism based

10/ p. 186
9/ p. 436

on one language was unacceptable, and this was the basis for his opposition to an "Anschluss" of German Austria to Germany. In the Emperor's view, Austria could never be defined in terms of Germanism. That would be, he believed, an impossibility, because Austria was something altogether different. It was not confined to one language, or to one ancestry. An Austrian he believed, could also be a person whose mother tongue was Slovak, Czech, Croat, Italian, German, Hungarian, or, for that matter, any other European tongue, and he could belong to any culture. The common denominator was to him, a union of Christian peoples whose aim was the betterment of their lot and that of humanity — a sort of commonwealth of nations. High ideals perhaps, but good ones, for they had sustained the Empire for over 640 years. They had to work too, he sincerely believed, for post-war Austria.(9)

The Emperor used his many contacts in Paris, London and Washington to expound his views that independence would work in German Austria's benefit, and that German Austria's "Anschluss" to Germany would not be in the best interest of the Entente, especially France. The Emperor succeeded in his lobby for at the peace treaty at St. Germain-en-Laye on September 10, 1919, "German-Austria" was declared an independent republic, and sometime later, had its name changed to just plain "Austria." This was perhaps, the Emperor's greatest achievement.

The peace treaty that the Entente powers forced on Hungary on June 4, 1920 at Trianon, established conditions in Hungary that were even harsher than those that had been imposed on German Austria. A large part of its eastern territory was ceded to Rumania, and its southern provinces to Yugoslavia. In addition, the vacuum left by the removal of Habsburg order, was quickly filled by the new socialistic order of Bolschevism, and a communist by the name of Bela Kun became President of the Council of Ministers. At the same time, Rumanian soldiers were pouring across their borders into Hungary, creating civil strife and disorder. Curiously, however, counter forces to restore order were found in the old aristocracy. The old Emperor Franz Josef's last admiral, Nikolaus von Horthy, was raising an army at Szeged in southern hungary, and Colonel Anton Lehar, brother to the famous operettist Franz Lehar, organized a force of soldiers in

9/ p. 456

western Hungary who were loyal to the old monarchy. Together, the two forces marched on Budapest, routed Bela Kun, and not only halted the Rumanians, but drove them out of Hungary. Upon the restoration of some semblance of order, the National Assembly in Budapest voted for a constitutional monarchy under the Crown of St. Stephen. However, they did not want a king, and elected Nikolaus von Horthy as their Regent. They had exchanged left wing terrorism for right wing dictatorship, for this is what their Regent in effect became.(10)

However, back at Prangins, the Emperor Charles was still undisputed King of Hungary, and the Empress Zita was his Queen. Although the Entente powers (France, England, Italy) had some reservations against the restoration of a Habsburg monarchy in Hungary, and although there was opposition from the little Entente (Czechoslovakia, Yugoslavia, Rumania) against such a move, the real test was the feeling of the Hungarians themselves. After all, Admiral Horthy himself had let the Emperor know in Prangins that he was his faithful servant. It is no wonder then that the Emperor and his Empress saw hope for a restoration, and themselves as monarchs in Hungary. Unfortunately, however, the Emperor Charles was soon to find out that the Hungarian military had sworn their allegiance to the Regent and not to the Monarch. And, furthermore, Admiral Horthy soon proved to be more interested in maintaining his own position of power, than in giving it to his King.(10)

Nevertheless, the Emperor Charles, against the advice of the Empress, thought that if he personally went to Hungary, the fact of his presence there would ensure overwhelming support for his person. The Hungarians would then accept him as their King, and the Entente oppositions, both big and small, would fall by the wayside. Furthermore, he had taken an oath before God back in 1916, which was also binding on his officers. By virtue of this oath the army would follow and serve him as their King. Thus, he went to Hungary.

The Empress Zita, who had born the Emperor a seventh child — the Archduchess Charlotte — on March 1, 1921, did not go with her husband on this first restoration attempt when he left Prangins on March 24th.

10/ p. 187-188

The Emperor crossed the border into France at an unguarded outpost, proceeded to Strassburg where he caught the Paris express to Vienna. Once in the old Imperial capital, he made his way to his old friend, Count Tamas Erdoedy, in the Landskrongasse, where he spent the night. Late the next evening, the Emperor, accompanied by Count Erdoedy, crossed into Hungary, and made his way to the ancient Austrian-Hungarian city of Steinamanger (now called Szombathely). Once there, they immediately went to the Bishop's palace where they found themselves welcome and in friendly hands. As it turned out, the Bishop had just finished supper and had as his guest, the Minister of Education in Regent Horthy's government — one Prelate Josef Vass. The two churchmen were thunderstruck, but immediately accepted their King. When told of the King's mission, they suggested that the King's old friend and loyal servant, Colonel Baron Lehar, be summoned. Colonel Lehar was commandant of an army contingent in western Hungary and was stationed in the city.(5) (11)

As soon as the Colonel arrived, the five men sat down and discussed the situation. What they needed was a game plan on how to approach the Regent and get him to turn over the reins of government to the King. A military expedition would not be appropriate because it would alarm the little Entente, who then might send in their own troops to defeat the King. No, it had to be done quietly, with no uprising and no bloodshed. But how? The answer, they concluded, was to use the intervention of Count Paul Teleki, the President of the Council of Ministers in the Regent's Government. He was close to Admiral Horthy, and he would know best his inner feelings and how to deal with him. And just coincidentally, Count Teleki happened to be celebrating the Easter Holy days at the home of his friend, Count Sigray, in Ivancz, a small town just 30 kilometers from Szombathely. They decided to send for him.(11)

It was two o'clock in the morning when their messenger knocked at the door of Count Sigray, and asked him and Count Teleki to immediately come to Szombathely on a most urgent matter. Teleki and Sigray thinking that something drastic had happened to Admiral Horthy, immediately complied. When they arrived in Szombathely, the two men were astounded to see the King there, and on being filled

5/ p. 146
11/ p. 309, 311

in on the purpose of his mission, they at first hesitated and then objected to taking part in it. But the King had no intention of abandoning his mission, and Count Teleki was asked to immediately go to Budapest and advise the Regent that the King would be there on the next day to take over government.(11)

It was six o'clock in the morning of that fateful Easter Sunday of March 27, 1921, when Count Teleki left for Budapest to advise Admiral Horthy that the King would shortly arrive in the Hungarian capital. The Emperor Charles, in the meantime, attended Easter Mass in Szombathely, and then, together with Count Sigray and two officers, left for Budapest. They arrived at two o'clock in the afternoon in front of the government buildings and made their way to the Regent's office.(11)

Now for some reason or other, Count Teleki had never arrived in Budapest, and this put the King into an unprecedented situation. He had to ask to see the Regent, rather than the other way around, which would have been what appropriate etiquette required. The fact that Horthy was not aware of the King's presence in Budapest, meant that Count Sigray had to approach Horthy. The King, in the meantime, waited in a small antechamber until Horthy came to him.(11)

When Admiral Horthy finally came to the King, he was very perplexed. "This is most unfortunate", he advised him, "You must immediately return to Switzerland." The King told the Regent that in coming here, he had burnt all his bridges behind him. He was there to take control of government, and he expected the Regent to turn it over. However, this was not to be.(11)

For two hours the King argued with the Regent, reminding him that some years earlier in Vienna when he was the Emperor's Admiral, he had sworn an oath to serve and protect the King. Now the Regent argued, he had taken an oath to serve the National Assembly in Budapest, and his oath, he told the King, superceded the earlier oath. No matter how hard the King tried, he could not persuade the Regent to hand over the reins of government. Horthy made all kinds of excuses, from enraging the little Entente and inviting their invasion, to the possibility of wholesale revolution breaking out within Hungary. Seeing that he was getting nowhere with Horthy, and

11/ p. 312, 313, 314-318, 321

realizing that he did not hold any trump cards in this confrontation, not even a revolver, the King eventually agreed to a status quo of three weeks during which the Regent promised to make preparations and feel out the Entente on its reaction. He promised the King, who had now offered to go back to Szombathely to await the Regent's call, that he would contact him in three weeks, and if everything was satisfactory, invite the King back to Budapest and turn the government over to him.

But as soon as the King left Budapest, Horthy sent a telegram to Colonel Lehar ordering him to immediately, upon the return of the King to Szombathely, escort him out of the country and over the border into Austria. The duo Horthy-Teleki had stabbed the King in the back and left Count Lehar with a devastating choice. It was now obvious that Horthy had no intention ever of turning his government over to the King, and this perception was now very evident to Lehar who advised his friend that the time was not now ripe for the King's repossession of his throne. Horthy's unyielding treachery had prevented the King from assuming his responsibilities, the carrying out of which the King had sworn before God on December 31, 1916.(11)

The King decided to yield this time, but he would neither forget nor give up. He told Colonel Lehar that he would be back when the time was right and changed from his Field Marshall uniform back into civilian clothes before leaving Szombathely. He also removed the highly decorated collar from his jacket, and left both with the Colonel. When Colonel Lehar would next receive instructions to "sew the collar back on", he would know the meaning of the message.(11)

The news of the King's journey into Hungary had by now been leaked to the Entente. So when the King's train, which had been assembled in Szombathely for his return trip to Switzerland, reached the Austrian border town of Frohnleiten, it was boarded by a detachment of British soldiers under the command of a British colonel. They were to provide the King protection, and also ensure that he would go directly to Switzerland.(11)

The train proceeded across Austria, and when it came to Bruck an der Mur in the Steiermark, a group of demonstrators organized by

11/ p. 314-318, 321, 324, 328

the Social-Democratic government in Vienna, halted the train and threatened the Emperor. The British troops quickly disembarked and cocked their rifles. The demonstrators dispersed, and the train continued on its way.(11)

When the train reached the Swiss border, the Emperor's military escort got off, and the train continued on to Buchs where the Empress Zita was waiting anxiously for her husband. It was now late evening, April 6, 1921, and as the sun set and the darkness of evening descended, the curtain fell on the first act of the Emperor's restoration attempt. His spirit rose however, as he took his Empress into his arms and vowed that the collar back at Szombathely would soon be again sewn on his uniform.(11)

Now back in Switzerland, the Emperor soon found out that the attitude of the Swiss government had changed — he was no longer welcome. It seems that Admiral Horthy had requested the Swiss to keep the Emperor under virtual house-arrest. As a consequence, the Swiss Parliament had passed a resolution by which each canton could have a veto as to whether or not the Imperial family could be granted asylum within its borders. In addition, the border provinces, including the cities of Zurich, Bern and Basel, could under no circumstances now give refuge to the Emperor. The Imperial family was thus forced to leave Prangins.(11)

A new place of residence was found for the family at Castle Hertenstein near Lucerne, for even the old ancestral home at Wartegg was no longer accessible to them. The family moved to Hertenstein, and it was there that the Emperor celebrated his 34th birthday on August 17, 1921. No one realized that this would be his last.(11)

During a conversation with one of his wartime ministers who had come to visit him, the Emperor remarked:

> *"I have been once again in Hungary, and I shall return a second time, a third time, and a tenth time, and I shall try again and again to regain my proper place at its helm, so that I can forge a strong Danubian federation. If I should not be able to achieve this goal, then a dismal future lies ahead for all these nations, since then, Germany will once again rise to dominate Europe, and the Soviets will threaten European civilization. And between these*

11/ p. 328, 329-330

> *two millstones, the small peoples in the Danubian plain will be*
> *enslaved and ground to dust.*"(11)

What gave this man the foresight to correctly prophesy the future as we have witnessed it since then? God? It is a pity that no one listened.

Thus, before even having settled in at Hertenstein, the Emperor Charles already began to plan his second restoration attempt. This was to take place in October 1921, and for this expedition he planned and organized every detail in advance. Nothing must be left to chance, he said. There was too much at stake.

In the meantime, back in Budapest, Admiral Horthy was consolidating his position and power. He had made himself virtually a dictator, and surrounded himself only with men he could trust. Anyone with the slightest sympathy for the Emperor was dismissed from his Cabinet. There was to be no opposition. In addition, the militia stationed in western Hungary and considered loyal to the Emperor, was recalled to the interior. It was thus, that the commander (Lehar) of the Royal Osztenburger Regiment, stationed in Szombathely, received orders to relocate his regiment to Budapest.

On October 13, 1921, a courier arrived at Hertenstein with the news of Horthy's latest moves, and the request that the Emperor should come immediately to Hungary, otherwise, it would be too late, the courier advised. It was time to sew the collar back on the uniform.

The Emperor immediately launched a plan that he had worked out beforehand. He was going to re-enter Hungary, but this time by aircraft, and the Empress let it be known that she was not going to let him go alone. Her responsibility as wife, she said, was higher than that as mother. The children would be left under the protection of their grand aunt Maria Theresia and the Countess Kerssenbrock.(10)

The eventful flight was to leave Switzerland on October 20, 1921. The Emperor had arranged to rent a Junkers transport aircraft from a Swiss airline company, and for the services of a German pilot familiar with the aircraft. When later asked why he undertook to fly such a dangerous mission, the German pilot, Wilhelm Zimmerman, said he was made an offer he could not refuse — namely 20,000 Swiss Francs. Accompanying the Emperor and his wife, were three other

---

11/ p. 329-330

passengers: two of Hungary's best aviators, Alexander Alexay and Oskar Fekete-Farkas, whose mission it had been to select the take-off and landing airports; and the Emperor's personal adjutant, Aladar von Boroviczeny.(10)

The aircraft, bearing the Swiss registration letters "59-CH", was a six-place monoplane with wicker seats. It was powered by a single engine in its nose, with the pilot peering through a raised windshield at the front of the cabin. Needless to say, when the engine was started, there was a lot of vibration and a lot of noise to which the Empress had not been accustomed. The plane took off from the grassy runway of the Duebendorf Airport in Switzerland at 11 o'clock in the morning. The field had just emerged from under a cloud of fog, and as the aircraft gained altitude, the weather suddenly cleared. The pilot headed at 3,500 meters altitude towards Austria.(10)

It was the Empress' first time in an aircraft and the altitude, vibration and noise made her somewhat ill at ease. Furthermore, she was in the fourth month of her eighth pregnancy. As she looked down at the checkered fields in her beloved Austria, she could not help but recall her happy childhood. Her life passed before her as she continued to watch the passing landscape below, oblivious to the uncomfortableness in her body brought on by the rocking of the aircraft and her pregnancy. Her will, however, determined her stamina, for she was happy to be with her husband on this day of ordeal.(10)

And then she saw below her the old Imperial City of Vienna. How small everything appeared. The Danube, its tributary the Wien, the railway yards, the inner city with its St. Stephen Cathedral, the magnificent Ringstrasse, the Belvedere and Schoenbrunn, and even the Laxenburg. It was all there now, as in the past, and as the urban panorama continued to pass she felt a tear in her eye, which she quickly dispersed as the Emperor smiled at her.(10)

And then, they came to the Hungarian border and on to the old Austrian-Hungarian city of Oedenburg (now Sopron). There, the pilot chose a suitable landing field, a stubby field which belonged to Count Josef Cziráky. As the aircraft rolled to a stop, a hoard of townspeople gathered in excitement at the strange happening in their midst. It was 24 minutes after 4 o'clock in the afternoon. The flight

10/ p. 196, 198-199, 201

had taken almost five and one half hours, and the passengers were anxious to get out of their confined cabin and once again set foot on solid ground — especially the Empress Zita.(10)

A messenger was immediately dispatched to Count Cziráky, who was celebrating the Baptism of his son, and had among his guests, Count Julius Andrassy, a loyal servant of the King, and during the war years, his Foreign Minister. When advised of the Royal landing, Count Andrassy felt as if he had been struck by lightning. He could not believe that his King had just come from Heaven. He immediately declared his services at the disposal of the King. Count Andrassy and the Royal party then motored to Sopron where they met with Stephan Rakovszky, the former Parliamentary President, and with Anton Lehar. The Emperor immediately established a provisionary government in which he appointed Rakovszky President of Ministers, Andrassy as his Foreign Minister, and Lehar as Minister of Defence. General Paul Hegedues, who was military commander of the garrison in Sopron, also swore allegiance to the King and was given command of his troops. Within 48 hours Hegedues was to prove himself a traitor.(10)

On October 23, 1921, a military expedition composed of some 2,000 soldiers who had sworn allegiance to the King, headed for Budapest by train, under the command of Hegedues. In attendance in a private compartment were the King and Queen of Hungary. At their departure, the local populations of Sopron, Raab, and Szombathely all voiced their support for Their Majesties. Garlands of flowers were attached to the train as it headed out of Sopron on its mission. Admiral Horthy, having learnt of the King's expedition, took stern countermeasures and had the railway tracks torn up outside Budapest. The train therefore could not proceed beyond Kelenfoeld, a suburb of the city.(10)

It was Sunday, and a field mass, attended by the King and Queen, was celebrated. Candles burnt at the altar, hastily erected among the railway tracks. The King and Queen knelt on the stony road bed, and took Holy Communion. In the meantime, further down the track in the direction of Budapest, fighting had already broken out. Horthy's troops were attacking the King. Under the pretext of reconnoitering

10/ p. 201

the front, General Hegedues left the King and made his way instead to see Horthy. He switched his allegiance to the Regent, and entered with him into a plan to deceive the King. When he returned to the King's ranks, Hegedues told the King that he had arranged a cease-fire with Horthy's troops, which was to last until the next morning, at 8:00 a.m. It would give the Loyalist forces a chance to rest and await reinforcements from Sopron. The King reluctantly agreed, and then used the cease fire to visit his frontline troops. Together with the Queen at his side, and under a white flag, they visited the front, encouraging the soldiers and comforting the wounded. There were still many hours left before the cease-fire was to come to an end. However, during the night, Horthy's forces had surreptitiously set up their positions on the high ground around the battlefield, and then at break of day, with still a few hours to go before the cease-fire was to end, Horthy's forces attacked. They overran the unprepared Loyalists, and the King was forced to retreat. The battle had been lost.(10)

Their Majesties sought refuge in the home of Count Esterhazy at Castle Totis. It was now October 24, and it was the first night since leaving Switzerland that the Royal Couple again obtained a full night's sleep. On the next day, they were driven to Tihanyi on Lake Balaton, where they were given refuge in a Benedictine monastery. There they remained until the Entente powers came to a decision as to what to do with their Royal charges. Horthy wanted them out of Hungary, and Switzerland declined to take them back. Neither France nor Spain would accept them, and Austria had long ago turned its back on its Imperial Habsburgs. Only Great Britian showed concern, and on October 26, 1921, its Parliament unanimously passed a resolution to help get the Habsburgs out of Hungary and into a safe place of exile.(10)

Now it just so happened that there was at that time a British warship in the Black Sea. It was a cruiser, the HMS Cardiff, and it would be used to transport the Emperor and his Empress to safety. But they first had to be brought to a place where they could board the warship. So on October 31, the Imperial couple were transported in a military transport vehicle, accompanied by three officers representing the Entente, from Tihanyi to the local railway station, and from there by special train to the city of Baja on the Danube. There

10/ p. 201-203, 204-205

they boarded the British monitor, HMS Glowworm, which took them down the Danube, to the Black Sea. At Salina, they were transferred to the British warship which was to take the Emperor forever away from Europe.(11)

The Empress Zita and her husband were guests of the British navy for almost three weeks. During all this time, as they steamed through the Bosphorus and Dardanelles into and across the Mediterranean, they were not told of, nor had they any idea of, their destination. Nor did they have any news of their children whom they had left many weeks before at Hertenstein, and who since had been taken by their great-aunt the Archiduchess Maria Theresia and the Countess Kerssenbrock to live at Wartegg with the Empress' mother, the Duchess Maria Antonia. It was not until the warship docked at Funchal, on Madeira, that the exiles knew their final destination, and it was there that they first learnt of the well-being of their children. It was still some time, however, before they could all be reunited.(10)

It was three o'clock in the afternoon on November 19, 1921, when the British warship that had carried the Emperor and Empress of Austria from the Black Sea to the Portugese Island of Madeira, dropped anchor in the harbour at Funchal. The population of the capital city on this relatively poor island in the middle of the Atlantic, some 2,000 kilometers off the coast of Morocco, had been made aware of their guests, and they turned out in great numbers to greet them. A small delegation of residents headed by its mayor, went out in a small boat to welcome the Imperial couple. As he was not in accord with the British captain who had planned to bring his charges to shore, the mayor insisted that this was now his function. As a result, the Empress and her husband were rowed ashore in a large fishing craft, and disembarked at the city's wharf to the jubilant cries and applause of the residents. Their smiling faces assured the Empress that they were at least in friendly hands, and this was confirmed by the local priest who added his welcome and blessing. Then, after almost three weeks at sea, they were taken to the Villa Victoria, a converted hotel, which became a very comfortable home. There they were allowed to stay and rest, and gather together their disrupted lives.(10)

10/ p. 208-209

After a few days of rest, the Emperor and Empress received the British Consul of Madeira who gave them a message, offering the Imperial couple the return of confiscated properties and a generous stipend from the United Kingdom, provided that the Emperor abdicate. His Majesty answered the Consul that the Emperor's crown could not be bought.(10)

Shortly thereafter, Their Majesties learnt that their six year old son Robert, who was still in Wartegg, was suffering from appendicitis and would have to undergo surgery. Empress Zita immediately undertook preparations for a journey to Switzerland, to be with her young son. At the same time she could then bring back to Madeira all her children who had been left at Wartegg with her mother. Count Hunyady who had been with the Imperial couple since they left Hungary after their last restoration attempt, moved Heaven and Hell and managed to obtain the necessary passport for Her Majesty. The Emperor, however, had to remain in Madeira. It was on December 9th that the Empress received the necessary passport. It had been made out in the name of the Countess of Lusace, and showed her residence as Lucca, Italy. She spent Christmas 1921 with her husband and then set out on the first ship for the continent.(10)

When the Empress arrived in Zurich on January 12, 1922, she went immediately to the Paracelsus Hospital where her son had successfully undergone his operation. She was also advised by the Swiss authorities that she had been allowed only a 14-day stay, and she was forbidden to move around Switzerland, not even to Wartegg which had been declared "out of bounds." Also, she was constantly watched by the police, which may have been for her own safety as well as to ensure the Swiss authorities that she would leave.(10) The Empress was allowed to live in the Hospital, and was given a suite of four rooms. It was here that her aunt, the Archduchess Maria Theresia, brought the children for their long awaited reunion with their mother. Unfortunately, however, fate would not allow them to leave Switzerland together.(10)

There was also another matter to attend to before leaving Zurich. The Imperial family's financial situation had descended to a record low. An international conference of foreign ministers was supposed

10/ p. 209-210, 212

to arrange some means of financial support for the new residents of Madeira. But now that the family was safe and far away in exile, all participants quickly forgot about their pledge for aid. Not one cent was collected for the support of the Imperial Family.

The Empress thus had to rely on the remaining family jewelry which had been left in the care of one Baron Bruno Steiner, a one-time financial adviser to the Emperor. This included the Order of the Golden Fleece, the Housecrown, a Rose necklace, a very valuable brooch, and a pearl necklace that had belonged to the Empress Maria Theresia. In addition, there was a Florentine diamond ring that belonged to the Emperor, and the Borso Bible of Crivelli that had been in the Family's possession for many years. But the Baron was nowhere to be found.(10)

In the short remaining time at her disposal before being forced to leave Switzerland, the Empress searched far and wide for the elusive Baron. But neither he nor the family treasures could be found. They disappeared forever, although the elusive Steiner turned up many years later in Germany, despondent and a pauper, and died without ever revealing the fate of the Imperial treasures that had been entrusted to him.(10)

The Empress left Zurich on January 21, 1922, and made her way across France to Spain, where she stayed as a guest for a few days at the Court of King Alfonso XIII. It was there that the children, in the company of the Countess Kerssenbrock, joined their mother. Then, on February 2nd, they all returned to Madeira. When they arrived at Funchal, the family celebrated its reunion by attending Mass and thanking God for the good news that they were again together. They also found some bad news. Since the Empress had left Madeira for Switzerland on December 9th, the Emperor appeared to have aged considerably.(10)

With their financial resources now extremely diminished, the first task the Imperial family undertook was to find cheaper accommodation. The Villa Victoria, although sufficiently spacious and comfortable, proved to be beyond their means. Through the generosity of a rather well-to-do Portugese resident of Funchal, the Imperial family was given the use of the Villa Quinta del Monte. It was, as its name

10/ p. 213-214

implied, situated high on the side of a mountain, overlooking Funchal and the sea. Unfortunately however, it was never intended as a winter residence, so when the family moved into it in mid-February, they found it very cold and damp in comparison to the Villa Victoria in the town below. Furthermore, it had no electricity, no hot water, and only one toilett facility. Access to and from the Villa Quinta was very difficult. To reach it, they had to make use of a large, winding mountain road. Furthermore, they were forced to negotiate the climb on foot, since they had no other means of transport. There was, however, a funicular or cable car which ran occasionaly but required a fare to be paid in each direction. It was therefore used only in emergencies.(10)

The view from the Villa Quinta del Monte, however, was magnificent, and there was lots of firewood for heating and cooking. However, there was not much with which to fill the pots, and there were many mouths to feed. The family now consisted of the Emperor, the Empress, who again was pregnant and in her fifth month, and seven children — Otto 9, Adelhaid 8, Robert 7, Felix 6, Charles Louis 4, Rudolf 3, and the baby Charlotte who was already one year old. In addition, there was the Empress's aunt, the Archduchess Maria Theresia, and the Countesses Mensdorff and Kerssenbrock who looked after the children with the assistance of one Ottilie Reuter (now Stern). They were helped by a small contingent of long-term, loyal employees who had dedicated their lives to the service of the family, and more often than not, did not receive any compensation for their services other than the family's sincerest thanks and appreciation. They included Franziska Kral who had served the Empress as midwife at the births of her seven children, the old chauffeurs Gregoric and Galovics, a Mrs. Hubalek who had served the family for many years, a servant girl named Neti, and Mrs. Gregoric, the chauffeur's wife who was the cook and whose job it was to thin the soup and to create appetizing meals from whatever was available. Meat, because of its cost, was very scarce, and she therefore had to get by with fresh eggs, lots of vegetables, and farinaceous dishes of many kinds. Fish, of course, was readily available and relatively cheap, and became the staple diet of the family and its entourage who were all now crowded into the Quinta, one room of which had been converted into a chapel.(9)

The worst about their new home, in addition to being too small, was that it was continually cold and damp, so much so that mildew seemed to grow everywhere. The Emperor, a great believer in the outdoors, had taken up daily outings into the surrounding country-side. On one of these outings, accompanied by his two eldest children, he caught a chill. He had decided to walk down the mountain to Funchal to buy a present for young Charles Louis, whose birthday was on the following day, and, as it was usually much warmer down in the village, he had dressed lightly and did not wear a coat.(10)

The weather in Funchal was exceptionally cold and damp that day, and by the time they returned to the Quinta, the Emperor had the symptoms of a bad cold. By late that evening he developed a cough and a fever. By the middle of March, the cold had developed into major influenza, and the village doctor was summoned. He came, and immediately called a second doctor. The two concluded that the Emperor had caught pneumonia, and that one of his lungs was affected. Within a short time his condition became worse — the second half of his lung had also become infected. The treatment for such a malady in those days was very ineffective, and His Majesty grew weaker day by day. The Empress now became very alarmed. Was it possible, she thought in horror, that the Emperor might die? After all, he was only 34 years old, and his eighth child was not due until June. Surely God would not take him from her now, she thought. How could He have taken them to such heights, and now abandon them in despair. This last Emperor, this last Habsburg, whose ancestors ruled over an Empire on which the sun never set. Would he now have to die a pauper? The Empress begged for his recovery and prayed for his salvation, and in the end resolved herself to His Will.(10)

It was the end of March. A priest was called to say Mass, and the 9 year old Otto was allowed to see his father. The other children were not privy to their father's grave illness and were sent to play outside. The Emperor, whose body was in great pain but whose spirit was high, told his eldest son he was called so that he might also know

9/ p. 518-519
10/ p. 215

some day, how to behave as a Catholic and as an Emperor. God, when you meet Him, he told him, does not expect a report full of triumphs — only the knowledge that one must always do his/her best for what one believes.(11)

On the morning of April 1, 1922, the Emperor's breathing became heavy and irregular. He received the Last Sacrament, made his last confession, and for the last time, received Holy Communion. A few minutes later, it was 12:23 p.m., he died holding a crucifix in his hands. That evening, the Countess Kerssenbrock assembled the servants and instructed them that from then on, they were to address the young Otto, as "Your Majesty."(10)

That night, at the hands of the local undertaker, the body was embalmed and exposed in the chapel of the Quinta. At 12 o'clock midnight of the second day, a Mass for the dead was recited by the local Bishop. On the third day, two doctors came and removed the heart from its body. It too was conserved and placed in an urn. On the fourth day, the Emperor's body, dressed in his field uniform, his shoulders covered with a white lace soutane, was exposed in a room of the Quinta. Many people from the village — the mayor, various officials and representatives, as well as many ordinary people from all walks of life — came to pay their last respects to this great man whom they had hardly known but about whom they had heard so much. They wanted to see him and touch his hands, as if he were a saint. All afternoon this adoration continued, with the family solemnly in attendance. The Empress did not cry. She did not, through any of her ordeal, ever lose her composure. She again showed, by her example to her grieving children, to her faithful associates and servants, and above all to the many people who came to pay their last respects, that she was truly an Empress. Her outward behaviour was impeccably correct, just as the Emperor would have wanted her to be. Within her heart, however, the gnawing and sorrow continued. What will I do without him, she thought to herself over and over again — and she prayed and accepted God's Will, as she had been taught to do ever since her childhood. Her faith strengthened her and supported her now. Her future was now in His hands, for only He knew why this was all happening to them, even though she did not.(10)

10/ p. 215-216, 219-233
11/ p. 353

On the fifth day following the death of the Emperor, the body was placed in a simple coffin and taken to the Church of Nossa Senhora del Monte near the Quinta. Heading the procession were the assembled clergy, including Father Zsambóki who had administered the last rites. Then came the coffin, transported on a sort of low-slung, two-wheeled hand wagon, something akin to a wheelbarrow with two wheels. It was supported and guided on its somber journey by six pallbearers — three on each side. They were the teacher Dittrich, the two chauffeurs Gregorić and Golovićs, and three residents of Funchal — a man by the name of Wagner who originally came from Austria and became a business man there, a Count Almeida, and the Count's brother-in-law whose son owned the Quinta. Immediately behind the coffin, walked the Empress Zita with her eldest son, the young Emperor Otto, then the Archduchess Maria Theresia with the Archduchess Adelhaid and the Archduke Robert, and then the Countesses Mensdorff and Kerssenbrock with the youngest children — the Archdukes Felix, Rudolf and Charles Louis, and the Archduchess Charlotte. They, in turn, were followed by the family's devoted servants, each carrying wreaths of flowers.(9)

Upon reaching Funchal, where it seemed the whole population had come out to watch and pay their last respects, the procession entered the local church of Nossa Senhora del Monte where a crypt had been prepared for the Emperor. Before commending the body to eternal rest the coffin was covered with the old Austrian-Hungarian flag, and then placed into its final resting place. Many flowers had arrived to adorn the church, and to honour the Emperor. One of the many wreaths bore a pennant with a Portugese inscription, reading "To the Martyr King."(9, 10)

9/ p. 519-520
10/ p. 219-220

CHAPTER 5

RETURN TO EUROPE (1922-1940)

On the morning of her husband's death, the Empress Zita had worn a soft, pink-coloured dress. It was the last time, her eldest son remarked many years later, that he saw his mother in colour, for ever since that eventful day on April 1, 1922, she was to wear nothing but black.(9)

"The King is dead, long live the King" is an old English expression that has become a traditional saying when a monarch dies. And so the Empress too took it upon herself to put the past behind her and to think of the future. All her strength and priorities would now be directed at the education of her children, and particularly towards the preparation of the Emperor Otto for his eventual hoped for, return to the Habsburg throne. Yes the Emperor had died, but his soul lived on, and it was the Empress Zita's determined belief that a time would come when again the nations of the old Danubian monarchy would call out to a Habsburg, and for this eventuality, the young Emperor had to be prepared.(10)

In addition to preparing for the future, the Empress also had to manage the present. She was in the seventh month of her eighth pregnancy, and she was determined to put her act together as quickly as possible. She could not remain at the Quinta del Monte — the house was not satisfactory as a winter residence, and the educational facilities for her children's growth and development were very limited. She needed to go to a place that promised security to her family. And with the Emperor Charles now dead and buried, the Great Entente could certainly no longer object to the Empress and her children now leaving exile. While the chancelleries of Europe pondered anew what they should now do with Austria-Hungary's first family, the Empress remembered her husband saying to her that if he died, she and the children could count on the King of Spain. After all, the Empress reasoned, Alphonso XIII was distantly related to her family and as a Bourbon of Habsburg ancestry, he surely would be willing and able to receive them.(5)

However, in order for this to happen, the Great Entente, (England, France, Italy) would first have to be in agreement. Some countries in Europe, and particularly the Little Entente (Czechoslovakia, Rumania and Yugoslavia) became particularly nervous at the thought of having a young Habsburg (the Archduke Otto) and his mother back in Europe, and objected to any change in the family's status quo. However, the fact that the Emperor Charles was no more, and since the King of Spain had agreed to host the Imperial family, permission to leave Madeira was granted.(5)

A Spanish ship, the "Infanta Isabel", en route to Cadiz, stopped in Funchal in May, and on the 19th day of that month of the year 1922, the Empress and her entourage left Madeira. In a way, it was difficult for Her Majesty to leave Funchal for she was also leaving behind her beloved husband.(5)

On May 21, the ship dropped anchor at Cadiz, where the travellers boarded the Seville Express to Madrid. The train sped northward over the plains of Andalusia, through the Murillo country to Cordoba, and then on to Guadalquivir. The train crossed the sheep pastures of La Mancha, and sped to the steel city of Toledo where El Greco had lived and worked almost three hundred years earlier. And then, in a few more hours, they came to Madrid. The King and his wife, the British-born Queen Victoria Eugenia, met them at the station. They were taken to the old Palace of El Pardo, which had been built by the Habsburg Holy Roman Emperor Charles V in the sixteenth centry, and which was put in readiness for the family of Emperor Charles I of Austria by the King of Spain, Alphonso XIII.(5)

The Imperial family had barely settled in at the Palace, when the Empress went into labour. In a large room, where Cortez had reported accounts of his discoveries of Gold in South America to his Habsburg King, a beautiful Habsburg Archduchess was born into the world. It

---

5/ p. 271-273

was May 31, 1922, exactly 60 days after the death of her father on Madeira.

With King Alphonso XIII as godfather, and the King's mother, Maria Christina as godmother, the new Habsburg Archduchess was christened. She was baptized Elisabeth Charlotte Alphonse Christine Therese Antonia Josepha Roberta Franciska Isabella Pia Marco d'Aviano, and Omnes Sancti. Fortunately, she had the strength to bear all these names, for God had given her eight and one half pounds at birth.(9)

With the birth behind her, the Empress Zita now had time to reflect on her present and on her future. Much had happened to her during her short life; rising to a throne at 24, she became an exile at 27, and a widow at 30. The greater part of her expected life span still lay ahead, and her future now centered around her children. She must provide them with the environment and the opportunity for growth, and she was not sure that El Pardo was the answer. Although King Alphonso and Queen Victoria Eugenia were most gracious and attentive to her needs, the Empress sensed that all was not well at the Palacio Real, the royal residence. The British-born Queen had shown great difficulty in adapting to the Spanish Court. Not only was the torrid temperature of Madrid hostile to her, but the rise of socialism on the Iberian peninsula which had already taken the lives of the Portugese King Dom Carlos and his son Louis Philippe, so affected the Queen that she dared not venture outside the palace any more. Internally in the Royal household, she had brought to Spain the dreaded dynastic ill of Haemophilia. This affliction, attacking only male descendants, but seemingly passed on through the female line, was characterized by profuse and uncontrollable bleeding of the slightest wound. Of the four boys that Queen Victoria Eugenia bore the King, three were afflicted with this disease. This fact caused great stress in the Royal household, and together with the Queen's immense difficulties in adjusting to the Spanish court, resulted in an atmosphere at Palacio Real that was, to say the least, not a happy one.(5)

The Empress Zita sensed the discontentment of her hosts immediately. This, together with her living conditions at El Pardo, which

---

9/ p. 526
5/ p. 281

were very uncomfortable under the intense heat of the Spanish summer, quickly caused her to look for greener pastures. Furthermore, the now budget-minded Empress quickly realized that she was living beyond her means at El Pardo. She would again have to move.(5) So when one day, a former Austrian Ambassador to the Court of Spain had found the family a more suitable home, the Empress was delighted. The new home was the Villa Uribarren at Lequeitio, which the Spanish Queen Isabella II had once used as a summer palace.(10)

Two weeks after the birth of the Archduchess Elisabeth, the Empress, accompanied by family and followers, took the Exprés del Norte. She left Madrid and headed through Aragon and Navarre, through old Castile, and into the Basque country. The landscape through which she passed, although poor in quality was rich in visual splendour. The train took them past hundreds of brightly coloured Spanish homes, adorned with shining glazed tiles and decorated with magnificent, overflowing flowerpots. The homes were surrounded by walls, overhung with aromatic jasmines and other exotic foliage. It was a breath-taking journey, past the waters of the Manzanares, and by that immensly impressive Escorial built by a distant ancestor, the Habsburg Philip II, as a burial tomb for the Spanish Habsburgs. With bewilderment and unbelieving eyes, the children gazed upon this vision of stone that rose beside them as the train sped by. Soon this structure of terraced magnificence, with its one hundred miles of corridors and 2500 windows, faded into the background. The train puffed on, ever northward, passing through the Goya country to Fuentedodos and Zaragoza (so named by the Roman Caesar Augustus), stopping briefly at Loyola, home of the Jesuit Order, and eventually arriving at their destination.(5)

Lequeitio is a small fishing village on the Gulf of Biscay. It then counted some 4000 souls, most of whom were hardworking fishermen who had built their picturesque houses around two old convents and one very old gothic church. The Villa Uribarren into which they settled, overlooked the sea at the foot of a small mountain, appropriately named Mount Calvary. Its name must have reminded the Empress of the many hardships and severe suffering that she had been forced to endure over the last five years. But then Jesus Christ had

5/ p. 287-291
10/ p. 221

died on a mountain by this name, and hopefully His Act of Salvation would now benefit the life of the Imperial family. Hopefully their lot would improve.(10)

The Villa was a two storey structure with some thirty rooms, and in considerable need of repair. The cracks in the walls allowed the sea air to enter and leave, and its 30 rooms required considerable repairs and painting. By the grace of God, all this was done, and the burgers of the village, together with financial aid from Hungarian, Austrian and Spanish admirers and friends, carried out the needed repairs. Then, except for a short interlude at the sea resort town of San Sebastian in June of 1923, the Empress remained at the Villa Uribarren for seven pleasant years — from August 18, 1922 to September 15, 1929.(10)

This period proved to be a peaceful one for the family, and allowed the development of the Empress' first priority, the education of her children, and particularly that of the young Emperor Otto. The education of Otto had two main thrusts: pretention to the Habsburg throne and contentedness with his status. He must, above all, be prepared to rule when again called upon by God to do so. There was no "if" in the mind of the Empress.(10)

Towards this end, the Empress selected the best teachers she could find for the young Emperor, as well as for his brothers and sisters. From the renowned Benedictine Abbey of Pannonhalma in Hungary, she obtained highly educated and dedicated teachers to instruct young Otto on culture, morality and responsibility. Among these outstanding pedagogues were Professor Jako Blazovich who instilled into the young Emperor a deep love for the old Danubian nations, and Professor Count Heinrich Degenfeld, a jurist, who taught him political science and law. A Professor Niederarcher taught Greek, German and Geography to the elder children, and a Miss Street taught them English. French lessons were administered by a Miss Sepibus, and the preliminary education of the youngest children was the responsibility of a Miss Maass.(10)

In order to ensure a proper curriculum for her children, the Empress Zita established a two-man educational committee composed of Max Hussarek, a former prime minister and cultural minis-

10/ p. 221-223

ter of old Austria, and Janos Zichy, a former cultural minister of Hungary. This duo, not only planned and guided the education of the young Otto, but also directed and supervised that of the other children. A typical day in the study plan started at 6 a.m. and finished at 7 p.m., with appropriate times for breakfast, dinner and homework. Superimposed on this rigid daily calendar was, of course, the children's religious training, which was directed by the Empress herself to ensure that the Roman Catholic Faith was and would remain the underlying focal point of their academic training.(10)

During all this time, the daily routine of the Empress also served as a model for the children. She rose daily at 5 a.m., and within a half hour, could be seen attending Mass in the Basilica at Lequeitio, in the company of the wives of the village fishermen. Then after returning home to the Villa Uribarren, she would repeat her act of devotion by again attending a Mass in the Villa's chapel with her children before classes began. Even the children's leisure hours were used to prepare them for the future. The language used in their daily household routines and at play was varied daily so that they could continually practice what they had learnt. On Mondays it was German, on Tuesdays Hungarian, on Wednesdays French, and so on.(10)

All this was financed of course, on a very meager budget which the Empress administered through Countess Kerssenbrock. There were now revenues coming from Hungary, Austria, and wherever else there was still something to be had. It was not much, but it was sufficient to pay expenses and to educate, particularly Otto for his expected role.

For seven years the routine at Lequeitio went on and only came to an end, when forced to do so by the limitations of the children's educational facilities. The young Emperor was already attending his first year at University, but this was not in Lequeitio, nor in the surrounding Basque countryside. It was in Luxemburg. The rest of the children too had outgrown the capacity of the Uribarren educational facilities, and something had to be done to accommodate their evergrowing need for knowledge.(10)

Furthermore, the Empress's financial capacity was being severely stressed by the need to bring teachers to the students. It was time to

10/ p. 224, 242

now bring the students to the teachers. The solution was to lie in Belgium. Not only was Queen Elizabeth, the wife of Belgium's King Albert I, the Empress Zita's cousin, but Belgium offered her family access to the renowned Catholic University of Louvain — the oldest and yet most modern university of the times.(10) (9)

Thus on September 15, 1929, the family moved to Brussels, and settled temporarily in a house furnished for their use by Count Hypolithe d'Ursel. The Count, a member of an ancient Belgium noble family, was proud to offer his home as a temporary refuge for the Empress of Austria.(30)

The search for a permanent home came to an end in January of 1930, when the French nobleman Marquis Jean De Croix, offered his Château de Ham in the small town of Steenockerzeel in Belgium, to the Empress. It was a beautiful structure, surrounded by magnificent ponds inhabited by countless ducks and swans. It was a picturesque castle, built first in the 16th century, and still mainly unchanged in character. It suited the Empress remarkably well, for not only was it comfortable (it had been completely refurbished by the Marquis, including central heating), but it was also close to schools and the University of Louvain, and the Empress was again close to her Emperor son to guide him towards his destiny.(10)

Steenockerzeel also gave the opportunity for Her Majesty to again enjoy life in a cultural sense. No longer was she an exile, no longer was she cut off from her peers, supporters, and faithful admirers in the Gotha of Europe. In a sense she had come home. She began to again attend theater and concerts, and participate in church and cultural activities. Her children, too, greatly benefited from their proximity to other children of their own age and kind, and they soon blossomed in the company of their new found friends and surroundings. However, one thing had remained unchanged, and that was the Empress' determination not to stray one little bit from the game plan that had been laid out for her children's development. Over their progress the Empress kept an everwatchful eye, personally supervising their daily lessons, and proofing them at every step. In this task, the Empress was aided by the Countess Kerssenbrock, the Count Degenfeld, and the loyal couple Gudenus.(10)

9/ p. 273
10/ p. 246-248

At Steenockerzeel, the Empress also again held court. When visitors came to pay their respects — and they came more and more often now — they were received always with appropriate protocol. A particular example was the celebration of the young Emperor's eighteenth birthday on November 20, 1930. The Emperor had reached his legal age and the Empress, who previously and since her husband's death had acted as a sort of regent, now suddenly declared herself no longer in that role. A special birthday Mass was celebrated by Bishop Seydl in the private chapel of Steenockerzeel, to which many guests, including delegations from both Austria and Hungary, had been invited. Then, following the religious celebration of this very significant event, a reception was held, and the Emperor, who had now come of age, received his guests with the Empress looking on. It was a moment of triumph for the Empress and a moment of significance for the young Emperor.(10)

Deep within her heart, the Empress still believed in an eventual restoration of the Emperor to the throne of a united Danubian monarchy, and she worked actively towards such an event. In 1931 she visited Pope Pius XI who granted her an audience lasting well over an hour. She also visited the King and Queen of Italy, and although there was no formal release of whatever was discussed, rumours had it that Papal and Italian support for a new restoration had been on the agenda.There were many other happenings in the political world in Europe during the early thirties that encouraged the Empress to lobby governments and people, so that when occasions permitted, her Habsburg plans would not be forgotten. The Empress continued her active participation in such activities until June 27, 1935, the day on which the Emperor completed his studies and graduated with a Doctorate degree, with great distinction, from the Catholic University of Louvain. From then on, it was he who took the lead in supporting the family's aims and in working for the family's repossession of its former wealth and rights from those governments that had confiscated their properties and taken away these rights. It was now he who would carry the banner of the Habsburg dynasty and lead the fight towards restoration. And slowly things began to change in his favour.(10)

10/ p. 247-249

Adolf Hitler had come to power in Germany, and pressures for national socialism were being felt in Austria, causing Austria much unrest. The Austrian social democratic movement was dissolved, and the balance of political power started to move from the extreme left to the extreme right. And although their numbers were not large, the monarchists did hold some influence through their positions in the civil services, the officer corps, and in industry. Through their key positions in the new conservative government — the Christian Democrats — the Legitimists worked for the benefit of their Emperor back in Steenockerzeel. With time, the legal chains binding the Habsburgs in Austria began to loosen. Total expatriation of family members from Austria, was recalled and resolutions were passed that were intended to return to the Habsburgs their private wealth, which had been previously confiscated. And in early 1938, some of the changes that were made actually bore fruit. Some palaces and other real estate holdings were released to the family, which thus found the means to sustain itself. However, before much could be achieved in this regard, the ambitions of Germany to swallow up Austria were realized. "So far and yet so near" must have been the thought uppermost in the mind of the Empress as she watched the events of March 12, 1938, the day German troops marched into Austria and extinguished, at least for the immediate future, her hopes for a Habsburg restoration.

Nevertheless, life back in Steenockerzeel went on. The Archduchess Adelhaid had followed her elder brother to Louvain where she earned a Doctorate degree in Economics. In Vienna at the time of the "Anschluss", the Archduchess Adelhaid together with her brother, the Archduke Felix, managed to flee the German troops by escaping to Hungary in a car provided by Margrave Alexander Pallavicini. From there she and her brother returned to Steenockerzeel.(9)

The Archduke Felix who had also studied in Louvain where he earned a degree in Law, went to the United States in 1939, and worked there to lobby the cause of Austria with American senators and with government. He also became the "quartermaster" for his Imperial mother who would soon be forced to flee Europe and seek refuge in the New World.(9)

10/ p. 251-253
9/ p. 157-158, 223

The Archduke Robert, after having earned his Doctorate degree in Economics from the University of Louvain in June 1939, went to London. There he represented his brother Otto and his family's interests, and lobbied for the eventual restoration of an independent Austria. He was in London when the German Army caused his family to flee Steenockerzeel.(30)

The Archdukes Charles Louis and Rudolf, and the Archduchess Charlotte, were undergraduates at the University of Louvain when they were forced to leave as the German armed forces overran Belgium. The Archduchess Elisabeth was a high school student at the time at Les Dames de Marie in Brussels, and had to interrupt her studies when news of the German invasion became a horrifying fact. It was May 10, 1940.(30)

BOOK 2
ESCAPE FROM EUROPE

CHAPTER 6

FLEEING BELGIUM (30)

It was May 9, 1940. A small celebration had been organized at the Château de Ham in Steenockerzeel in Belgium to celebrate the occasion of the 48th birthday of the Empress. The Empress was surrounded by her immediate family, with the exception of the Archduke Felix, who had travelled to America to organize help and assistance for the thousands of homeless Austrian refugees; the Archduke Robert, who had gone to London to ensure that the best interests of Austria would not be forgotten by the British; and the Archduke Otto, who was in Paris, having just returned there from America.

With her at Steenockerzeel were her two youngest sons — the Archdukes Charles Louis and Rudolf, and her three daughters — the Archduchesses Adelhaid, Charlotte and Elisabeth. The Empress also had in her care at Steenockerzeel the four children of her brother Prince Felix of Bourbon-Parma. They were the Princesses Elisabeth, Marie Adélaide, and Marie Gabrielle of Luxemburg, and their brother, Prince Charles of Luxemburg.

All afternoon of that beautiful, sunny, spring day, visitors arrived from Brussels and from Luxemburg to pay their respects and extend their best wishes to Her Imperial Majesty. The guests included various ministers of the Governments in these countries, and also the Empress's brother, Prince Felix of Bourbon-Parma, and his wife the Grand Duchess Charlotte Adelgunde of Luxemburg. The occasion was almost festive except that the threat of a German invasion was hanging like a sword of Damocles over Steenockerzeel. A German invasion of Belgium could happen at any time.

The family however, had prepared for such an eventuality. Ever since the German take-over of Austria in March 1938, the outbreak of war between the allies and Germany had been expected. In preparation for such a happening — because Belgium lay between the warring adversaries, France and Germany — the Imperial family had long ago removed all their private and highly confidential documents from Steenockerzeel to France. It was there, in the Castle Bostz, owned by the Empress's brother Prince Xavier de Bourbon-Parma, near the city of Moulins, deep in the interior of France, that the Imperial family had made provision for refuge should the German armies decide again to overrun Belgium.

And so, on that beautiful spring afternoon of May 9, 1940, the festivities honouring the Empress were cheerfully continued. The family revelled in its togetherness, and took comfort in the belief that God had spared them so far. Surely He would look after them, if the worst had to be. Overlooking the preparations of the festivities were the Countess Kerssenbrock, the Count Degenfeld, the Empress's secretaries — Mesdemoiselles Dobler and Possawad, and the Dufek family — of which the man served as chauffeur, the wife as cook, and the daughter as servant.

Late that same evening on May 9, when all the guests had returned home, the Imperial family received a warning from King Leopold III in Brussels that a German attack was imminent, and that they should prepare themselves accordingly. Then, at 1 a.m. on the following morning, a telephone call from Prince Felix of Bourbon-Parma confirmed the fact that German tanks had crossed the border into Luxemburg. The anticipated overrun of the Netherlands had begun.

The Empress immediately put into effect the pre-planned preparations for an exodus. Last minute packing ensured that personal belongings needed for the flight would be taken along. At half past four in the morning, the roar of overhead aircraft, and the explosion of falling bombs not far from the château, pressured the activities that were already under way. The children were aroused from their sleep and made ready. They could see from their windows the fires that were burning only a few kilometers away. Concern became urgency, for now there was real physical danger to the inhabitants at

Château de Ham. They were, after all, sitting in one of the largest targets in the area. All packing was hastily completed and by early morning, the cars that were available to the Imperial family were made ready for departure. Before leaving the château, one of the servants even telephoned the school which the Archduchess Elisabeth had been attending, and left word for the teacher that the Archduchess would not be attending classes that day.

There were five cars in their caravan; four belonging to the Imperial family, and one, a chauffeur driven limousine, belonging to the House of Luxemburg. It was a large Buick sedan, and was driven by a chauffeur named Nicklow, who was employed in the service of Prince Felix and the Grand Duchess Charlotte. They had entrusted their children to the Empress with instructions that in the event of an invasion, their children would flee to France with the Imperial family. In the chauffeur driven sedan carrying the Luxemburg contingent were the Princesses Elisabeth, Marie Adélaide, and Marie Gabrielle, the Prince Charles, and a governess who accompanied the Royal children.

The Imperial contingent consisted of four cars: a large Chevrolet sedan driven by the chauffeur Dufek, a large American Plymouth driven by the Archduke Rudolf, a French Renault driven by the Archduchess Adelhaid, and a small Austrian Steyr driven by the Archduke Charles Louis. Riding as passengers in the Imperial cars were the Empress Zita, the Archduchesses Charlotte and Elisabeth, the Countess Kerssenbrock, the Count Degenfeld, the Empress's secretary Herma Dobler, and Madame Dufek with her daughter.

When the caravan, fully loaded down with passengers and baggage, left the Château de Ham at Steenockerzeel, it was almost 9 a.m. The route from Steenockerzeel, led through the town of Tervueren in the Province of Brabant, by-passed the City of Brussels, and moved in the direction of Ostende on the English Channel. Around Brussels they ran into very heavy southbound traffic. Trucks and cars loaded with refugees and their personal possessions, crowded the highways and made the caravan's eastward movement slow and difficult. They therefore stopped for a while at the home of a friend who had an estate outside Brussels. It was the Villa of Madame Frans

Wittouck, an Austrian lady whose maiden name was Brandeis, and who was living in Belgium. Her husband was an important industrialist in Brussels, and she had invited the Imperial family to stay with her, should they ever wish to do so.

As it happened, the Imperial entourage only remained there for a few hours. After some nourishment and a little rest, the caravan continued on its eastern journey to the sea. As German planes flew overhead, and fires could be seen in almost every village which they passed, the little caravan, protected no doubt by St. Christopher himself, made its way along the highway to the coast. At Aalst, a little town west of Brussels, they ran into a column of advancing British troops. Although their smiles and happy-go-lucky attitudes encouraged the Imperial fugitives, it further slowed down their progress. Eventually they passed the column and continued on their way. The noise of war was everywhere. Bridges were being attacked and villages were set on fire by the hundreds of enemy aircraft overhead. Again St. Christopher safely guided the caravan which eventually passed the old medieval city of Bruges, and reached Ostende. From there they turned south and crossed the border into France at Depanne. They had made a large detour on their journey south, but the French defences along its northern border with the Netherlands, made this eastward trek necessary. When they crossed the border into France, it was 11 o'clock in the evening of May 10. They spent the night in a small inn near Dunkerque, tired but safe.

Early the next morning, somewhat refreshed, and in the light of day, the caravan continued on its way. This time, it headed away from the coast and moved east towards Laon. There they stayed with an old friend, the Baron Coppee. He owned the Château de Fourdrain which was situated near the small village of La Fère, just west of Laon. The Baron had long ago invited the Imperial family to make use of this Château in the event of need. It was a large estate and it now offered the Imperial entourage a welcome repose. They stayed there a few days to assess the military developments in the north, and to contemplate their next move. However, as history has shown, the German armies overran Belgium in less than 10 days, and King Leopold III was forced to capitulate to save his country from total destruction. And as history also showed, the German armies did not stop in Belgium. They quickly broke through France's Maginot Line defences which the French Government had thought impregnable, and continued their advance southward.

The Imperial family was therefore once again forced to flee from the rapidly advancing Germans. They headed for Bostz, where the Empress's brother, Prince Xavier of Bourbon-Parma had a castle. Surely they would be safe there, and that became their next destination. Count Degenfeld had in the meantime left the Imperial entourage and headed for Paris to join the Archduke Otto who was busy working the problem of the thousands of Austrian refugees who had descended on France.

When they arrived at Bostz, the Empress was welcomed by her brother Prince Xavier of Bourbon-Parma with open arms. The Prince had been a colonel in the Belgium army, but when that country was overrun by the Germans and King Leopold III capitulated, the King had given Prince Xavier permission to give up his Belgium commission and fight for France.

At Bostz, the Imperial family felt comfortable and safe, for they were now in the middle of France. Nevertheless, security was again an illusion. The German advance continued ever southward, and in "blitzkrieg" fashion, so that within a few weeks, the Imperial family had to again flee to escape the advancing German armies.

William C. Bullit, American Ambassador in Paris, and friend of the Emperor Otto, suggested to the family that they should get out of France as quickly as possible. He thought that they would be safe in America, and suggested that they should immediately send their secret papers, documents and personal belongings to Bordeaux, from where the last American ship was about to sail for the United States. The family accepted the Ambassador's recommendation, and the Archduke Rudolf immediately made his way to Bordeaux with the family's private documents which it did not want to see in German hands. When the documents were safely on board the American ship, the Archduke Rudolf drove back to Bostz and rejoined his family which was preparing to resume its exodus from France. The Emperor Otto, until then in Paris, now also joined the fam. ,, whose main objective now was to get as quickly as possible to America. The safest way to America was then through Portugal, and thus when appropriate Portugese visas had been obtained, the family left Bostz.

The German war machine had by that time reached Paris, and the French Government had declared Paris an "open city", thus sparing it from certain destruction from German guns and bombs. By this act of international agreement, Paris was spared the ravages of war that had and would befall many other European cities before the war would end. The French government left Paris and set up its operations in Bordeaux, and the Luxemburg government, until then having found refuge in Paris, moved on to Portugal and later to London.

The Imperial family, now intent on reaching Portugal, moved south to Lamonzie-Montrastruc, a small town near Bergerac, not far from Bordeaux, where the French government had placed the Château de Bergerac at the disposal of the Grand Duchess of Luxemburg. When they arrived at the Château, the family was welcomed by Prince Felix and the Grand Duchess Charlotte of Luxemburg, who had also just arrived there with their children from Paris. However, the family reunion at the Château de Bergerac was again to be a short one, for the Luxemburgs had decided to move to Portugal, and the Imperial family, still keeping one step ahead of the advancing Germans, also wanted to reach safety in Portugal. But to get to Portugal, the family first had to cross into Spain.

It was June 18 when they reached the Spanish border which had been closed to all traffic from both sides by the Spanish authorities. There were long line-ups of refugees, many of them Austrians, all wanting to get into Spain. The caravan stopped at Hendaye, the last village in France, and the Archdukes Otto and Charles Louis walked up to the Spanish border guards and asked to see the officer in charge. When they finally met with him, they learnt, to their amazement, that this was the same man that had been the Colonel in the Civil Guard in charge of their protection at Lequeitio, eleven years earlier. He was very friendly, and when the Archdukes told him who they were, and that the Empress of Austria was waiting to be let across the border, he immediately gave the necessary permission. He could not do otherwise, he told them, for he remembered them as children back in the Basque country where he, with a small guard, had been responsible for the Imperial Family's safety. With that, the "Empress from Lequeitio" as he called her, and her entire entourage, passed across the border into Spain. The entourage however had by this time swollen to considerable numbers, for accompanying the Imperial automobiles on foot, were a large number of Austrian refugees. The good Colonel saluted the Empress as she passed by, and looked the other way as the dozens upon dozens of Austrians fleeing from the Nazis, made their way to freedom.

The Imperial caravan continued to Irun, a small Spanish border town where they stopped briefly to thank God for their good fortune, and then carried on to Burgos, a city on the old road connecting Madrid to the Bay of Biscay. They spent the night in a small inn in Burgos, and the next day continued on to Portugal and Lisbon. In Lisbon, they made their way to the home of a Count Saldanha, whose wife was an Austrian noble woman by the name of Eltz and who the family had previously known. Senora Saldanha was also the sister of Count Henry Eltz who sometime later also came to Québec as a refugee.

Count Saldanha owned a beautiful seaside hacienda in Dafundo, not far from Lisbon. It had a beautiful view of the Atlantic Ocean, and it was here as the Count's guests, that the Empress, her family, and her entourage were to remain until arrangements could be made for their voyage to America. The accommodation was very comfortable, and the seaair, with its cool evening breezes, was a pleasant welcome to the Imperial family in the month of June 1940.

Whereas the rest of the Imperial family settled down in Dafundo to await permission to enter the United States, the Emperor Otto, who already possessed an American Visa, immediately made his way to America. There he, together with his brother the Archduke Felix who was already in the United States, made arrangements through the American Foreign Office and President Roosevelt for the necessary visas.

Meanwhile, not far from Dafundo, the Luxemburgs had found refuge at Cascais at the home of a mutual friend, the Marquis Spiritus Sanctum. He too had a beautiful Villa overlooking the ocean, in which Prince Felix, the Grand Duchess Charlotte, and the Luxemburg princes and princesses passed away the hours while arrangements for their visas to America were also being processed.

CHAPTER 7

FLYING THE ATLANTIC (30)

It was mid-July, 1940 when the American Consul in Lisbon advised the Empress that visas for Her Majesty and for her family had arrived, and that they could now go on to America. He also provided them with airline tickets for the transatlantic Pan American Airways clipper to New York for Her Majesty , for the Archdukes Charles Louis and Rudolf, and for the Archduchesses Adelhaid, Charlotte and Elisabeth. There was also an airline ticket for the Countess Kerssenbrock, but the rest of the party had to travel by sea.

The Pan American Airways clipper which took the Empress of Austria and her young family to America was a Boeing B-314 aircraft. It was a huge flying boat with a wing span of 120 feet and a length of 106 feet. It weighed 42 tons and was powered with four wing-mounted, Wright engines, each delivering 1500 horsepower. It had a crew of eleven and could carry 70 passengers in comfort equivalent to that on a sea-going ship.(29)

The clipper's normal air speed was 150 miles per hour. This would be delayed on westbound flights due to headwinds, and improved on eastbound flights. From take off at Lisbon to landing at New York, the trip was normally scheduled to take some 27 hours, including two stops en route — one in the Azores and another in Bermuda. The distances covered from Lisbon were 1053 miles to Horta in the Azores, 1612 miles from the Azores to Darrel's Island in the Bermudas, and another 772 miles from Bermuda to New York, a total flying distance of 3437 miles. Thus the clipper, leaving Lisbon at 9 a.m. on a Monday morning (GMT) would arrive at New York on the following day, a Tuesday, at 6 p.m. (EST).(29)

Literally, called a "flying boat", the aircraft had more the physical characteristics of an ocean liner and railway pullman car, than those of a modern-day aeroplane. It was in effect a boat with wings arranged like a pullman car. The hull was divided into an upper and a lower deck. The upper deck housed the control cabin used by the Captain and First Officer, and by their navigational and engineering officers, and the lower deck was divided into individual passenger compartments, a dining room-lounge area, a galley and washroom facilities. The flight crew totalled six officers, and in addition there were five attendants to look after the welfare of the 70 passengers. Each of the passenger compartments, which could accommodate a maximum of six people, was equipped with comfortable fauteuils which the attendants could convert into beds. There was also a utility cabin on the upper deck for passenger luggage and for life rafts and other emergency equipment. A one-way transatlantic fare per person cost $425.00 and a return fare could be bought for $765.00.(29)

It was mid-July when the small Imperial family group boarded the transatlantic clipper in the Port of Lisbon. It was 9 o'clock in the morning when the huge flying boat taxied out of the harbour and made its way into the wind on the open sea. Slowly at first, and then faster and faster, it skimmed over the waves, finally lifting its great weight into the air. It turned and headed west to America, leaving behind the troubled Europe that had so harshly treated the Empress Zita and her family.

In those early days of transatlantic flying, Pan American Airways assigned to each passenger a consecutive number to indicate his/her historic position as a pioneer transatlantic passenger. The Imperial family were assigned two digit numbers, indicating that they were among the first 100 passengers who pioneered Pan Am's transatlantic service.(29)

All in all, the voyage was quite comfortable. Each of the family had his/her own bed, and the trip was divided into three parts. Their first destination, after flying 1053 miles was the Azores where they landed in the late afternoon of the same day. The stop at Horta, the capital of the Azores, had been scheduled to last two hours. However, since a storm warning had been sounded, and the weather was rapidly closing in, the Captain of the aircraft decided to cut short his stay and continued the flight west as quickly as possible. Therefore, after refuelling and resupplying provisions, the captain took his aircraft out of the protected harbour into the open sea for take-off. The winds from the oncoming storm had by then whipped the Atlantic into large, threatening waves, which the Captain still judged manageable for take-off. Then, with the four engines roaring, the huge aircraft skimmed and bounced over the rough sea, and finally rose slightly from the water. But as the passengers uttered sighs of relief, the big machine suddenly fell back and hit the water with a huge thump and shudder, before again becoming airborne. This sudden collision with the now huge waves, damaged one of the fuel tanks of the aircraft, and this caused the Captain to abort the flight. He turned the aircraft around and headed back to the Azores. However, because of the very rough seas that had developed, he landed the airship within the Harbour itself rather than on the open sea. This was a rather tricky manoeuvre because of surrounding hills, the necessity for a quick descent, and the rather short length of water at his disposal for stopping the aircraft. Nevertheless, he skillfully succeeded in carrying out a safe landing, and without further damage, returned to the Pan American dock.

The passengers were allowed to disembark from the aircraft which was listing noticeably to one side, while the captain and his crew proceeded to survey the damage to the aircraft. In a feat that would be hard to imagine nowadays, the Captain had sand bags placed on the opposite wing to counterbalance the list, and then changed into swim trunks and dove into the water to inspect the hull below the water line and determine the extent of the damage. Unfortunately the damage was more extensive than what was first thought, and the Captain decided not to continue the flight with that aircraft. As a result, the passengers were put up in local hotels in Horta, and had to wait in the Azores for 48 hours until a replacement airship became available to pick them up and thus allow them to continue their journey.

On the evening of the third day after leaving Lisbon, the Imperial party boarded the replacement clipper that Pan American Airways had sent to the Azores. They taxied out of the harbour of Horta and again headed into the open sea, which, by then, had calmed. To the accompanying roar of the four powerful engines, the big plane quickly lifted from the rolling waves and headed into the Atlantic sunset. As darkness fell and the airship droned ever westward, the family, looking out of their cabin windows, could see the reflection of the moonlight on the white-capped water far below, and the glitter of the millions of stars that lit the July night above. Once in a while, the brilliant path of a shooting star would flash across their view, reminding them of the Star of Bethlehem that guided the three wise men on their journey westward, almost 2000 years before. Where were these stars now leading them, and what manger would they find in America? These questions must have passed through their minds as they said their evening prayers high in the night sky over the dark Atlantic on that July night in 1940.

Tucked in their beds, high above the Atlantic, the Imperial family slept the night away. And then, in the early morning hours, as daylight slowly again evolved, they got up, dressed and looked forward to their next destination — the Bermudas. Almost eleven hours had passed since leaving the Azores, and they were anxious to once again set foot on mother Earth. The steward quickly re-converted their beds back to comfortable daytime fauteuils, and brought them fruit juices and coffee with which to greet the day. Then far below and far ahead, they glimpsed land. Many islands gradually appeared, in vivid green amongst the deep blue sea, surrounded on all sides by sandy beaches. The plane started its descent, and as the blue waters of the Bermudas came ever and ever closer, the panoramic view greatly impressed the Imperial travellers. They had never before seen such vivid greens mixed with cerulean blues, framed by coral sands. It was 9 a.m. Atlantic time, when the huge plane touched down on the blue waters of the islands, broken only by the gently rolling white caps, and greeted by the subtle curtsies of the Palms as they bowed in reverence to the Empress peering from the window of her cabin. The plane then settled in the warm water and slowly taxied to the dock where the Pan American representatives welcomed the passengers to the Island. During the two hour stop, while the aircraft was being refueled and serviced for the last leg of its flight to America, the passengers were allowed to disembark and avail themselves of the temptation of an American breakfast of sizzling bacon, ham and eggs and myriads of sweet breads and pastries. Being used to the much more somber offering afforded by a continental breakfast as had been their custom in Europe, the family seemed bewildered by the abundance that lay before them. However, the long journey behind them, and the fresh morning sea air, quickly brought forth a sense of appetite, particularly among the children.

Following their hearty breakfast, and anxious to proceed with their trip, the passengers again boarded their aircraft. It was now late morning in the Bermudas, and the rest of the journey to New York was to be in daylight. At 11 a.m., the clipper again taxied out to open seas,and after take-off, again headed west, keeping just ahead of the sun which was now high in the heavens overhead.

The flight to New York lasted five more hours. But before sighting the American landmass, the travellers once again lunched in the sky. The dining room, which was large enough to accommodate 24 diners at a sitting, extended the width of the fuselage of the flying boat and offered first class meals served on china. The tables were covered with damask tablecloths and decked with silver utensils. There was a choice of meat or fish, assorted vegetables and salads, and appropriate wines. Waiters in white jackets attending the passengers, ensured prompt and proper service from the galley to the tables.

By 6 p.m., Eastern Standard Time, the clipper came in sight of New York. The skyscrapers of lower Manhattan were a sight to behold, — an unbelievable panorama of steel and stone, reaching into the sky from which the clipper came. Landing in the Upper Bay between the Narrows and Manhattan, the flying boat taxied passed the Statue of Liberty and made its way to the Pan American dock on the East River. There the transatlantic crossing came to an end. It had taken them almost 96 hours to cover the 3437 miles from Lisbon, but they were safe and they were finally in America. Here, there would be no more running from the advancing German armies. Here they could rest and continue their life, and prepare themselves for whatever challenge lay ahead.

When they finally had docked and walked off the flying boat, the Imperial family was greeted by the Emperor Otto and the Archduke

Felix, and by a Maître Parker who had been commissioned by the American Government in Washington to ensure that their arrival would be smooth and uneventful, and to welcome them on behalf of President Roosevelt. He also provided them with transportation to Number 10 Park Avenue, which was the home of the Archduke Felix who had come to New York some six months earlier.

After some 48 hours of rest and relaxation, which included a quick sightseeing tour of New York, the Imperial family moved on to Royalston in Massachusetts. Royalston is a small town near Athol near the border between Massachusetts and New Hampshire. Calvin Bullock, a New York City banker who the Archduke Felix had befriended, owned three houses at Royalston, one of which he made available to the Empress and her family. It was a large house with plenty of rooms, and provided the Imperial family a comfortable, secluded place to stay until such time as their plans would take them elsewhere. As it happened they stayed there for the rest of the summer, during which time the Empress made plans for a more permanent home and for the education of her children. It was not the last time that Calvin Bullock would come to the aid of the Imperial family. It appeared that St. Christopher was still on the side of the Habsburgs.

BOOK 3
QUEBEC

CHAPTER 8

FINDING A HOME (31)

The uppermost problem occupying the Empress at Royalston was completing the education of those of her children whose studies had been interrupted by the German invasion of Belgium. The Archduchess Adelhaid, who had received her Doctorate in Economics at the Catholic University of Louvain, could stay in New York and work with her brother the Archduke Felix. But the two Archdukes and the Archduchess Charlotte still had to earn their university degrees, and the Archduchess Elisabeth first and foremost had to complete her High School curriculum before being able to study at a university.

Complicating the situation for the Imperial students is that their studies in Belgium had been in the French language, and that their knowledge of the English language was insufficient to allow them to continue their studies in English without losing at least a year. Furthermore, the Empress's desire that the educational facilities should if at all possible be Roman Catholic in nature, further complicated the choices available to the children's continuing education. But then, the answer came to them, for in Québec City to the north, there was a French university situated in a Roman Catholic environment, and to serve as the icing on the cake, the Dean of Philosophy at that French-speaking university was a professor who had some years earlier come to Québec from the University of Louvain and was not unfamiliar to the Empress. He was Professor Charles De Koninck and was familiar with the exact courses that the Imperial children had studied at Louvain, and his guidance in bringing the children up to speed in their new environment and curriculum at Québec would be invaluable. The Empress, who in her daily prayers had asked for Divine guidance in resolving the educational option to be followed in America, suddenly felt that her prayers had been answered. She resolved to try and go to Canada, and chose the Université Laval in Québec City as the preferred place of continuing education, and therefore Québec City as her preferred new home and base of operations. From Québec, it would also be possible to easily keep in touch with the Emperor Otto in Washington and with the Archduke Felix in New York. Contact with her one remaining son in Europe, the Archduke Robert in London, would be a little more difficult.

Through her New York and Washington connections, the Empress asked the American Government to enquire from the Canadian Government as to the possibility of the Imperial family moving to Canada and Québec. The American Government graciously complied, and Mr. Pierre Casgrain, then Canada's Minister of the Interior, was given the responsibility of settling the Empress and her family in Québec.

As it happened, the Minister had a cousin, Miss Marguerite MacDonald, who spent the winter months teaching English at the University of Toronto, and the summer months at her home in Québec City. As she had not yet returned to Toronto that summer, the Minister telephoned her in Québec and asked her if she would take on the job of settling in the Empress and her Imperial family.

Miss Marguerite MacDonald was a very capable woman. She knew almost everyone of influence in Québec, and immediately started to make appropriate contacts. She called upon Maître Stanislas Germain, a prominent Québec City lawyer to assist with the necessary legalities, and contacted the Archbishop of Québec, the Most Reverend Monseigneur Cardinal Villeneuve to explore ways and means of meeting the educational and living requirements of the Imperial family — at least in the interim until some permanent arrangements could be made.

In the meantime, back at Royalston, the Empress had been informed of happenings in Ottawa and Québec. In order to assist Miss MacDonald, the Countess Kerssenbrock soon came to Québec City to better acquaint herself with the surroundings in that city, and to help out with selection criteria and the family's needs when evaluating available accommodation. The two ladies hit it off immediately and quickly became good friends. The Countess then returned to Royalston, and Miss MacDonald set out to look for a suitable residence for the Imperial family.

Québec City in the 1940's was not the Québec City it is today. There were no tall buildings, no highrise apartments, no tall hotels other than the imposing Château Frontenac which dominated the city from the cliffs and overlooked the river below. The City of Québec was then concentrated on a peninsula protruding eastward between the mighty St. Lawrence river flowing to the sea, and its small tributary, the St. Charles river, whose banks served as a natural harbour for the numerous goelettes that transported logs and pulpwood to the mills of Québec, and whose shores housed the many industrial establishments of the old city. About 250,000 inhabitants lived in the city at the time, and an electric street railway system transported its passengers up and down the steep streets that characterized the city. Its suburbs Sillery and Ste. Foy were still remote, and the city's roof line was pierced by numerous church steeples whose bells tolled the time of worship and called the faithful to prayer. It was a city adorned with age old convents of which the Ursulines is the oldest, an imposing Basilica, a seminary for the education of youth, an imposing hospital founded by the sisters of the Hôtel Dieu, the colleges of the Jesuits and the Recollets, and the Université Laval which was the first institute of higher learning in New France and is the oldest university in the Americas. There were also many imposing private homes that Québec's successful merchants and intelligentsia had constructed for themselves since the early 1800's.

This was the city which the Empress was about to call home, and in this city, Miss Marguerite MacDonald set out to find the Empress a house. Between her contacts in the real estate market, and advertisements in the Québec Gazette and Le Soleil, she visited whatever sounded suitable. And when she had selected three or four such possibilities, she contacted the Countess Kerssenbrock who would then come to Québec City to approve or reject each potential residence.

There were a number of such trips made by the Countess to Québec
that summer, so that she and Miss MacDonald got to know each other
quite well. On one of these trips, Miss MacDonald showed her the
house of a gentleman whose wife had just left him. When they arrived
at this house, the two ladies found to their dismay that the old
gentleman had tried to drown his sorrow in drink, and as a result
became quite amorous towards the Countess. Needless to say, the
two ladies quickly left and crossed his address from their list.

On another visit to Québec, this time accompanied by the Archduke Charles Louis, the two ladies visited a house that offered
possibilities, but was terribly decorated. The furniture was dilapi-
dated and the floor and wall coverings were well worn and scratched.
Everything needed repair and cleaning. Following the inspection of
the premises the two ladies were asked by the proprietor for whom
the house was required. For an European family, they told him. To
which the proprietor remarked that in that case, he would have to
remove all his lovely furniture, for these Europeans certainly would-
not look after them the way he had done. The two ladies quickly left
for they could hardly contain their laughter, and the Archduke remarked that now he had heard everything.

At another place, an old gentleman whose wife had just died, was
showing the house to the two ladies. As the place was not too clean,
he apologized to them for the dirt and disarray that was evident
everywhere. You know, he said, they had a live-in governess for
years who was not very clean but who they liked very much. She was
Austrian, he apologized, and these people are not always clean, he
added. The two ladies did not embarass the old gentleman by telling
him who the house was intended for. Again they left and laughed and
kept on looking.

As it happened, there was a house that showed great promise. It
was situated in Sillery, a suburb of Québec, in an isolated grove of
Maple and Elm trees, and belonged to the sisters of Ste. Jeanne d'Arc,
a religious order in Sillery. It was known as "the Villa Saint Joseph"
and was being used as a home for old priests. It even had a small
chapel. After having first talked to the sisters, who thought they could
find other quarters for the two or three old priests who were living

there at the time, Miss MacDonald went to see Cardinal Villeneuve at the Bishop's Palace. He was agreeable and gave the necessary permission to the sisters of Ste. Jeanne d'Arc to make the house available to the Imperial family.

The house of course needed some work, and above all furnishings. The sisters remarked that they had about 16 or 18 adult beds and mattresses in storage at their convent. These beds had been used in place of the much smaller beds normally found in the student dormitory, to serve visiting teachers from English-speaking Ontario who used to come to Québec in the summer months to learn French at the convent. With the permission of the Mother Superior, these beds were made available to Miss MacDonald for use at the Villa Saint Joseph.

However, the Villa still needed chairs and tables and bureaus, and these were found through private donations and at auctions. And so the Villa eventually received all the furniture, rugs, and accoutrements that were needed to turn it into a home for the Empress Zita, for her student children, and for her entourage which would includ ed the Countess Kerssenbrock, the secretary Miss Herma Dobler, and the Chauffeur Dufek and his wife and daughter who now also were in America, and who would continue their loyal service to the family.

CHAPTER 9

ARRIVING IN QUEBEC (31, 32, 33)

While the Imperial family was still at Royalston, the Countess Kerssenbrock was making arrangements for their arrival in Québec City. In addition to visiting and evaluating residences, the Countess also had concerned herself with making the educational arrangements for the Imperial children.

Among others, the Countess called on the Archbishop of Québec, Cardinal Villeneuve, who not only had the final say over the use of the Villa Saint Joseph, but also directed the Countess to Monseigneur Alphonse Marie Parent, Secretary of the Faculty of Philosophy at Université Laval, and to Father Georges Henri Lévesque who was the founder of the Faculty of Social Sciences at the university in 1938.

It was with Father Lévesque that the Countess Kerssenbrock discussed the status of the Imperial children's past education and the requirements for their continuing education at Laval. Entrance to university studies required a baccalaureate degree with proficiency in certain subjects that did not exactly parallel the academic requirements at Louvain. The required baccalaureate was based on the classic sense of the old educational system of the Province of Québec. As a result, the Archdukes Charles Louis and Rudolf and the Archduchess Charlotte, who had completed their university entrance studies in Louvain, were admitted to the Faculty of Social Sciences at Laval on the condition that they also undertook certain extra studies, particularly in philosophy, which their curriculum at Louvain had lacked. These extra requirements were discussed by the Countess with Professor Charles De Koninck, Dean of the Faculty of Philosophy at Université Laval. Professor Charles De Koninck, who had first come to Université Laval as a visiting Professor of Philosophy from the Université Louvain in 1935, had become Dean of the Faculty by the time the Imperial students arrived in Québec.

The Archduchess Elisabeth however, who had not completed her pre-university studies in Belgium, still had to earn her baccalaureate degree before being admitted to Laval. For these requirements, the Countess Kerssenbrock made arrangements at the Collège Jésus-Marie in Sillery, a suburb of Québec City. Furthermore, because the children of the Empress's brother, Prince Felix of Bourbon-Parma and the Grand Duchess Charlotte of Luxemburg had also sought refuge in America and wanted to continue their studies in Québec, the Countess Kerssenbrock also made arrangements for Prince Jean of Luxemburg to attend university with the two Archdukes, and for Princess Elisabeth of Luxemburg to attend the Collège Jésus-Marie with the Archduchess Elisabeth. The three remaining Luxemburg children, Princesses Marie Adelaide, Marie Gabrielle, and Alix, only joined their sister and cousin at Collège Jésus-Marie, one year later, in September 1941.

The first member of the Imperial family to arrive in Québec City was the Archduchess Elisabeth. She had come ahead of the family in order to start classes at the Collège Jésus-Marie where she had been enrolled by the Countess Kerssenbrock. It was a Sunday afternoon, September 12, 1940, when Miss Marguerite MacDonald first met the young Archduchess who had come alone from Royalston, at the railway station. The two ladies then took a taxi to the Collège Jésus-Marie in Sillery. There they met with the Reverend Mother Marie-des-Anges, who was the Mother Superior of the convent and who had been expecting them. Arrangements had been made that the young Archduchess — she was then 18 years old — would stay at the Pension des Dames. This was a residence for students and ladies that had been added to the convent in 1922, and included, in addition to numerous dormitories, a few private suites and simple rooms. It was one of these that was assigned to the young Archduchess on that Fall day in September 1940. It was to be her home for a full year, while she completed her courses that were required to enter university.

arch. Elisabeth   Insp. Toth   arch. Charlotte   Ing. Rudolphe

17. Arriving in Québec.

18. The Collège Jésus-Marie in Sillery.

19. The Archduchess Elisabeth and her cousin the Princess Elisabeth at the Collège Jésus-Marie.

20. The Archduchess Elisabeth with her troop of Girls Guides.

21. The Emperor Otto visiting Archduchesses Charlotte and Elisabeth and
the Archkuke Charles Louis in Québec.

22. The Archduke Rudolf upon graduation from Université Laval.

23. The Archduke Charles Louis upon graduation from Université Laval.

24. The Imperial students with Père G.H. Lévesque at Université Laval.

25. The Villa Saint Joseph in Sillery.

26. A family portrait in the Villa Saint Joseph.

27. The chapel in the Villa Saint Joseph.

28. After Mass at the Villa Saint Joseph.

29. The Archduke Rudolf visited by the Archduke Felix and the Emperor Otto.

30. The Emperor Otto visiting his brothers in Québec.

31. The two Zitas.

32. The De Koninck residence at 25, Avenue Sainte Geneviève.

When the Mother Superior was first presented to the Archduchess Elisabeth in the parlour of the convent, Mother Marie-des-Anges invited the young Archduchess to participate in a Benediction to the Blessed Sacrement that had been arranged in her honour in the chapel of the convent. This chapel, which was inaugurated in 1900, had been dedicated to Our Lady of the Sacred Heart. It was of beautiful wood construction, decorated in white, blue and gold, and built in the "Québec-Gothic" style that had been developed and became popular in New France since the early 18th century.

The Mother Superior wanted to make use of the occasion to introduce the young Archduchess to her future comrades, and told her that a special prayer kneeler had been set up in the choir of the chapel for her use. At this the young Archduchess began to weep, exclaiming that she had never had any special treatment in church when she was in Belgium, and that she preferred to be treated like any one of the other students. The Mother Superior explained that it was necessary, however, that the other students know who she was, and that after the ceremony, she would be a student no different from the others. And so it came to pass. The Archduchess began her classes, made new friends quickly, and soon found that she became to her comrades, just another student.

Three days after the arrival of the Archduchess Elisabeth in Sillery, two more royal visitors arrived. They were Prince Jean of Luxemburg, and his sister, the Princess Elisabeth of Luxemburg. As with her Imperial predecessor, the Princess Elisabeth had to complete her baccalaureate and had been registered for this purpose by the Countess Kerssenbrock at the Collège Jésus-Marie in Sillery. She therefore joined her cousin, the Archduchess Elisabeth in the Pension des Dames. Prince Jean was given temporary residence in the facilities of the Dominican Fathers on Grande-Allée boulevard.

A short time later — it was near the end of September 1940 — the two Archdukes, Charles Louis and Rudolf, also arrived in Québec City. They joined their cousin, Prince Jean of Luxemburg, at the Monastery of the Dominican Fathers on Grande Allée where they stayed for some three weeks. The three young men occupied the visitor's apartment at this monastery which was situated near Bourlamaque Avenue and next to the Plains of Abraham (now Québec's Battlefield Park). It was also at this monastery that Father Georges Henri Lévesque, Dean of Laval's Faculty of Social Sciences, was living.

One night, when the three young men were about to retire in the visitor's apartment of the monastery, they received a knock at their door. The unexpected visitor was a Father Leduc from Beauharnois, Québec, who, whenever he came to Québec in the past had stayed in the visitor's apartment at the monastery. When one of the Archdukes answered the door, the visiting priest was astonished to find the apartment already occupied, and asked the three young men who they were. The noble residents introduced themselves as "Charles Louis of Habsburg", "Rudolf of Habsburg", and "Jean of Luxemburg." The priest, thinking they were joking, said "and I am Leduc of Beauharnois", excused himself, and found another apartment. The next morning, when the three young men were having breakfast with Father Lévesque, they told him of their experience of the night before. They remarked that they were surprised to find out, when the good Father introduced himself to them, that there were also members of the nobility in Québec. After a good laugh and an explanation by Father Lévesque, the four continued their breakfast.

It was October 20, 1940 when the rest of the Imperial family arrived in Québec City from Royalston. There, while waiting to come to Québec, they had been joined by the mother and sister of the Empress, the Duchess Maria Antonia of Bourbon-Parma and the Princess Isabelle of Bourbon-Parma.

Because their permanent residence to be, the Villa Saint Joseph, was not yet ready for them — it was still being put in order and furnished for their use — the Empress Zita, the Archduchesses Adelhaid and Charlotte, the Duchess Maria Antonia, the Princess Isabelle, the Countess Kerssenbrock, and the Empress's secretary, Miss Herma Dobler, were put up at the Pension des Dames of the Jésus-Marie Convent.

On the morning of the next day, October 21, 1940, the Empress and her entourage called on His Eminence Cardinal Villeneuve, the Archbishop of Québec, to pay their respects and to thank him for his kindness in allowing them the use of the Villa Saint Joseph, as well as for the assistance the family had received in solving the problems of their continuing education.

After a pleasant exchange of formalities and some personal pleasanteries, the Cardinal said to Her Majesty:

"Madame, je vous dis qu'ici à Québec, il y a deux saisons — c'est l'hiver et le mois de Juillet."

("Madame, I want to tell you that here in Québec, there are two seasons — Winter and the month of July").

This piece of advice, though humerous to those uninitiated in Québec winters, made a deep impression on the Imperial family members and was to come to their minds again and again in the coming year as they learnt to experience the truth of the Cardinal's remark.

That night, back at the Collège Jésus-Marie, the Imperial and ducal family members were honoured at a convocation attended by Monseigneur Camille Roy, Rector of the Université Laval, by Mère Marie-des-Anges, the Mother Superior of the Convent, and by all her teaching staff, collegiates and pensioners. The special convocation took place in the Salle Sainte-Cécile, which was situated in a new wing of the convent that had been added in 1905 to the original central structure which dated back to 1870. The Salle Sainte-Cécile replaced the original Salle Mozart as the grand concert hall of the convent for convocations, graduation ceremonies, theatrical presentations and concerts.(18)

The assembled students, teachers, educators and clergy, welcomed the Empress to Québec, and paid homage to Her Majesty the Empress of Austria and Queen of Hungary. Monseigneur Camille Roy offered the homage of the University to Her Majesty in the most appropriate terms and with the highest respect and elegance. In closing the formalities, a choir of student voices, accompanied by the piano, sang the Imperial Austrian Anthem composed by Josef Haydn — "Gott Erhalte." Although the evening was a great honour for all the collegians and pensioners that were present, it was also a very emotional one for the Empress Zita. After so many years, and thousands of miles from her homeland, she received once again this outstanding homage to her person, to her family, and to her country.(18)

On the following day, October 22, the Empress Zita, together with her mother, the Duchess Maria Antonia of Bourbon-Parma, her sister Princess Isabelle of Bourbon-Parama, the Countess Kerssenbrock, the Archdukes Charles Louis and Rudolf, and the Prince Jean de Luxemburg, visited the motherhouse of the Sisters of Ste. Jeanne d'Arc. It was this congregation of Sisters that administered the Villa Saint Joseph which the Imperial family was to occupy. Since the good sisters had used it as an old-age home for retired priests, the house had been divided into two parts — one part being a residence for the old priests and one part for the sisters who had been assigned to look after them. It was therefore ideal for the Imperial family. One part could be used by the Empress Zita and her family, and the other part which was segregated from the Imperial quarters, could be used for servants and visitors. These circumstances, plus the rather remote location of the villa in Sillery — it was then in the middle of a large woodlot and still some distance from its nearest neighbours, made it an ideal solution as a place of residence for the Imperial family.(20)

Her Majesty arrived at the Ste. Jeanne d'Arc convent at 11 o'clock on the 22nd day of October. The entire religious community of the convent had assembled in its noviciate hall, where they welcomed and paid homage to the Imperial family of Austria. In his welcoming address, Father P. Maurice Gagnon, chaplain of the convent, reminded the congregation that the Emperor Charles and his family had been persecuted by the free masons and socialists of Europe, and that he had suffered his torment and endured his painful exile always in a manner true to his faith. He then quoted from one of the Emperor's biographies which read:

> *"Christian and Catholic, the Emperor Charles I was a sovereign of another age among the workings and diplomacy of modern governments. Progressive Europe could no longer tolerate a Catholic monarch among its midst, and has therefore degenerated."*

> *"The extent of the degeneration", he added, "could be observed by the happenings in Europe today (i.e. 1918 to 1940), which is as a result, suffering the terrible consequences".(20)*

Finally, Father Gagnon congratulated the Empress for the tremendous show of faith that she and her children had demonstrated in these troubled times when misfortune seemed stronger than ever, and stressed the honour that had come to Québec and to their institute through the coming of the Imperial family to the Villa Saint Joseph.(20)

Her Majesty, after thanking Father Gagnon, and being told a little bit of the history of the Sisters of Ste. Jeanne d'Arc, expressed her wish to meet each and every one of them. In a reception line composed of the Imperial family members, the Mother General of the Convent presented each Sister personally to Her Majesty and to each member of her family. The Empress personally greeted and thanked each Sister in a manner that the congregation later described as warm, graceful and charming. As each Sister's hand touched the hand of the Empress, the simplicity and grandeur of this great lady was transmitted to them in a manner that they would never forget. The ceremony closed with a song in honour of Saint Joan of Arc:

> *"Femmes, pourquoi perdre courage? Est-ce que Dieu n'a pas promis qu'une humble fille du village qui garde encore ses brebis conduirait, quelque jour, l'armée à la victoire? Et pourtant nous sentons que faiblit notre foi: À la prédiction comment saurait-on croire quand l'ennemi partout jette en nos rangs l'effroi?"*

> *("Women, why lose courage? Did God not promise That a humble girl of the village Who still guards her lambs, Would one day lead the army to victory? And yet when we feel that our faith is weakening: How could we believe this prediction, When the enemy, attacking on all sides Spreads terror among our ranks?")*

Those of the Sisters of Ste. Jeanne d'Arc who to this day remember that eventful day of October 22, 1940, still speak of the intense rays of ardent faith that emanated from the soul of this great Lady whose remarkable courage and inbred Christianity assisted her in carrying the burden of her heavy cross. The ordeals suffered by their own Jeanne de Lorraine, they thought later, must have been a premonition of the sufferings that were forced upon this great Lady of the House of Habsburg-Lorraine. Had God in his wisdom, entrusted the protection of the Emperor Charles into her hands, as He had entrusted their Jeanne d'Arc to protect King Charles VII of France?(20)

It was October 24, 1940, when the Imperial family and its retinue moved into the Villa Saint Joseph. Joining the Empress in her new home, in which she was to pass almost ten years of her life, were the two Archdukes, the Archduchess Charlotte, the Empress' mother — the Duchess Maria Antonia, and the Empress's sister — the Princess Isabelle, the Countess Kerssenbrock and Miss Herma Dobler. They were soon joined by others who had crossed the Atlantic by ship and made their way to Québec. These included the three members of the Dufek family, and Count Henry Eltz, Count Degenfeld, and a friend of the Archdukes by the name of Franz Laizner.(30) The Archduchess Elisabeth remained a pensioner at the Collège Jésus-Marie with her cousin the Princess Elisabeth of Luxemburg, and Prince Jean of Luxemburg took up residence in private quarters in Sillery.

CHAPTER 10

AT COLLEGE JESUS-MARIE

It was the 12th day of September 1940 when the Archduchess Elisabeth entered the Collège Jésus-Marie in Sillery to complete her university entrance studies. The Collège had been associated with the Université Laval since 1925, and it provided its students with a baccalaureate degree in the classic sense of the old educational system of the Province of Québec. Its teachers were Sisters of Jésus-Marie, a teaching order introduced into Sillery by the Abbé Joseph Honoré Routhier in 1849. The Abbé had wanted to establish a second order of teaching nuns in Québec — the first being the Ursulines — and chose to do so some eight kilometers west of Québec City along the old Chemin St. Louis, which was the old king's highway linking Québec City with Montréal, some 260 kilometers to the east. He also wanted a site that was accessible by both road and water, since there was, at that time, no bridge linking the north and south shores of the St. Lawrence, and a ferry boat provided services between Québec, Sillery and New Liverpool (St. Romuald).(17)

The site for the new convent was chosen therefore near the intersection of the Chemin St. Louis and the Côte de l'Eglise which connected upper Sillery to the ship's landing at Pointe-à-Puiseaux. The site, which included a very fine villa known as "Sous-les-bois" because it was surrounded by a beautiful stand of old maple trees, was purchased in 1849 by the Abbé Routhier from a Québec notary whose name was Errol Boyd Lindsay, and given to the Sisters. The Villa Sous-les-bois housed the first sisters, their chaplain Abbé Octave Audet, and a handfull of student "pensionnaires."(17)

Construction on the permanent convent, which was designed and built after plans drawn up by the Québec architect Ferdinand Peachy, was completed by September 1870. Some five additions to the original structure saw the convent considerably enlarged when the Archduchess Elisabeth first came to the Sillery on September 12, 1940. The convent had also been elevated to the status of "collège" on February 25, 1924 when it became affiliated with the Université Laval. It became known as the "Collège Classique, le Couvent Jésus-Marie de Sillery", or, in shorter form, "The Collège Jésus-Marie." Unfortunately however, the convent suffered a disastrous fire on the night of May 13-14, 1983, and was completely destroyed. It has since been re-built and continues to serve as a collège of the highest distinction for young ladies from Québec, from the surrounding country side, and from many foreign lands where the teaching quality of the convent and its collège has become famous.(17)

Life at the collège in the 1940's did not leave the students much time for personal pleasures other than their work. The girls were invited to attend Mass daily at 6:00 a.m., and although it was not obligatory to do so, the Archduchess Elisabeth made it her daily morning routine to attend Mass and take Holy Communion.(33)

After Mass, it was breakfast, and then morning classes started at 8:30 a.m. and ended at 11:30 a.m., when the lunch break began. After a light lunch and a short rest, the students would commence their afternoon classes at 1:30 p.m. These would continue until 3:30 p.m. when a "goûter" of light refreshments would sustain the students for the rest of the afternoon, including a study period in their rooms. Supper was served at 5:30 p.m., and was followed up by a short recreation period, after which homework assignments in their rooms completed the day. Bedtime was early because the next day's morning bell would sound at 5:30 a.m., calling the students to Mass and into another day. Saturdays and Sundays were free and the students could participate in organized sports and other recreational activities, or go home if feasible.(33)

The collège curriculum followed by the Archduchess Elisabeth included courses in sociology, philosophy, religion, science, mathematics, chemistry, French literature, music and etiquette. The classes were small and usually included not more than half a dozen students. In the class of 1940-41, six young ladies wrote and passed their university entrance examinations. They were the Archduchess Elisabeth, and Mesdemoiselles Suzanne Casgrain, Judith Duclos, Thérèse Lemay, Gilberte Violette, and Madeleine Gingras.(18)

The relationship between the students and the Archduchess was always formal. Communication between them was never on a first name basis, and the Archduchess was addressed by the teachers by Madame Elisabeth. However, uniforms were "de rigueur" (i.e. compulsory) and were the same for all students. They consisted of a navy-blue tunic worn over a white blouse having a round collar and long sleeves with cuffs. Affixed to their navy-blue tunics and over their hearts was the collège crest, one half of which showed three antique golden lamps on a field of azure blue, and the second half, a golden flowering lilly on a field of darker blue. In the centre of the crest was a smaller silver crest bearing the azure blue initials "JM."(33)

During her sojourn at Collège Jésus-Marie, the Archduchess felt and was treated like any other student. If anything, she received there a little more freedom than she might have had at home, where formalities with her mother, the Empress, always dominated an otherwise loving relationship. Like the other Imperial children, she always approached her mother with deference, and, except for the most intimate moments, usually through the Countess Kerssenbrock. Respect for her mother, the Empress of Austria, was instilled in her at an early age, and paralleled her respect for God and the Church. Her mother was the matriarch of the House of Habsburg, and she, Elisabeth, was her most devoted servant. This respect for formality, and the ingrained knowledge that she was an Archduchess first and foremost, at once became very apparent to her classmates. Unlike the rest of her friends at the collège, she once said there were only three men in the existing world whom she could someday marry. And she later married one of them.(33) (45)

In addition to her studies, the young Archduchess also had a passion for sports and the outdoors. She eagerly participated in various sport programs offered at the collège and became an active

Girl Guide. In this activity, she found herself enrolled in the Eighth Company of Girl Guides of Notre-Dâme de Québec, of which she later became Deputy Leader. She loved nature and the outdoors and amazed her comrades with her knowledge of flora and fauna, and with her love for the many birds and animals that roamed the Québec countryside which the troop would explore whenever time and weather permitted.(35)

And so the year passed. When the final examinations were written, the Archduchess returned to the Villa Saint Joseph where she enjoyed the summer outings and the endearing company of her brothers and sisters.

When the summer was ended and the Archduchess had been admitted to the Faculty of Social Sciences at Université Laval, she returned one more time to the college which she had learnt to love and through which she had made many friends. It was the occasion of the graduation ceremony at the Collège Jésus-Marie, and the Archduchess and her "Class of '41" were about to receive their diplomas.(18)

It was October 25, 1941 when the ceremony of honouring the graduating students took place. This ceremony, which was normally a very solemn occasion, was on this day particularly grandiose, not only because the Archduchess Elisabeth of Austria was going to receive her Baccalaureate in Arts, but because the Empress of Austria herself was going to participate in the festivities. Among the honoured guests were the Reverend Monseigneur Camille Roy, rector of the Université Laval; Her Royal Highness, Madame the Duchess Maria Antonia of Bourbon-Parma, mother of the Empress; Their Imperial and Royal Highnesses, the Archduchess Charlotte, and the Archdukes Charles Louis and Rudolf; Her Royal Highness, the Princess Isabelle of Bourbon-Parma, sister of the Empress; His Royal Highness, the Prince Jean of Luxemburg; Madame Therese Countess von Korff Schmising-Kerssenbrock; and Their Royal Highnesses, The Princesses Elisabeth, Marie Adelaide, Marie Gabrielle, and Alix of Luxemburg. In addition, there were present numerous professors and dignitaries from the Université Laval, the good Sisters of the Jésus Marie, many students of the collège, and their parents.

The activities started with an acknowledgement of the Empress by Miss Suzanne Casgrain, a fellow student of the Archduchess Elisabeth, and class valedictorian. In her address to the Empress she remarked:

"At this time last year, the good Angels who accompanied the Imperial family on its arduous voyage, saw fit to allow Her Majesty and her Imperial family to visit Notre Dame de Sillery.

We are reminded of the first snowfall, the soft snowflakes falling slowly, covering the Villa Saint Joseph and its surrounding trees and bushes with a white blanket.

And while the Villa with its solitary avenues and somber quiet, which reminds one of a Benedictine monastery, had welcomed the Imperial family, the Collège de Sillery sadly regretted the loss of its illustrious visitors and began to live on memories.

Each morning in the chapel and again in the evening, the students used to see the grand ladies praying devoutly. But now, the purple prayer kneelers with their praying figures are no longer there.

During the days, even without seeing them, we knew that they were there. Their invisible presence gave us joy and reminded us of their faith and humbleness.

And in this very hall, one evening just a year ago, the Collegians of Sillery assembled to welcome, and see with their own eyes, the direct descendents of the Emperors and Kings of Catholic Europe.

When on October 24, 1940 the Archangel Raphael brought these noble refugees to our door, he left in our college, two charming princesses, and with them the hope in our hearts that this great lady would someday return to us and again grace our souls.

It is therefore with our sincerest thanks to our noble companion and to your dear child, Madame, that we now have the honour to receive from your hands our scholarly rewards, and we extend to Your Majesty our humble homage and deepest gratitude.

Only providence knows what the future holds, and no one knows better than you do, Your Majesty, that we must be thankful for whatever divine providence may hold for us.

Today, when so much benevolence invites daring, may the youth of Sillery again hope to see you in this hall, or if I may be more daring, could we hope that some day Your Majesty will deign to address us? What a marvelous teacher of history we would listen to with all our utmost attention.

The community of Jésus-Marie, the collegians and their parents, again wish to express to Your Majesty, their sincerest admiration."(18)

Following Miss Suzanne Casgrain's homage, Her Majesty rose to accept a bouquet of chrysantemums from Miss Judith Duclos, a classmate of the Archduchess Elisabeth, while a chorus of voices sang in French, the Beautiful Blue Danube. The text was very apropos:

"Mighty River with waves so blue,
Reflecting the sky and dazzling the eye.
Who can not wish to gaze upon its beauty?
And greetings to Hungary, the country of Magyars.
This cherished land full of courage and art."

Then, one by one, Her Majesty gave to each graduating student, her academic prizes and her Baccalaureate in Arts degree.

Following the formalities, the students presented a play written by Mr.Henri Ghéon, called "The Sultan's Daughter and the Good Gardener."

Assisting in this presentation were Miss Louise Gauthier as the Sultan, Miss Simonne Mousseau as The Amber Pearl, Miss Madeleine Doyon as The Gardener of the Sultan, Miss Réjane Poulin as the Sister "tourière", and Miss Suzanne Casgrain as The Good Gardener.

Miss Patricia Poitras, who received her Baccalaureate in Singing that evening, then sang an appropriate song for Her Majesty:

"The land of a sovereign
Who made our laurels flourish

Also proclaims
Honour to my melody!
And on the day when we have to
Leave these hallowed halls with regret,
We call upon a blond Archduchess,
And her admirable Mother,
To show us the way
Into this valley,
By graciously bestowing upon us
Our baccalaureates from Laval."(18)

After a bouquet of red roses was presented to Her Majesty by Miss Madeleine Gingras, Reverend Monseigneur Camille Roy addressed the assembled gathering. In his remarks, he included the following reference to Her Majesty:

> "Madame, your presence at this academic gathering adds a very special prize to the graduates who today are receiving their graduation diplomas from the Collège of Sillery. The graduating class of 1941 is additionally honoured to have in its midst, Madame the Archduchess Elisabeth, and to have received from the hands of Your Majesty the precious documents which attest to their having received their Bachelor in Arts degrees.

> If there is honour in receiving their degrees today, let me assure you that these honours are not obtained "honoris causa." Madame the Archduchess and her companions have won their honours "laboris et meriti causa", i.e. through hard work and merit.

In his remarks and in closing the graduation ceremony, the Abbé Alphonse Marie Parent, Secretary of the Faculty of Philosophy at Université Laval and Professor of Philosophy at the Collège Jésus-Marie, reviewed the history of the collège over its last 30 years. he remembered the historic first meeting between the faculty and students with Her Majesty and with her Imperial family on the previous October 21, 1940. He remembered the first visit of Madame the Grand Duchess Charlotte of Luxemburg and her husband, Monseigneur the Prince Felix of Bourbon-Parma, and the coming to Sillery of their children the Princesses Marie Adelaide, Marie Gabrielle, and Alix, to take up their studies at the Jésus-Marie and follow in the footsteps of Madame the Archduchess Elisabeth, who had now graduated from the collège. In closing, Monseigneur Parent thanked Her Majesty for the confidence she had given to the Collège Jésus-Marie and to the Sisters who had taught her Imperial and Royal Highness, the Archduchess Elisabeth.(18)

The last activity on the Program was the confering of prizes by Her Majesty to the most deserving students. Twenty-four students in all faculties, including the Archduchess Elisabeth, received prizes from the hands of the Empress. Those won by the Archduchess Elisabeth included: the prize for morality, the prize for logic, the first prize for university physics, the first prize for plain and analytical geometry, a prize for practical chemistry, and the second prize for algebra and trigonometry.

In addition, the Abbé Arthur Lacasse of the Royal Society of Canada, dedicated his latest work, "Le Défilé des Heures" (The Unwinding of the Hours) to the Archduchess Elisabeth, and last but not least, the Archduchess received special mention for her respectful deference to authority, for her always friendly obligingness, and for her never-failing punctuality.(18)

And so, the chapter closed for the Empress and her immediate family at Jésus-Marie. Her memory and good deeds, however, remain at the Collège to this day. Those who knew her personally, of whom there still are a few around, loved her with devotion and respect, and those who came later to the convent, both Sisters and students, speak of Her Majesty with the highest respect and reverence. It can be said she deeply left her mark, and even though the old hallowed halls which saw the Empress of Austria in her Imperial and Royal person in 1940 and 1941 have since burnt to ashes, the spirit of the Empress still reigns supreme in that modern building of the 80's that now is the Collège Jésus-Marie.

CHAPTER 11

AT UNIVERSITE LAVAL

As already mentioned, three of the Empress's children were admitted upon their arrival in 1940, into the Université Laval. Their qualifications had been presented in advance to the University by the Countess Kerssenbrock to Father Georges Henri Lévesque, Dean of the Faculty of Social Sciences. The three students were the Archdukes Charles Louis and Rudolf, and the Archduchess Charlotte.(32)

The Archduke Charles Louis, born on March 10, 1918 had begun his academic life at the Jesuit College of St. Michel in Brussels in 1929. He studied there for 9 years, obtaining his university entrance requirements in 1938. He then entered the Catholic University of Louvain outside of Brussels where he registered in courses leading to a Law degree. His studies included Sociology and Economics, but were interrupted by the events of May 10, 1940 when the German armies began their invasion of Belgium.(9)

The Archduke Rudolf, born September 5, 1919 had also attended the Jesuit College of St. Michel in Brussels, where he followed courses in the Humanities until 1935. From 1936 to 1938 he studied for his Matura (High School Leaving) in the Duchy of Luxemburg, undertaking courses according to the Austrian curriculum. These courses were in preparation for his anticipated studies at the Schottengymnasium in Vienna. This center of learning, whose name can be roughly translated into "Celtic College", was established in the middle of the 12th century by the Babenberg Duke Heinrich Jasomirgott, who invited a Benedictine order of Irish monks to come to Vienna and establish a monastery. This monastery, whose name honours their memory, became the city's first religious center of learning, and remains, to this day, a renowned center of classical education. It was in this college that the Emperor Charles had also studied, and it was in this college that the Archduke Rudolf had hoped to continue his studies. However, because Austria had in 1938 been annexed by Hitler's Germany, the young Archduke had to change his educational plans, and instead attended the Catholic University of Louvain in Belgium. He thus followed in his older brother's foot-steps, and enrolling in courses leading towards a degree in law, also studied economics and sociology. However, his studies there were also interrupted by the hostilities that suddenly befell Belgium.(9)

The Archduchess Charlotte, who was born March 1, 1921 began her academic studies in the Couvent des Dames de Marie in Brussels in 1933, and continued there until 1936. Also, anticipating to con-tinue her studies at the Viennese Schottengymnasium with her brother, the Archduke Rudolf, she too followed a course of studies designed to allow her access to that ancient and renowned Viennese center of learning. Her preparatory studies were undertaken at Steenockerzeel under the guidance of a private tutor by the name of Ernst Sieber.(9)

However, when in March 1938, Austria was suddenly occupied by Hitler's troops, the educational plans of the Archduchess Charlotte also underwent drastic revision. She then continued her studies in Louvain where she worked towards a degree in Economics. How-ever, when the German armies invaded Belgium, the Archduchess fled with her family and began her fateful journey to America.(9)

In Québec, the two Archdukes and the Archduchess Charlotte enrolled in the Faculty of Social Sciences under Father Georges Henri Lévesque. At the time the faculty had not yet been divided into its three fundamental parts as it is today, — namely Sociology, Economics, and Political Science. It was then still a young faculty, affiliated with the Faculty of Philosophy, and its students therefore received a good general grounding in all of the three disciplines outlined above, rather than in only one of the three disciplines as practicality and progress dictated in later years.(32)

The Imperial students thus received broad instructions in the main courses in Sociology, in Economics and in Political Science, and therefore received the benefits that such broad scope, and much

---

9/ p. 437, 449-450

smaller classes than today's, allowed. The additional courses that constituted the "missed" subjects in Humanities, were administered through the department's affiliation with the Faculty of Philosophy, and this in turn allowed the development of a close personal relationship between the Archdukes and their "private" teacher, Professor Charles De Koninck.(32)

Father Georges Henri Lévesque, Dean of the Faculty of Social Sciences in 1940, remembered his Imperial students with great admiration. "They were very agreeable and very well-mannered", he recalled. "In addition, they were very serious and very dedicated to their studies. My first impressions were also those of every one who came in contact with them. All the students, all the professors, all the faculty, were very impressed with them, and they in turn, seemed very pleased to be with us here in Québec. They were simple and considerate, not arrogant at all", Father Lévesque remembered, "and they quickly became friends with the other students and with the faculty."(32)

"When she first came to discuss their entrance into the University", Father Lévesque added, "the Countess Kerssenbrock asked if it would be possible to have the Archdukes seated in the front row of their classes." And he said to her, "I pray Madame that you do not insist on this. We are a democratic country, and we give everyone the right to choose where they may wish to sit. It would be a catastrophy for both the Princes and for the students if we were to do as you ask" he continued, "because it would be a kind of segregation."(32)

And then the Countess asked if it would be possible for the other students to address the Princes as "Monseigneur"? Again Father Lévesque said "Please do not ask this if you want the Princes to be happy." "Eventually, everyone called the Princes by their first name, and they sat amongst the other students wherever they wanted, and they were happy", Father Lévesque remarked. He later told this story to the Archdukes and they were not only happy but very thankful. They were delighted to be considered just like anyone else at the university, and thrived in the university atmosphere.(32)

During their first winter in Canada, the Archdukes quickly learnt that the winter season in Québec could not be fought; it had to be joined. And so they participated eagerly in many of the student's winter sports activities. They even learnt to drive an automobile on Québec's winter streets, which in those days was not an easy matter. Québec City has considerably more snow than any comparable city in Canada, and the fact that it is built on hills, makes winter driving there quite an art, normally left only to taxi and street-car drivers and other hardy professionals.(31)

And so it was that one day, just before Christmas of 1940, the Archduke Rudolf volunteered to deliver a small Christmas present that the family had concocted to Miss Marguerite MacDonald and her mother, who were living about two kilometers from the Villa Saint Joseph in Sillery. (Miss MacDonald was the lady who Canada's Minister of State, the Honourable Pierre Casgrain, had contacted to assist in settling the Imperial family in Québec).(31)

When the Archduke arrived at the MacDonald home, he arrived just in time to see Miss MacDonald leave the house for a dental appointment in downtown Québec City. He offered to drive her, as her dentist was located on rue de la Fabrique, in the old city. The young Archduke skillfully manoeuvered his vehicle and passenger through the slippery snow-bound streets of old Québec, and finally arrived at the Dentist's building. "How long will you be" he asked his passenger. "About an hour" she replied, and then the Archduke said, "I'll wait for you", and he did. When the Archduke had later safely deposited his passenger back at her home in Sillery, Miss MacDonald could not help but recall, "and to think it had to take two wars and one revolution for me to be driven around by an Archduke."(31)

The Archdukes also eagerly participated in the normal student activities of the day, and made many friends. One of these was Jean Bussières who accompanied the young Archdukes one summer to Western Canada. It was customary for the students at Laval to spend some of their summer vacation helping farmers in Western Canada gather their crops. With many young men enlisted in Canada's armed services, labour on the farms was difficult to obtain, and so the farmers often welcomed the assistance of willing students with their wheat harvest.(32)

And so it was that one year, in the summer of 1941, the two Archdukes and their friend Jean Bussières found themselves in Alberta helping a local farmer with his harvest. As the Archdukes insisted they wanted to be known as just two students from Québec, their employer was not advised of who they really were. But at the end of the season, after the work had all been done and the students were about to return to Québec, someone let the farmer know who his guests were. And on the day the students were to be paid for their efforts on the farm, the farmer remarked that since they were princes anyway, they probably did not need the money, and he did not pay them. The two Archdukes therefore had to borrow money from their friends so that they could eat on their return trip across the continent to Québec. However, their sojourn in the western Canadian sun did leave the young men healthy and happy, and when they returned to Quebec's second season, they felt strengthened and wiser, even though somewhat disillusioned.(31)

Once again back on campus, the Archdukes quickly picked up their camaraderie as well as their studies. Another one of their classmates was Doris Lussier who later became famous in Canadian dramatic circles as "Père Gédéon" in the Radio Canada — CBC production of "La Famille Plouffe" — a television series that played for many years on both French and English television throughout Canada.(32)

One day, on the occasion of Father Lévesque's anniversary, the students wrote and presented a play called "The Day of the Dean." It was a satire on a day in the life of Father Lévesque and personified the Dean's day in humorous anecdotes, starting from his rising at 5:30 a.m.and retiring late in the evening. Father Levesque's role was played by Doris Lussier, and he apparently touched on all aspects of the good Father's daily life, to the great amusement of all the students. The Archdukes, notwithstanding, laughed at the exaggerated antics of their beloved Dean as much as anyone — and Father Lévesque even today tells the story of that long ago farce with great delight and with a broad smile.(32)

"The Archdukes were there" he said, "and they greatly enjoyed participating in the student's activities." This showed that the informal familiarity that existed between the students and their professors was also enjoyed by the two Archdukes. Nevertheless, the faculty members, in deference to their station, always addressed the Archdukes as "Monseigneur" and the Archduchess as "Madame", even when their discussions were on a one-on-one basis.(32)

The Imperial students also actively participated in one of Quebec's famous spring past-times, the sugaring-off party. This is were maple sap is collected in buckets hanging on maple trees in March of each year, as it rises in the heat of the spring sun. The sap is then boiled down in especially constructed "sugar shacks" and condensed about 40:1 into maple syrup. The product is then eaten as a sweetener on pancakes, bread, or ham, or made into delicious sugar pies, maple butter, and maple candy — all of which were highly favoured by the Imperial students, even though not necessarily beneficial to the Imperial teeth.(32)

On another occasion the Imperial family members accepted an invitation to go hunting on the farm of Monsieur Léonce Lévesque, brother of Father Georges Henri Lévesque. Monsieur and Madame Léonce Lévesque had a farm in the Roberval area of Lac Saint-Jean, some 300 kilometers north-east of Québec City. It was the Fall of 1941, and the magnificent pine forests covering the landscape, as well as the gastronomic delights of the region, made the outing sufficiently rewarding, even though the Imperial party came across neither moose nor bear in Québec's hunting and fishing paradise. They enjoyed instead learning of the region's history — that in 1725, explorations by one Georges Baptiste le Gardeur de Tilly, opened up the area as a chief source of lumber for France's naval and marine requirements. Since 1838, following incursions by the first trappers, missionaries and adventurers, the region gradually opened itself to the needs of agriculture, and a characteristic culture greeted the Archdukes Charles Louis and Rudolf, the Archduchesses Elisabeth and Charlotte, and the Countess Kerssenbrock when they arrived at their host's farm on that Thanksgiving weekend in October 1941. This culture, which treats the Lac Saint-Jean region almost as if it were a country within a country, has its own flag, its own history, its own archives, its own folklore, and its own legends. But above all it has its own faithful "citizens" who are jovial, hospitable, and extremely friendly, as well as its own culinary specialties consisting of a cuisine unlike any other in the province. It was no wonder then that the Archdukes and their Imperial sisters, even today still remember that outing in highly cherished terms.(32)

As already mentioned earlier, during the times that the Archdukes were attending classes at the Faculty of Social Sciences at Université Laval, they were also taking private courses from Professor De Koninck. These courses, taken "after hours" were mainly courses in Philosophy. They were the traditional courses any student would have had under Québec's old classical educational system before being admitted to University. They included studies in traditional philosophy, and included the works of St. Thomas Acquinas, certain philosophical studies, some traditional metaphysics, physics, and some elements of theology.(32)

Professor Charles De Koninck gave these courses to the Imperial students mainly in his home at No. 25 rue Ste. Geneviève, and this home eventually began to be lovingly referred to by the Archdukes as the "Université De Koninck." It was a beautiful classical home that lent itself graciously to the needs of the De Koninck family and to the academic needs of the Imperial students who spent many pleasant, interesting and productive hours within its walls. The nature of the house, its history, and its characteristics are described in more detail in another part of this book.(36)

Because he was a great Christian philosopher, and because he was known to the Empress Zita from his work at the Catholic University in Louvain, there soon developed a special affinity and respect between Professor Charles De Koninck and the Empress Zita. This affinity was due in large part to the immense piety of the Empress, and the fact that Professor Charles De Koninck was a man of great faith. They found in their common devoutness the bonds that allowed them to communicate together on a very high plane. Both had a stong devotion to the Blessed Virgin, and their high moral ideals contributed not only to their own close friendship, but also to unbreakable ties that still hold the Imperial and De Koninck families together to this day. These ties have been reinforced by specific sponsorship commitments between certain members of the Imperial family and certain members of the De Koninck family in the form of godparent-godchild relationships. Such and similar relationships are more clearly defined under "Epilogue" in this book, and specifically under the "De Koninck" and under the "Germain" families.(36)

The tutorials given by Professor Charles De Koninck to the Archdukes also resulted in close ties between the students and their teacher. Although the Archduchess Charlotte as well as Prince Jean of Luxemburg participated in these tutorials, the closest ties forged were those between Professor De Koninck and the Archdukes — particularly with the Archduke Rudolf. Their academic interests and their respective personalities resulted in the forging of strong personal bonds between these two men. They joked a lot, understood each other extremely well, and their friendship continued even after the Archdukes completed their studies and left Québec. Their bonds were further strengthened over the years through continued correspondence and particularly through periodic visits by the Archduke Rudolf to Québec. This bond would not be broken until the sudden death of Professor Charles De Koninck in 1965.(36)

And so, with the help and support of Professor De Koninck, the make-up courses were achieved, and with four full semesters behind them at the Université Laval, the two Archdukes, Charles Louis and Rudolf, and their younger sister, the Archduchess Charlotte, completed their academic programs. It was then the Spring of 1942, and the world was still in turmoil. There was neither the time then, nor the luxury, to remain in Québec and study for their Doctorate degrees, as they might have done had there not been a war on. So first things first. There was other work to be done and such studies could be undertaken later. The priorities at the moment were to fight against Hitler — to get personally involved in the allies' military operations, and to help work the strategic task of ensuring a free and independent Austria and Hungary when the fighting ended. The Archdukes therefore left the Université Laval with a License degree in Social Sciences. The Archduchess Charlotte similarly graduated, but went on to Fordham University in New York where she further specialized in sociology.(30)

CHAPTER 12

THE EMPRESS

With the Archdukes Charles Louis and Rudolf, and the Archduchess Charlotte living "at home", the Empress Zita was usually fully occupied with their well-being. As she had already done for most of her life, she occupied herself with budgeting the meager resources available to her for the optimum good of the family. It must be remembered that the Empress had also under her roof, her mother the Duchess of Bourbon-Parma, her sister the Princess Isabelle, the Countess Kerssenbrock who had been with her since 1918, her secretary Herma Dobler who had served her faithfully since 1931, and a small number of servants who had come with her from Europe. In addition, there were a few other refugees who had fled to America and who had gravitated to the Empress in Québec. These were mainly old and faithful acquaintances and included the Counts Degenfeld and Eltz. The former had been with the family since 1918 as governor and private teacher to the Imperial children, and Count Eltz who was the brother of the wife of Count Saldanha, in whose home in Portugal the family had stayed while waiting to leave for America. Both Counts were Austrian by birth, and had lost all their family property and possessions when the National Socialists gained control of Austria in 1938. They had also found refuge in Québec where they worked for the Imperial family as best they could under the trying circumstances that providence had bestowed upon them.(30)

At times therefore, the Villa Saint Joseph must have seemed quite crowded and its larder somewhat over-streched. But the Empress had been accustomed over the years to "water the soup" when the occasion required it, and although her meager resources did not allow her any extravagances, no one under her shelter ever suffered from hunger either. Her "miracles of multiplying loaves and fishes" to meet the needs of the occasion, were greatly helped by the generosity of her benefactors, among whom was Québec's Cardinal Villeneuve and the good Sisters of the Congregations of Jésus-Marie and Ste. Jeanne d'Arc.(36)

There was also some financial assistance from friends and supporters in London and Washington, as well as from some more well off Austrians who had fled their homelands in 1938. Among these was the former Austrian Chancellor Dr. Kurt Schuschnigg, whose assistance Count Degenfeld acknowledged in a letter in 1942. He wrote:

> "I wish I could express to you how very much Her Majesty and all their Highnesses are always moved by your affection and loyalty,and how they pray that God will reward you for all that you have done and for all that you are always doing. And may He also repay you a thousandfold for your constant loyalty."(10)

By means of such assistance and the good will and help of the religious community in Québec, the Empress Zita managed not only to make ends meet, but also to help others who were less fortunate than she was. Countless refugees from her homeland who had managed to make it to freedom in America, beseeched her for her help. Such help was sought not solely for money, but also for assistance in finding work and shelter.(36)

Monetary assistance also came from her sons, the Emperor Otto and the Archduke Felix, who were working in New York and Washington for the freedom of Austria, and who themselves were committed to helping any and all of their countrymen who had made it to America and who needed help. Their work with the Austrian National Committee, which was dedicated to the re-establishment of an independent Austria, also required funds. And for these, and for the support of his Mother the Empress, the Emperor Otto often went into debt, obligations which he eventually repaid through proceeds from lecture tours throughout the United States and Canada.

During her early days in Québec there is a story to be told of how the Empress of Austria appeared to some children. They were the children of Maître Stanislas Germain — two girls 8, and 10. One day their father told them that their house was being honoured by a visit from an Empress and two princes.(35)

The two young ladies became excited and began to imagine what an empress might look like. They had read all the children's stories about kings and queens and princes and princesses, and so they expected a Cinderella-like person, all dressed up in a long shining dress and wearing a crown. The only princes they had ever known were always in shining armour and on horseback. So when on a dismal Fall day in 1940, the Empress and her two sons came to their house, the young girls were very disappointed. The lady before them, although she wore a long dress, was all in black. There was no crown, no sparkling jewelry, no silver slippers, just a plain lady, all dressed in black. And the two princes did not look at all like princes, they were just two young men with no armour and not even a horse.(35)

The two young girls, now grown up, remembered looking at the Empress through the bannister of the staircase behind which they were hiding. The Empress suddenly appeared to them as a very motherly person, so kind in every manner, and gentle of voice. She had no pretensions, they recalled, and certainly not at all stuck-up for an Empress and a Queen. She radiated charm and simplicity, and her humanness was quite impressive. And when they were presented to the Empress by their father, the little girls made little curtsies and quickly fell under the grand lady's charm. They felt no longer shy, and quickly accepted this updated version of their old fairy tales. Recalling the event today, one of the children now grown up, still remembers the ease with which she talked to this most motherly Lady who had expressed interest in her school work and in her dolls. This Grande Dame of Europe sure knew how to find her way into a little girl's heart, they recalled, and she has stayed there to this day.(35)

And so, the Empress became a resident of Québec, and except for a short sojourn in New York City where she underwent a thyroid operation at the Doctor's Hospital in April of 1942, remained by and large, in Québec. Her sons had left in the Summer of 1942 for the United States, and her daughter, the Archduchess Charlotte, on completing her studies at Université Laval in the Spring of 1942, had also gone to New York to join her sister, the Archduchess Adelhaid, in social work. Her older sister had left Québec in 1941 to pursue courses in sociology at New York's Fordham University, and work as a social worker in East Harlem.(10)

With her family then mostly in the United States (the Archduchess Elisabeth was still studying in Québec), the Empress found herself with more and more time on her hands which she devoted to charitable works. During the Summer of 1942 she was, however, still convalescing from her thyroid operation, and had by her doctor's order submitted herself to some needed rest. She had to sleep 9 hours every night, rest for one hour every morning, and rest for another three hours every afternoon. She however quickly adapted her daytime rest periods to contemplate the problems of her "empire" and started making plans for the future.(10)

She began an extensive correspondence program, addressing her concerns for a re-established free Europe to whoever would listen, and debated her views and objectives with those in power and with influence . Her objectives were clear: to save the lands of her old Danubian empire, and above all Austria, from the clutches of Josef Stalin; to re-establish an independent Austria; and to restore, if at all possible, the Habsburg monarchy. Her means to accomplish these immense tasks, were to continually serve God, to sanctify herself, and to neverbecome discouraged.(10)

The positions she took, supported and lobbied for, included: not ceding the Trentino (the South Tirol) from Austria to Italy; the returnof Triest (Austria's pre-1918 sea port on the Adriatic Sea) to Austria; and countering the proposal of the Czechoslovakian Prime Minister in Exile, Eduard Beneś, that national minorities be exchanged between Czechoslovakia and Austria (it was Benes who had said "Better Hitler than Habsburg", and later lead his country into the shadow of communism).(10)

The Empress also spent considerable time and effort, advising and supporting her son, the Emperor Otto, who was busy lobbying the president of the United States for an independent Austria, and with her son, the Archduke Robert, in his similar lobby with Winston Churchill. She also maximized an opportunity during the Québec

Conference between Churchill, de Gaulle, Roosevelt and Stalin in August of 1943, when she met with Sir Winston Churchill to discuss the future of her old Danubian lands. She did the same thing with President Roosevelt when she met him in Washington in September of the same year. In all these discussions, she ceaselessly warned against the emergence of the Soviet Union's political power and its growing influence in Europe.

She foresaw Soviet influence gradually spreading across Eastern Europe and slowly extinguishing the hopes and freedoms of the peoples she so loved. "Is it not amazing" she wrote later, "that the Soviets were already using the same tactics that had been used by the Nazis. At first they asked for nothing more than the security of their own borders. But then this already included White Russia and the Ukraine, and then suddenly they expanded their demands to include pan-Slavic solidarity. And they did not stop there, for they then demanded influence over Poland, Hungary, Yugoslavia and Rumania."

In a September 1945 meeting at Hyde Park with President Roosevelt, the Empress lobbied for the support of the United States for the restoration of Hungary. The President promised her then that he would help this country which he also loved, and which had been so harshly treated by the Treaty of Trianon in 1919. But all these promises were to fall by the wayside at Yalta, when Stalin, Churchill and Roosevelt carved up Europe which laid the foundation for the "iron curtain" that was to separate the victors of 1945, and divide nation against nation and brother against brother for generations to come.(10)

In the meantime, back in Québec, the Empress Zita greatly increased her own personal crusade of help for the unfortunate victims of the war in Europe. She began speaking tours to raise money and support for her European charities, and together with Count Degenfeld, the Countess Kerssenbrock, and her faithful secretary Herma Dobler, began to collect clothing, food and medical supplies for the thousands upon thousands of homeless, displaced peoples of Europe. She remembered only too well from personal experience how it was in 1918, and forsaw the inevitable suffering that was bound to follow at the end of the war. She organized CARE packages and begged for public support, delivering over fifty speeches in Canada to whoever would listen in Ladies Clubs, convents, and schools. In Canada alone she gathered together relief material that was to fill over 200 large containers. In the United States she did likewise, and in all collected over $35,000 (in 1945 dollars) worth of clothing, food and medical supplies, constituting some 25,000 "CARE" packages.(36)

Because all her North American family members had by then gravitated to New York City and Washington, the Empress decided in late 1949 to also move to the United States. She did, however, return to Québec on a number of occasions after that, and maintained her friendships in that city with the various religious and lay friends that she remembered from the wartime years.(30)

Her New York headquarters became Tuxedo Park, a New York suburb in which their old family Friend, Calvin Bullock, had provided them with a villa. This villa, which is described more fully in another chapter of this book, was at first rented and later purchased by the Archduke Rudolf, and served as the family base from which the eventual return to Europe would be launched.

All in all, family life at the Villa Saint Joseph had been quite pleasant. During their student days in Québec City, the four youngest children lived mainly with their mother, except for the year that the Archduchess Elisabeth had spent as a border at the Collège Jésus-Marie (Chapter 10). They nevertheless maintained a certain etiquette amongst themselves. At home, the Empress Zita was first and foremost "the Empress", and secondly "the mother", and this fact was substantiated by an episode related by Miss Marguerite MacDonald when she once visited the Villa Saint Joseph.(36)

During a conversation between Miss MacDonald and the Empress who was seated on a divan, the Archduchess Charlotte suddenly entered the parlour. As there was no place to sit at that moment except on the divan next to her mother, the Archduchess hesitated, until she was invited by her mother to sit on the divan. She would not by herself, Miss MacDonald explained, have sat down at the same level as her mother.(31)

This deference to station and etiquette was again demonstrated when the Archduchess Elisabeth came down one day with appendicitis and had to be taken to the St. Sacrement Hospital in Québec for an operation. Although the operation went off in routine order and without any problems whatsoever, the surgeon performing the operation was asked for permission to allow one other member of the family to also attend the operation. It was tradition in the Austrian Court and in the dynasty, that a Habsburg would never be operated on without another member of the family being present. Needless to say, the wish was granted.(36)

The deference to station and etiquette was nevertheless balanced by the great sense of humanity, the simplicity and the warmness of heart possessed by the Empress. On one occasion, when Her Majesty had been invited to a reception at the house of Maître Stanislas Germain, one of the Germain children who was then only six years old, surreptitiously crept up behind Her Majesty and slapped her backside. With his mother watching in horror, the Empress turned to face the little boy and burst into laughter. "Hello Louis" she said to him with a big smile and lovingly patted him on the head. The Empress had shown she knew how to be a mother.(35)

At another reception in the same house, but some years later (1969) when the Empress had occasion to once again visit Québec, the serene dignity and delicateness of the Empress was once again demonstrated. When the conversation referred to the Empress's eldest son, who after the death of the Emperor Charles in 1922 would have inherited the throne had Austria remained a monarchy, the Empress referred to her son always in a manner relative to whom she was addressing. When speaking to Professor Charles Engel of the Université Laval whose background was Austrian, Her Majesty referred to her son as "The Emperor." When speaking to a Hungarian count who happened to attend the reception, the Empress referred to her son as "The King." And when the Empress was talking to Madame Germain or to Madame Engel, both of whom were mothers, she referred to her son as "my son." This story not only characterized the Empress as a sensitive and dignified Lady who deeply loved her Danubian homeland, but also as a loving mother who clearly understood the warmth, strength and weakness of a mother-son relationship.(37)

Many people who knew her in Québec, still reflect on her serene piety, and agree that she was truly a "Grande Dame." She was a great Lady in the sense that she stood morally tall over many of her regal peers. Her stature was extremely impressive even though her build was slight. Her courage and serenity outshone her outward simple bearing.

Professor Charles Engel, who once was present when the Empress was leaving to return to Europe from New York, described her outward simplicity as follows:

> "We had taken one of our children, who was leaving for Europe, to the ship's dock in New York. And there stood the Empress, also about to make a crossing. She was dressed unobtrusively in black and carried a very modest little suitcase in her hand. It was not an expensive crocodile suitcase, nor was it even a leather suitcase, it was a simple woven suitcase, unadorned and not at all pretentious. It was a typical example of the humility and simplicity that characterized the Empress of Austria. Yet she radiated a serene charm, the like of which no other living being could emulate."(37)

Father Georges Henri Lévesque recalls being invited to the Villa Saint Joseph for dinner. The occasion was a visit to Québec from the Emperor Otto. There were a few other guests, including Madame De Koninck, and the conversation revolved on many things. And then at one point the Empress, looking at her eldest son, leaned over to Father Lévesque, and said "I am very happy." It was the "mother", not the "Empress" who was speaking, Father Lévesque recalled.(32)

Madame Zoe De Koninck recalls the Empress in glowing terms. She was always kind and thoughtful, had an extraordinary memory for names. Even after many years when Her Majesty again visited Québec, she remembered the first names of all the De Koninck children, their ages, and their likes and dislikes. "Her eyes were always very much alive", Madame De Koninck recalls, "but they were also sometimes sad, especially when she talked about her husband." "I always felt", Madame De Koninck continued, "that the

Empress never overcame the terrible drama in her life when she lost her husband".(36)

The Empress always showed a great deal of interest in everything that was going on. She often talked about the poor people whom she called "le pauvre", and was always talking about how they needed help and how she might help them. In her many journeys through Québec and Ontario, she visited many religious congregations whose mission it was to help the poor.(36)

One of these was the Hungarian Order of Social Service Nuns in Montréal, who then had their headquarters at 3629 Ste. Famille street. It was a large, graystone building, set slightly back from the street, and approachable through a small iron gate and a small external staircase. The building still stands today but is now an apartment house, the Nuns who used to live there having moved their quarters closer to a new Hungarian church that was built in the north end of the city. The old Hungarian church, no longer in existence, stood on Clarke street between Milton and Prince Arthur streets, not far from where the Hungarian Nuns used to live. (The author used to frequent this church as a child, and remembers the gray habited nuns and Father Nicolas Horvath who was their pastor, and the pastor of the Hungarian community in Montreal from 1937 to 1960).

The Empress's interest also touched upon religious happenings in and around Québec. She liked to visit religious communities, and in one of these, at Ste. Anne de la Pocatière, a small village about 100 kilometers east of Québec City, she noted that the piano used to accompany the students at the local school, was in much needed repair. So when sometime later, someone offered her a good used piano, Her Majesty immediately sent it on to the school at the little village.

While in Québec, the Empress also liked to visit the "Musée Chinois", a private collection of oriental art that had been collected by Father Joseph Lavoie, a Jesuit priest who had spent many years as a missionary in China. It was a personal collection of artifacts and mementos, and belonged to this missionary priest who had been living in China until the communist takeover of that country in the thirties forced him to flee. He brought his private collection with him back to Québec, and because of the interest it generated there, Father Lavoie organized it into a permanent exhibition and museum. It was situated on Grande-Allée Boulevard, not far from the home of the then Prime Minister of Canada, the Right Honourable Louis St. Laurent. The museum, whose proceeds from admissions were used to finance other Catholic missions, no longer exists today. It was closed upon the death of Father Lavoie, and the artifacts and mementos were distributed to other religious institutions and museums in the Québec City area. The Musée did however provide many hours of pleasant pastime for the Empress and her family in those early years of the 1940's.(32)

CHAPTER 13

THE LOYAL LADIES

Among the many loyal ladies that had devoted themselves to the Empress's service in the ensuing years between 1916 and the present, there were only two that came with the family to Québec in 1940. They were Countess Therese von Korff Schmising-Kerssenbrock and Miss Herma Dobler.

It would however not be appropriate or just, to not mention some of the other very loyal and devoted ladies who over the years gave themselves into the service of Her Majesty, even though the family's financial conditions at times precluded them from receiving any financial compensation. They shared with Her Majesty and Their Highnesses the good and the bad, the joys and the sufferings, and the attention and isolation that the Imperial family lived through in their times of happiness and sadness. They shared with the Imperial family feast and famine, and thus consecrated their lives in many ways to this last great Empress.

Two of the earliest Ladies in Waiting that attended the Empress shortly after Her Majesty and the Emperor Charles inherited the thrones of Austria, Hungary, Bohemia Croatia, Slavonia and Dalmatia, were the Countess Agnes Schoenborn (who later married the Emperor Charles' adjutant Aladar von Boroviczeny) and the Countess von Kally. These two ladies, both of whom came from the Hungarian nobility, were joined in 1917 by the Countess Kerssenbrock, whose main responsibility was to look after Her Majesty's children. The ever increasing demands made on the Empress by the affairs of state, made such help a necessity.

When the end of hostilities forced the Imperial family to leave Vienna for Eckartsau on November 11, 1918 the two Hungarian

Ladies and the Countess Kerssenbrock also moved to Eckartsau. However in that family owned castle near the border between Austria and Hungary, the Countess von Kally left and was replaced by the Countess Bellegarde as Lady in Waiting to the Empress.

When on March 23, 1919 the political circumstances in Europe forced the Imperial family to leave Austria and go into exile, the Countesses Kerssenbrock and Bellegarde, as well as the Countess Agnes Schoenborn moved with the Empress to Prangins in Switzerland. It is interesting to also note that in the entourage that arrived at Prangins, there were also nine other servants, of whom five were women. It is also interesting to note that they came from five of the earlier Danubian lands that was the empire: a chambermaid, Amalie Dvorzák, from Czechoslovakia; a cook, Marcia Golović, from Yugoslavia; a child nurse, Anneliese Lamisch, from Poland; another chambermaid, Therese Linhardt, from Bohemia; and an unnamed servant girl from Hungary. It was truly a representative sample of the old empire that then surrounded the Empress in exile.(9)

Three years later, when the Emperor was forcibly exiled to Madeira after carrying out two unsuccessful restoration attempts from Switzerland to Hungary, the female entourage surrounding Her Majesty changed somewhat. Although the Countess Kerssenbrock was still attached to the household, the financial strains on the family and the remote location of Madeira made some changes necessary.

While still at Prangins, the Imperial family was joined by two ladies who were to be of great help to the Empress in the years to come. One was the Countess Viktoria Mensdorff, and the other was Miss Ottilie Reuter (Stern).

The Countess Mensdorff was the daughter of Austria-Hungary's last Ambassador to Great Britain in 1914, Count Albert Mensdorff, and his Portugese wife, the Countess Maria Rosina Mensdorff-Pereira. It was the Countess Viktoria Mensdorff who accompanied the children from Switzerland to Madeira to joing their parents who had been sent there directly from Hungary following their second unsuccessful restoration attempt. It was also the Countess Viktoria Mensdorff who, during the tragic days before the Emperor Charles' death on Madeira on April 1, 1922 nursed the family and staff who had come down with a serious outbreak of influenza. And it was the same Countess Mensdorff who relieved the Empress during those last days of March 1922 when the Emperor lay dying in the Quinta del Monte on Madeira.(9)

Countess Viktoria Mensdorff stayed with the Empress throughout her Spanish sojourn, being present at El Pardo and Lequeitio. It was at El Pardo that the Countess cut up some of her own clothes to make much needed clothing and diapers for the Archduchess Elisabeth, born there on May 31, 1922.(9)

Miss Ottilie Reuter also joined the family at Prangins and followed them to Madeira. She was born in Innsbruck, Austria, where she attended the Convent of the Sisters of Charity. When she was 21 years old, she was asked by the good Sisters of that convent if she would consider employment by the Empress Zita as a children's nursemaid. She was told that the position would be on Madeira, and that the job did not pay well, it was, expressed in the currency of the time, about six dollars a month. Nevertheless, she accepted, and soon joined the family on Madeira. She stayed with the family for two years until April 1924, when her mother's health back in Innsbruck required her presence. Miss Ottilie Reuter, eventually married and became Ottilie Stern. She remembers her stay with the Imperial family in endearing terms, even though her working conditions on Madeira were much more difficult than she had expected.

Also assisting the Empress on Madeira and in Spain was an older Hungarian lady by the name of Franziska Kral who acted as mid-wife at the birth of the Archduchess Elisabeth, and two other ladies, a children's nursemaid by the name of Hubalek, and a kitchenmaid called "Netti."

When the educational requirements of the children finally caused the Empress and her family to move to Steenockerzeel in Belgium in September 1929, the family was still accompanied by the Countesses Kerssenbrock and Mensdorff. They were also joined by a couple named Gudenus who became in effect managers of the household. Whereas Baron Gudenus was charged with the responsibilities of the family's finances and with its administrative functions, his wife the Baroness Gudenus, occupied herself with managing the household.

9/ p. 519, 524

And because the Empress was occupying more and more of her time re-activating her relationship with the Gotha of Europe, a secretary was hired to deal with the ever-increasing volume of correspondence and paper work that came across the Empress' desk. Her name was Anni Possawad, and she was later joined by a second secretary, Herma Dobler from Vienna.

There were of course other servants, who over the years, served the Empress faithfully and diligently, but only two of these, came to Québec. They were the Countess Kerssenbrock and Miss Herma Dobler.

THE COUNTESS KERSSENBROCK:

Countess Therese von Korff Schmising-Kerssenbrock was born in the Kingdom of Bohemia under the old Austrian Monarchy in the year of our Lord 1887. She joined the Imperial family in Laxenburg, near Vienna, on February 1, 1917 as adjutant (Aja) to the Empress, and initially as governess to her four children (Crown Prince Otto, age 5; the Archduchess Adelhaid, age 3; and the Archdukes Robert and Felix, ages 2 and 1 respectively). Having inherited the throne in 1916, as well as a horrible war, the Imperial couple suddenly found themselves extremely occupied with affairs of state, and this left the Empress with very little time to devote to her young family. This task therefore had to be delegated to someone else, to someone of impeccable morals with a strong will and inexhaustible patience. Of the many ladies at court and in the nobility of the times, the Empress chose the Countess Kerssenbrock. Her choice was to be proven a wise one, for the Countess turned out not only to be an excellent governess for the children, but eventually also a most cherished and faithful confident to Her Majesty. She was to be with the Empress for 55 years, until her death in 1973.

One month after having been engaged as "Aja" to the Empress, the Countess attended Her Majesty at the birth of her fifth child, the Archduke Charles Louis. It was March 10, 1918 and the place was the Imperial Villa in Baden bei Wien, a famous "Spa" resort some 20 kilometers south of Vienna. Two days later, the Countess Kerssenbrock was to carry the young prince to the Cathedral in Baden for his Baptism.(27)

After the collapse of the Austrian Monarchy on November 11, 1918 the Countess remained with the Empress throughout Her Majesty's exodus from Vienna and her exile to Switzerland and Madeira. She proved to be a valuable support to the Empress Zita throughout her life, and became both loved and admired by the children who dearingly called her "Korffi."(9)

As a person, the Countess was highly respected. Always polite and proper, she became the go-between, the door to and from the Empress in Québec. Not only did she make all the necessary arrangements with the Collège Jésus-Marie for the Archduchess Elisabeth, with the Université Laval for the Archdukes Charles Louis and Rudolf and for the Archduchess Charlotte, but also for the Imperial family's accommodations in Québec. It was the Countess Kerssenbrock that one approached when one wanted to see and to talk to the Empress, and it was the Countess Kerssenbrock who expressed the wishes of the Empress to third parties. Yet she was always discreet, and quickly bowed out of any private conversation with the Empress once a contact had been made, or once a visitor had been brought to the person of Her Majesty. She received and wrote the correspondence that the Empress carried out from Québec, and was the children's confident when they needed to communicate with the Empress. There were of course many occasions when the normal mother-child relationship was left to run a natural course. In short, the Countess was the Empress' social as well as business secretary. She was Her Majesty's spokesperson and agent, as well as her best friend and advisor.(36)

As a person, she was robust but not overweight, stern but always pleasant, and sometimes tired but always energetic. The Countess was very cheerful, she laughed readily and had a good sense of humor. She loved the Imperial family and they loved her. She had for many years been considered by the family as one of them, and always considered herself as such. Nevertheless, she always maintained protocol, and always treated Her Majesty with the highest respect.

9/ p. 452-453
27/ p. 103

The Countess filled her day with her appointed duties, and liked to read and attend to the garden in back of the Villa Saint Joseph. It is said, she grew the most beautiful roses in Sillery, among which were also to be seen heads of lettuce, rows of carrots, and here and there some other vegetable that could be made use of in the cooking pot.

The Countess is remembered in Québec City by some people who were children at the time, as a person with a very deep voice. When she telephoned and asked to speak to someone, one of the grown up children recalls today, they would answer "One minute Sir", and the Countess would answer in her deep voice, "This is the Countess Kerssenbrock", and the children would turn red with embarassment.(35)

The Countess Kerssenbrock served the Empress in Vienna, Eckartsau, Prangins, Madeira, El Pardo, Lequeitio, Steenockerzeel, Lisbon, New York, and Québec City. In her later years she returned with the Empress via Tuxedo Park to Europe, and her last residence was at Zizers in Switzerland together with the Empress. It was there that she shared an apartment at the Johannes Stift with the Empress Zita and the Princess Isabelle, until she died on February 10, 1973 at the age of 86. Considered as part of the family, the Countess was laid to rest in the Habsburg crypt in the Benedictine monastery of Muri in Switzerland.

Other than the Countess Charlotte Fuchs-Mollardt, who served the Empress Maria Theresia first as Governess and later as Lady in Waiting before being laid to rest in the crypt of the Capuchins in Vienna, the Countess Kerssenbrock is the only other person of non-Royal blood to ever be laid to rest in a Habsburg crypt.

MISS HERMA DOBLER:(38, 33)

Herma Dobler was born on October 13, 1901 in Vienna. It was the end of an era that saw Vienna greatly transformed from an old walled city to a modern metropolis. The old Emperor Franz Josef I had just completed his dream, the realization of a multi-lane Ringstrasse which circumvented the old city by using the torn-down battlements as the route for a grand, tree lined boulevard. New buildings framed it on all sides, and gave the city that certain elegance matched only by Paris. It was a time that saw Austrian music, art and culture rise to new heights, giving birth not only to the new Vienna Opera House, Burgtheater, Parliament, splendid hotels and parks, together with their new electrification, but was also a time that signalled social, cultural and political changes to come.

The murder of Crown Prince Rudolf at Mayerling in 1889, followed by the natural death of his successor, the Archduke Karl Ludwig in 1897, left the Archduke Franz Ferdinand of Sarajevo fame as next in line to the throne of the aging Emperor. The Emperor's wife, the Empress Elisabeth, lovingly known as "Sissi", was then murdered in the Fall of 1899 by an Italian anarchist at Geneva in Switzerland. Where not all these omens, warnings of the bad times yet to come?

They were augmented by somewhat less tragic, but nevertheless equally mourned deaths: namely the musicians Franz von Suppé and Anton Bruckner in 1894, Johannes Brahms in 1896, Carl Ziehrer, Johann Strauss (son) and Joseph Milloecker in 1899, and Hugo Wolf in 1903.

These sad events underlined the times into which the child Herma was born. Her father was Leopold Dobler and her mother, his second wife was Herma Stixner. They too were Viennese, and lived in the radiance of the "good old times" as most older Viennese refered to the reign of Emperor Franz Josef (1830-1916).

Leopold Dobler brought up his children in the strong Catholic tradition prevalent at the time. Herma was educated by nuns from whom she learnt the Christian virtues and the love of God. She was a good student and had a talent for languages. In addition to the Latin and Greek that every student had to learn in order to graduate from the gymnasium, she also studied French, Italian, English and Russian, which with her native German gave her above average language skills which in later life were to prove very useful.

When still a young girl, her mother died, and Miss Dobler, together with her other young sisters, moved into the house of her paternal grandmother. This Mrs. Dobler happened to own a sort of large building that had been subdivided into small apartments, or "kabinets" as they were called in German. And from these, the grandmother and the young Herma Dobler received revenues which made their life considerably easier, and allowed young Herma to continue her education. She studied practical business courses, and these, together with her language skills, helped her to find a good job after graduating from the convent school which she had been attending during the war years of 1914-1918.

After war's end, she got herself a secretarial job in Vienna, and worked diligently to sustain herself in those hard times in what was left of Austria after Saint Germain and Trianon. She eventually met a young man and fell in love. They became engaged to be married, when Herma Dobler saw and answered an advertisement in a Viennese newspaper. It was the time of the great depression and more money would be needed to set up a home and start a family.

The advertisement that Herma Dobler answered was for the secretarial services of a young lady having just the qualifications she possessed. It did not say for whom or where the job was, only that it was for a very private person and that the applicant had to be diligent, dedicated and very discreet. She was called for an interview.

Young Herma Dobler was now almost thirty years old and thinking of a future with her young man. However, they had no money. So when she sometime later was advised that she had been chosen for the secretarial job and was told who her employer would be, she was faced with a great dilemma: stay in Vienna and get married under the harsh financial realities of the time, or become personal secretary to the Empress of Austria. She chose the latter, and went off to Steenockerzeel in Belgium, leaving her fiancé behind. She would return when she had made her fortune, a hope that many Austrian emigrants of the 1930's could attest to. And like many Austrians who had chosen to leave their homeland in those most difficult times, she was never to return permanently to Vienna.

And so she became understudy to Anni Possawad at Steenockerzeel, and when the former secretary left the employ of the Empress to return to Vienna in 1940, Herma Dobler became the principal secretary. She was with the Empress on May 10, 1940 and joined her in her flight across France and through Spain to Portugal. Unlike the Countess Kerssenbrock, who flew across the Atlantic from Lisbon to New York, Herma Dobler, together with many other refugees who fled to America, crossed the Atlantic by ship. When she arrived in New York, she made her way to Massachusetts where she joined the Empress at Royalston. With her many language skills, Herma Dobler had no difficulty in making her way through either English speaking America, or French speaking Canada.

In October 1940, she came with the Imperial family to Sillery, and settled in with them at the Villa Saint Joseph. There she continued her service to the Empress, and remained her loyal and faithful servant until Her Majesty left Québec in December 1949.

It was at that moment in time that Herma Dobler made the second great decision of her life — she chose to remain in Québec when the Empress left for Tuxedo Park and Europe. The war had destroyed everything that tied Herma Dobler to Europe, and there was no longer anything there to attract her. She had survived the destruction of two World Wars and could see no end to the chaos that had been her homeland. She was a monarchist, and Austria had again become a socialist republic. Furthermore, she had found a new life in Québec, had made many friends, and in general appreciated the old-world atmosphere that characterized this most European city in America. In short, she felt "at home", in Québec, and at her mid-life age she did not want to again traverse the globe and start a new life.

When the Empress left Québec, Herma Dobler moved back into the Pension des Dames at the Collège Jésus-Marie and began her new life in her new home — Québec. She had to find a job, and here her language skills again helped her. She gave German lessons.

One of her pupils at the Jésus-Marie was Sister Charlotte Genest. The good Sister taught music at the convent, and since many of her students were studying singing, a knowledge of the German language would be very beneficial to the Sister. Sister Charlotte Genest recalls the German lessons with great joy. "It was a beautiful language" she recalled, "and so expressive in song." Herma Dobler also taught her some German literature, and the two became good friends. "She taught me not only the language", Sister Charlotte Genest said with a smile, "but she also taught me to love to speak it. She was an excellent teacher."

She soon had a small group of 4 or 5 students who came to her regularly for German lessons. Among these was the Prince Charles Hugues of Bourbon-Parma, the son of Prince Xavier, brother of the Empress. The young prince, who also studied in Québec in his youth, later married Princess Irene of the Netherlands, who was the daughter of Queen Juliana, who had also found war-time refuge in Canada. The Duke now lives mostly in the United States and is the head of the House of Bourbon-Parma.

Although Herma Dobler's "little German school" at the Jésus-Marie brought her some revenue, it was not sufficient. She had to pay for her apartment at the Pension and for her board, and she therefore had to look for another job. Her friend, Miss Marguerite Barry, worked as a nurse for the Donohue family at La Malbaie (Murray Bay), some 150 kilometers downriver from Québec on the north shore of the St. Lawrence River. The Donohue family owned a paper mill at Clermont, Québec, and needed a secretary, and Miss Barry recommended her friend Herma Dobler for the job.

The Donohues lived in a big house at La Malbaie and had their offices at Clermont. They needed an experienced secretary with language skills and the qualifications offered by Miss Dobler met all their requirements. She was hired and moved to La Malbaie which was situated only a few kilometeres from Clermont. She travelled between home and work by bus, and earned a comfortable living for herself. She so pleased her employers that one day the Donohues told her that if she had someone in Austria that she wished to visit, they would pay for her trip.

And thus she returned to Austria in the Summer of 1958, her first trip back to her place of birth in almost 30 years. She obviously enjoyed her return immensely and wrote the following letter to her friend Marguerite Barry on July 14, 1958:

> "The flight was wonderful, and I endured the trip very well. After I had circled the sights in Vienna -the Opera, the Burgtheater, as well

as other music halls and stages, I made a trip into our beautiful mountain country. Unfortunately, however, from all the walking, my appetite improved and I have already gained a few pounds. It is too bad that you can not be with me."

Herma Dobler had often told her friend Marguerite Barry of the beautiful mountains in Austria, and how people there "wandered" (walked on foot) among them, over fields and valleys, and stopped to rest and eat at inns along the way. When she read Miss Dobler's note, she could almost hear the yodling, she recalled.

In the mid sixties, when Herma Dobler had reached retirement age, she left the Donohues and returned to Sillery. She again took up residence at the Pension des Dames, and spent her declining years at that hospitable institution. Her pleasures were a cigarette and a glass of white wine -the kind one drinks in Austria. She began to smoke a lot -often 40 cigarettes a day -and she began to show signs of anxiety. Her health began to deteriorate after 1975, and the years between 1977 and 1979 were particularly hard on her. She had contracted Alzheimer's disease.

Miss Marguerite MacDonald, who was then still teaching at the university in Toronto, would occasionally stay at the Pension des Dames when she visited Québec. On one such stay, she recalled being in a room next to that of Miss Dobler, and noticed that Miss Dobler had begun to experience severe bouts of anxiety. "She began to imagine things" she recalled. "Everytime I used the telephone, Miss Dobler would become very upset. She would think I was talking to the Gestapo, and she feared that they were going to come and take her away." These fears, Miss MacDonald thought, were probably due to the intense experience that Miss Dobler lived through in her flight across France to Spain -always being just one step ahead of the advancing German armies, and never quite sure that she would be safe.(31)

For a while the good Sisters at the Pension des Dames cared for the ailing Herma Dobler. But there eventually came a time when the Sisters could no longer cope with the problems of their ailing friend, and Miss Dobler was transferred to the Centre Hospitalier St. Sacrement, a chronic hospital in Québec City. There she received the care and attention that could no longer be provided by the Sisters at the Convent Jésus-Marie, and there Miss Dobler has lived as a chronic patient ever since, confined to her bed. Whenever a member of the Imperial family later visited Québec, Miss Dobler would also receive a visit. The staff at the hospital recall how Miss Dobler's eyes would light up with excitement on such occasions. However, at the time of this writing, the faithful secretary to the Empress lies there, no longer cognizant of her surroundings or visitors, and awaits the call of God to join Him in eternal life.

Before leaving the story of Herma Dobler, there is one more tribute that must be made. It is to praise the Sisters of the Jésus-Marie convent, and particularly Sister Monique Fournier, who has taken it upon herself to care for the well being of Miss Dobler. The Sisters visit her weekly, do her laundry, look after her affairs, and make sure that everything that can be done is done, to make the life of the severely incapacitated octogenarian as comfortable as possible.

CHAPTER 14

THE COUNTS AND THE COMMONER

As it was appropriate to mention the names and lives of some of the ladies who had devoted their lives to the Empress, it is also fitting and proper to recall some of the men who lived in the shadow of the Imperial family and gave of themselves in its support. Two of these men came to Québec and are the subjects dealt with in this chapter. They are the Count Heinrich Degenfeld, and the Count Henry Eltz who married a Miss Janet Ann Stevenson in Montréal.

COUNT HEINRICH DEGENFELD:

Count Heinrich Degenfeld was born and educated in the Austrian Tirol. He came from an old Austrian noble family whose academic influence on the princely families of Austria was renowned. His father, Count Ferdinand Degenfeld had been tutor to the Archduke Franz Ferdinand, who was the nephew of the Emperor Franz Josef and uncle of the Emperor Charles.(14)

Young Heinrich Degenfeld attended the Jesuit College of Stella Matutina in Feldkirch in the Austrian Tirol, a school that was recognized as one ofthe most unusual as well as best academic institutions in Europe. It was renowned for some of the graduates it produced -among them Prince Loewenstein of Bavaria, Prince Henri of Bourbon-Parma (the Empress Zita's paternal uncle) and many other prominent university professors, Austrian chancellors, statesmen and academics.(9)

Like his father, young Heinrich Degenfeld became a jurist and teacher to the nobility. He had already been associated with the

Imperial family during its exile in Switzerland, and upon the death of the Emperor Charles on Madeira, was again called into the service of the Imperial family.

The Empress had made young Otto's education her primary task, and as soon as she had settled at Lequeitio, the Empress began to select the best possible teachers for her Emperor son. One of these, and perhaps the most important in her judgement, was Count Heinrich Degenfeld. He was the man, she felt sure, who could educate and guide the young Emperor in the old tradition of the Austrian-Hungarian monarchy.(10)

And thus, Count Heinrich Degenfeld became the young Emperor's constant companion. He began to instill in the young man the best tradition of excellence in the Humanities, Sciences, and International Law, which later was to characterize the mature Emperor Otto as a most remarkable young man. Degenfeld's protégé proved to be highly intelligent and willing to work hard, and when he became of age (18 years old) he was ready to assume the position as Head of the House of Habsburg, a function which his mother had carried out since the death of her husband on April 1, 1922. He had developed according to his mother's wishes, thanks mainly to the talents and guidance of Count Heinrich Degenfeld, Her Majesty's most loyal servant.

Like the Countess Kerssenbrock, Count Degenfeld eventually also became a trusted confident of the Empress and a life long advisor to Emperor Otto. He had been with them in Steenockerzeel, and was with the family on that fateful May 10, 1940 when their flight to America unwittingly began. And when his protégé was in Paris in those early days of the war, Count Degenfeld was by his side, providing him with guidance and support.(30)

Count Degenfeld later followed the Imperial family to America, and ended up assisting them wherever and whenever he could. After a short stay in Québec City with the Empress Zita in 1940, Count Degenfeld went to Washington to assist the Emperor Otto and the Archduke Felix who had made the United States their diplomatic battleground for the liberation and independence of Austria.(30)

Also while in Washington, Count Degenfeld received and accepted an offer from Georgetown University to give lectures in Political Science and European History. He did this for some years and until such time as the Emperor Otto returned to Europe. Count Degenfeld, always loyal to his protégé, returned to Europe with him. He continued to serve the Emperor until he died. He is buried at Poecking in Bavaria, and remained until his last breath, a loyal servant to the House of Habsburg. Having served three Emperors of Austria, Count Degenfeld has found eternal rest in the shadow of his protégé, his lifelong student, and his last Emperor, Otto von Habsburg.(30)

COUNT HENRY ELTZ:(39)

The second Count addressed in the trilogy of this chapter is Count Henry Eltz. He was born on January 24, 1896 in the garrison town of Ollmuetz, in the Kingdom of Bohemia. His father, Count August from and to Eltz, was an officer and gentleman in the service of the Emperor Franz Joseph I. His mother was Lady Margaret Frankenstein, a member of a noble German family whose name has been indelibly written on the pages of history through the exploits of a fictional creative scientist.

Young Henry Eltz was the third of nine children that the Countess Eltz bore her husband. When the family returned to Austria from Bohemia, they settled at their ancestral home, the castle Tillysburg near St. Florian, and when young Henry was eight years old, he was sent to Feldkirch to attend the Jesuit College of Stella Matutina, the same place of learning that Count Degenfeld had attended as a child. From Feldkirch, Henry Eltz went to Innsbruck where he studied Law, and where he eventually obtained his Doctorate degree. Following graduation, he took a commission in the Imperial Army, which he kept until the armistice of 1918 disbanded Austria's military forces.

After World War One, Count Henry Eltz returned to Castle Tillysburg and practiced law. And there he stayed until 1938, when the National Socialists took over Austria and confiscated the family estate. Count Eltz fled Austria and made his way to Switzerland and

France, and then to Lisbon in Portugal where he had a sister, the Countess Saldanha, whose husband hosted the Empress Zita and her family just prior to their flight to America in July 1940. Count Eltz then joined numerous other Austrian refugees who made their way across the Atlantic to America.

While waiting in Lisbon for passage across the Atlantic, the Count often told the following story to his friends:

> He was a tall man, over six feet in height, and he possessed big feet. So one day when he went into a shoe store in Lisbon to look for a pair of shoes, he asked a small Portugese salesman if he had any extra large shoes. The salesman threw up his arms in disgust and demonstrated various shoe sizes with his hands, saying: "The English want shoes so big, and the Americans, they want shoes so so big, and you, you want shoes that are bigger still? Do you think we are all giants here?"

Eventually Count Eltz made his way to Québec where he joined the Empress and her family in Sillery. However, like so many other refugees of Aristocratic blood who had come to North America, Count Eltz quickly found out that his Doctorate in Law degree was not of much use in earning a living in Canada. He therefore undertook all sorts of odd jobs which could provide him with some revenue. At first he worked part-time for Price Brothers Lumber in Québec City, surveying and estimating lumber in the bush. Although he was a tall man, he was not a big man, and his health was not too good. Some of his World War One wounds were still bothering him, and the cold Québec winter was just too much for his frail condition.

While in Québec, he helped the Empress with her correspondence and also looked for another job, something more appropriate for his excess of knowledge but lack of brawn. And so, being fluent in six languages, but not being able to practice Law, he moved to Montréal and began to teach French at a school for immigrants. This led to an appointment at Loyola College (now the Loyola Campus of Sir George Williams University) where he taught languages in the Faculty of Arts. He remained there for nine years, until his sixty-fifth birthday in January of 1965 forced him to retire and leave his job.

33. The Archduke Rudolf in Alberta.

34. Hunting in Roberval.

35. Visiting the Musée Chinois with Père G. H. Lévesque.

36. In the foyer of the Musée Chinois.

37. Visiting the Hungarian Sisters of Social Services in Montréal.

38. The Empress Zita and friend.

39. The baptism of Natalie Germain.

40. The Luxemburg family in Québec in 1942.

41. A visit from Prince Xavier.

42. The Venner Mausoleum in Québec.

43. The Archduchess Elisabeth and Prince Heinrich von Liechtenstein.

44. The Princess Yolande de Ligne and the Archduke Charles Louis.

45. The Princess Regina von Sachsen-Meiningen and the Emperor Otto.

46. The Countess Xenia Czernichew-Besobrasow and the Archduke
Rudolf.

47. The Princess Margherita of Savoy-Aosta and the Archduke Robert.

48. The Archduchess Charlotte and the Duke Georg von Mecklenburg.

49. The Princess Anna Gabrielle von Wrede and the Archduke Rudolf.

50. The wedding reception for Miss Janet Ann Stevenson and the Count
Henry Eltz.

MISS JANET ANN STEVENSON:(39)

In 1941, when he moved from Québec to Montréal to accept a teaching job, Count Henry Eltz met a young lady whom he eventually married. She was Miss Janet Ann Stevenson, daughter of Mr. Peter Stevenson of Bathgate, Scotland and Mrs. Ann Crichton Stevenson. They met at a dinner party and were immediately attracted to each other. Both were tall, and both were alone in Canada, and they soon developed a close friendship. This was interrupted in 1943 however, when Janet Stevenson, who had joined the Canadian Armed Forces, was sent to England.

Although she was injured in Europe and discharged, she remained in England for 10 years. It was only after her parents had died that she returned to Canada. During all this time, Janet Stevenson and Count Eltz had kept up a faithful and steady correspondence, and when Miss Stevenson again landed in Montréal, it was not long before the couple became serious and decided to marry. The Count was then 60 years old and his fiancée was 14 years his junior.

The wedding took place on December 17, 1955 at St. Antony's Church in Montréal. It was a festive occasion and the wedding guests included a number of prominent people, some old Canadians and some new Canadians who had only recently arrived from Europe. They included Count Michael Andrassy who gave away the bride, attended by Mrs. Peter Martin, and Count Robert Keyserlingk who acted as best man. Among the guests were Count William Resseguier, the Marquis and Marchioness Edward Pallavicini, Count Gyula Andrassy, Colonel and Mrs. Thomas Guerin, Countess Michael Andrassy, Mr. Peter Martin of Glasgow, Scotland, Countess Sigrid Keyserlingk, Mr. Dennis Milch, Mr. and Mrs. Victor Cleyn, Mr. and Mrs. Franz Laizner, Mr. and Mrs. Alfred Czurka, Mrs. Gordon Drummond, Mr. and Mrs. George Garnham, Mr. and Mrs. Gerald Audcent, and Colonel and Mrs. Francesco Bitossi.(40)

After the ceremony, Mr. Nandor Loewenheim, formerly of Budapest and then Austrian Consul General in Montreal, and his wife, gave a reception for the newlyweds at their home on Bellevue

Avenue in Westmount, Québec. (Mr. Loewenheim was the Austrian Consul General, in Montréal until his death in April 1989).(40)

The couple lived in Montréal for many years and made many friends. It was not until 1967, after the Count had lost his teaching job at Loyola, that they decided to return to Europe. Being past the age of 65, the Count found the going rough, and when he received an invitation from a nephew in Bavaria to move there and stay with them, the Count and his Countess sold all their household possessions and moved to Engelskirchen on the Rhine in Bavaria. His newphew's family had a castle there called Schloss Ehreshoven, and it was to this castle that the couple moved and set up house. They lived there happily until the Count died. He was laid to rest in the cemetary at Augsburg in Bavaria.(39)

His wife, the Countess Janet Eltz, continues to live at the Castle to this day, and maintains the memory of her beloved husband in high esteem. The Archduke Rudolf, who has kept in touch with her these many years, remembers the Countess as an exceptionally fine person who sacrificed much of her life for the happiness of her husband. Through her love and devotion, he added, the Countess succeeded in bringing Count Eltz a few years of happiness after his many years of sorrow.(30)

BOOK 4
AFTER QUEBEC

CHAPTER 15

AT WAR AND WORK

THE ARCHDUKES:(30)

Having received their License in Social Sciences from the Université Laval in 1942, the Archdukes Charles Louis and Rudolf left Québec and made their way to New York to enter the war effort and to work for a liberated, independent Austria. Their older brother, Felix, had for sometime been established at number 10 Park Avenue in New York and it was to him that the two Archdukes then made their way.

The three Archdukes then joined the Armed Forces of the United States and were sent to Indiana where they underwent basic training and received their commissions. As officers, it was their hope and intention to establish a battalion of fighting men composed mainly of Austrian nationals and refugees from Hitler's Europe, under the command of the American Armed Forces. Unfortunately, however, their plans for an Austrian battalion were never realized. The socialistic views of the many refugees who had fled to America, and their determination not to support the reestablishment of an independent Austria, much less the restoration of the monarchy, made such a battalion impossible.(9)

Following a discussion with President Roosevelt in 1943, the Emperor Otto sent the Archdukes Rudolf and Charles Louis to Portugal to undertake discussions with the Legitimist Government of Hungary under Prime Minister Kallay. Their negotiations with Budapest, through the Hungarian Embassy in Lisbon, led to an agreement that the Emperor could be empowered as Hungarian Head of State, if and when Admiral Horthy (who was still governing Hungary as Regent), would resign his self-imposed mandate. These discussions however were soon to fall apart when German troops occupied Hungary in March 1944. Hitler had learnt of the Habsburg initiative, and had taken steps to forestall it as quickly as possible.(9)

As their dreams of establishing an Austrian battalion and their hopes of turning Hungary against Germany collapsed, the Archdukes resolved to fight the only way they had left, i.e. to get personally involved in the campaign on the battlefields. They joined the Austrian resistance movement.(9)

Things were not rosy in Europe those days. France was still occupied, and Austria not only did not exist as a separate country, but had become an integral part of Germany. Nevertheless, the Archdukes were equipped with false papers by the French underground and made their way across France, Switzerland and into Austria by travelling mostly by night and on foot.(9)

The Archduke Rudolf, who was then 23 years old and travelling under the name of "Johann Weber" was soon arrested by the German military police near the Austrian-Liechtenstein border and taken to German headquarters for interrogation. His youth, and not being in uniform when most of Europe was at war, had given him away.(9)

However, while being held for interrogation at the German headquarters, he suddenly made a dash for freedom. He jumped through an open window, ran away, and found refuge in the Capuchin Monastery at Feldkirch. There he lay low until the search for him had been given up. He subsequently sought and made contacts with the Austrian resistance movement, and soon participated in their activities.(9)

His activities, together with those of his compatriots in the Austrian underground became increasingly important after the allied invasion of Normandy began in June of 1944. They occupied themselves in their war of liberation, mainly in the North and South Tirol. The latter area of operations became increasingly significant to them,

---

9/ p. 438-439

because word from London led them to believe that the South Tirol would, after the war, again be returned to Austria.(9)

Many of the Archduke's partners in those adventurous days were Austrian legitimists, who together with quite a number of Italian compatriots, were anxious not only for an independent Austria, but also for the return of the South Tirol to Austria. In May of 1945 when the tide of war had changed in favour of the advancing allies, and the retreating German armies were blowing up their bridges behind them, the Archdukes and their comrades in arms fought desperately to save as many strategic bridges and other facilities as possible.(9)

The Archduke Felix had in the meantime left America and spent the last year of the war with his brothers Charles Louis and Rudolf in the Austrian resistance movement. The remaining brother, the Archduke Robert, continued to operate as the Emperor Otto's ambassador in London, lobbying Prime Minister Winston Churchill and the British Government on behalf of Austria's eventual, hoped for independence.(30)

However, when the French armies finally succeeded in liberating Tirol, the Archduke Rudolf again found himself under arrest, but this time by the French. The French General de Lattre de Tassigny had not believed that an Austrian resistance movement existed, and looked upon the men fighting in the Austrian underground as rabble-rousers and deserters. It was not until William Bullit, the American Ambassador to France, intervened and corroborated the position of the Archdukes and their band of merry men, that the French General gave in and allowed the captured Austrians and Italians their freedom.(9)

Following the collapse of the German war machine, the Archdukes made their way to eastern Austria. Again with forged papers, they were able to get through Soviet lines and reach Vienna. There they met with some trusted and sympathetic contacts, and immediately began to work for the return of an Austrian monarchy. They soon learnt however, that the same strong socialistic forces that had worked against the Habsburgs in 1918, were again active, occupying high positions in the provisional government, and working against the interests of the Habsburgs.(9)

9/ p. 438-442

When the newly established Republic re-activated the old "Habsburg Laws" that prevented the Archdukes from remaining in Austria, the Archdukes left Austria and returned to America. It was 1946.(9)

THE ARCHDUCHESSES:(30)

The Archduchess Adelhaid left Québec shortly after arriving there. She had received her Doctorate in Sociology while still at the University of Louvain, before coming to America. Therefore, arriving in New York in early 1941, she had no difficulty in establishing herself in her chosen field. In addition to doing social work in East Harlem, she also taught Sociology at New York's Fordham University.

The Archduchess Charlotte, after receiving her License in Social Sciences at Université Laval in 1942, also attended Fordham University in New York where she studied Sociology. In 1943 she joined her sister as a social worker in East Harlem.

The Archduchess Elisabeth, after completing her Baccalaureate in Arts at the Collège Jésus-Marie, attended Université Laval where she studied Social Sciences with the Reverend Professor Georges Henri Lévesque. Upon receiving her License in 1944, she too left Québec and went to NewYork where she joined her sisters. However, unlike her sisters, she could not obtain a work permit from the American authorities because she had been born in Spain. She therefore occupied herself through volunteer work, and worked as a secretary for her brother, the Emperor Otto, who was working feverishly for the reestablishment of a free and independent Austria.(9)

9/ p. 440-442, 450

CHAPTER 16

TUXEDO PARK (41)

While her family was still scattered throughout Europe and America, participating in the Allied war effort, influencing Allied governments, and helping the less fortunate, the Empress Zita remained in Québec. She kept herself busy addressing ladies clubs, church groups, and anyone else who would listen, on the needs of charity for the suffering in Europe. She organized the collection and sending of countless CARE parcels to the unfortunate victims of the war -on both sides -and especially to the suffering peoples of her old Danubian monarchy.

However, when hostilities ceased in Europe and the Archdukes returned to America, she found the center of her family interest suddenly concentrated in the New York City area. Although she kept her home at the Villa Saint Joseph in Québec City for a few more years, the pressures to join her family in New York became ever-increasing, and she therefore moved to join them just before Christmas of 1949. She had been in Québec for just a little over nine years, and when she left, she left with some sorrow in her heart. But none were more sorrowful than the many friends she left behind, -the good sisters at the Jésus-Marie and Ste. Jeanne d'Arc convents, and the good Fathers, teachers and priests, who had consoled her and her family in those troubled times of the 1940's. She was however to return to them again,some years later, as a visitor.

Meanwhile, in New York, the Archdukes Charles Louis and Rudolf had, through their contacts with Calvin Bullock who had also been their benefactor upon their arrival in New York almost a decade before, found a house not far from New York. It belonged to a Mr. and Mrs. Henry Cole — Mrs. Cole was the daughter of Calvin

Bullock. The house was situated in a suburb called Tuxedo Park, some fifty kilometers northwest of NewYork, tucked in between Sterling Forest Gardens and the Palissades Interstate Park.(30)

Tuxedo Park is an exclusive, gated town that gave men's formal wear its name. It consists of about 300 family homes nestled in garden-like surroundings around a small lake, and has its own country club. It was at this club, some 100 years ago, that the event happened that made the name "Tuxedo" a household word in the Western World's more formal circles. At the Autumn Ball of the socialites of Tuxedo Park in that year of 1886, one Griswold Lorillard created a sensation by appearing at the Ball with the tails of his dinner jacket cut off. The idea, at first bizarre, caught on, and men's dinner jackets just about everywhere are now called "Tuxedos."

Tuxedo Park was built as an off-season retreat where families like the Juillards, the Pells and the Astors could while away their leisure times in the peace and quiet of the Appalachian foothills, only a few kilometers from downtown New York.

Legend has it that the Park was planned by Lorillard's father and a NewYork architect named Bruce Price. The plan consisted of a modest proposal for some 20 "cottages" of 20 rooms each, with a clubhouse and a gate, a sewer system, and 45 kilometers of roads. With 180 laborers imported mainly from Italy and Eastern Europe, the park was completed by the Spring of 1886.

It was in this Park that Calvin Bullock offered a house to the Empress. It was a rather large house built in 1903, that originally belonged to a lady named Alice Voss. In 1907 the house had been rented to one Mark Twain, the writer and humorist. He used the house as a base for his quiet routines of dictation and mild social pleasures, and wrote there many works which have become classics in the annals of American literature. He also prepared in its large library the famous introductory remarks he made to a meeting of the Robert Fulton Memorial Association in the Summer of 1907, when he was asked to introduce the guest speaker. The event was attended by such prominent personalities of the times as Cornelius Vanderbilt, John Jacob Astor, Andrew Carnegie, Cleveland Dodie, and Samuel Clemens. When introducing Rear Admiral Harrington, the guest speaker for the occasion, Mark Twain is reported to have said:

> "I will say that the same qualities, the same moral and intellectual attainments, the same graciousness of manner, of conduct, of observation and expression, have caused Admiral Harrington to be mistaken for me, and I have been mistaken for him."

This then was the house, whose walls Mark Twain's humour had shaken with merriment, into which the Empress Zita and her family had moved into in early 1950. The house, which had initially been rented by the family from Henry Cole and later purchased by the Archduke Rudolf, received some well-needed renovations from the hands of the Archdukes themselves. They sawed and nailed and varnished and painted, and made the house their home. One room was converted into a chapel, and the remaining rooms provided a haven, not only for the Empress and her immediate family, including the Countess Kerssenbrock, but also for the occasional visiting priests and nuns and friends from Québec. And as it was her custom to always share what she had with those in need, the Empress also had with her for some time, some ailing Hungarian nuns for whom she cared and with whom she shared her fortunes.

The Empress loved Tuxedo Park, for not only did she find there the peace and privacy which her lifestyle had come to cherish, but because she was also close to her sons and daughters who were working in New York. She often travelled to New York to visit and spend a day with her children, or to do some shopping. The trip could be made quite easily with the subway, whose line provided a service under the Hudson River from Yonkers to Manhattan.

On one such trip, the story is told, the Empress stopped along the way to pick up some laundry. There she met a famous Hungarian author, Franz Molnar, who had just complained to the laundry manager that he had to come and pick up his laundry. "Why couldn't it be delivered" he asked. To which the manager replied "If the Empress of Austria can come and personally pick up her laundry, why can't you?"(10)

It was in Tuxedo Park too that the Archduke Rudolf married the Countess Xenia Czernichew-Besobrasow. The wedding took place in the Church of Our Lady of Carmel on June 23, 1953 at a time when the area was in full bloom. The nuptial mass was said by Bishop Fulton Sheen.

Although the Empress Zita made a number of return trips to Europe while a resident of Tuxedo Park, she returned for the first time in 1949 while still a resident of Québec. In September of 1949, she attended the wedding of her daughter, the Archduchess Elisabeth to Prince Heinrich von Liechtenstein. Following the wedding, which took place at Lignières in France at the home of Prince Xavier of Bourbon-Parma, she also visited her other brother, Prince Felix of Bourbon-Parma, at Castle Colmar-Berg in Luxemburg. She stayed there for a few weeks, enjoying the rest and relaxation in the company of her beloved brother from whom she had been separated for so long.

The Empress then returned to Tuxedo Park, where she stayed for a few more years. During this period, she made a number of additional trips across the Atlantic, usually to attend family weddings. The next crossing was in January 1950 when she attended the wedding of the Archduke Charles Louis with the Princess Yolande de Ligne in Belgium. The following year saw another crossing when she attended the wedding of her eldest son, the Emperor Otto, to Princess Regina of Sachsen-Meiningen in Nancy, France. She again crossed the Atlantic to attend the wedding of her son Robert to the Princess Margherita of Savoy-Aosta at Bourg-en-Bresse, France on December 28, 1953. One of her last crossings was in 1956, when her daughter the Archduchess Charlotte married Duke Georg von Mecklenburg in Poecking, Bavaria, on July 25 of that year.(30)

As a result of all these transatlantic crossings, the Empress developed quite a preference for certain ships and shipping lines. Among these was the S.S. Stadendam of the Holland-America Line. The Dutch operated four or five similar ships, and whenever the Empress travelled, she asked for space on one of them. They were relatively small ships, but very comfortable, and always very friendly, so that the Empress lovingly referred to them as "Pensions de Famille." They were truly family style boats, and she like the informality that they usually offered.(30)

However, on one such trip, as her reservations were being made for her by her son, the Archduke Rudolf requested the captain to safeguard her identity by keeping his mother's name off the Passenger List. This request seriously bothered the captain of the Dutch ship, whose own Queen Juliana he held in the highest esteem. Not to give royalty its due, was he believed, not the thing to do. And so the Archduke suggested that in order that Her Majesty at least have some safeguard of anonymity, she could be listed as just "Madame de Bar", a title which she actually possessed but which was not as grandiose as "Empress." The captain was still not convinced and replied, "But that is extremely difficult. How can you call an Empress just "Madame de Bar". To which the Archduke replied "Because that's the way she wants it."(30)

And so when later the Empress boarded the ship and came across the Passenger List, she noted the captain's solution with humour and resignation. He had listed her as "Her Majesty, Madame de Bar."(30)

And on another crossing with the Holland-America Line, the Archduke asked the captain if there might possibly be a priest on board, since Her Majesty was accustomed to attending daily Mass, and perhaps this could be arranged on board the ship. "No problem" replied the captain. "There are a number of such men on board on this trip, and I am sure it can be arranged." He immediately went to see the religious passengers and explained to them the Archduke's request.(30)

When he reported back to the Archduke that the religious men on board "refused to say Mass", he was dumbfounded and told Her Majesty of their refusal. They were both very disappointed and somewhat bewildered. But then the ship's bell rang the departure and the Archduke had to leave the ship. It was not until Her Majesty arrived in Europe and wrote to her son that he learnt the explanation for the refusal of the men in black to say Mass. "The notable Catholic religious men", wrote the Empress, "were teaching brothers." And thus the Archduke knew why they had "refused to say Mass."(30)

The Empress remained at Tuxedo Park for a number of years, and only returned her domicile to Europe when the health of her mother had deteriorated severly. The Duchess Maria Antonia had already some years earlier gone to Europe, and was living at the home of her son, Prince Felix, at the Castle Colmar-Berg in Luxemburg. The Empress decided to move to Colmar-Berg to take care of her mother.(30)

The Empress returned to Tuxedo Park whenever she later visited America, and the Archduke Rudolf maintained the house for another 16 years. Finally, after he too had re-located to Europe and there was no more need for a New York residence, he sold the house in 1970 to Doctor Ralph Capella and Mrs. Cecilia Capella. They are still to this day living in Tuxedo Park and enjoying this famous house that had sheltered not only Mark Twain, but also the Empress of Austria.(30)

CHAPTER 17

WEDDING BELLS (26 & 36)

ARCHDUCHESS ELISABETH:

As already mentioned, the first of the Imperial children to marry was the Archduchess Elisabeth. She had once confided to a classmate at the Université Laval that there were only three men in the world whom she could marry. One of these was Prince Heinrich von Liechtenstein, and she married him on September 12, 1949. The Empress Zita was then still living in Québec, and the occasion was to bring her back to Europe for the first time since the war.(45)

The Archduchess Elisabeth had gone to Europe for a vacation in 1948. It was there at the home of her uncle, Prince Xavier of Bourbon-Parma in Lignières, France, that she first met Prince Heinrich von Liechtenstein. Lignières is a small town in County Berry, south of Paris, and possesses a beautiful Château that dates back to the XVII century.

The Château de Lignières was built in the style of Louis XIV and is one of many imposing châteaux situated in this part of France. It has been a Bourbon possession since it was first built, and was at the time of the Archduchess Elisabeth's engagement, the home of Prince Xavier of Bourbon-Parma and his wife, the Princess Madeleine of Bourbon-Busset.

The wedding took place in the parish of Lignières. The church, which dates back to the XII century, was decorated in Bourbon blue and white, and was adorned with bouquets of white lillies. Present at this auspicious occasion were the Empress Zita, who had just arrived in Europe for the first time since the war, and her son the Emperor Otto. The bride, wore a simple gown of ivory satin, adorned with a long flowing veil that had been worn by the Empress Elisabeth (Sissi) when she married the Emperor Franz Josef I. The wearing of the veil was to become a Habsburg tradition to be repeated at the subsequent marriages of other daughters of the House of Habsburg.

With their nuptials behind them, the newlyweds settled down in the Prince's castle at Waldstein in the province of Steiermark in Austria. Princess Elisabeth von Liechtenstein is the only one of the Empress Zita's children who has made her domicile in Austria. The Princess Elisabeth von Liechtenstein has presented her husband with five children, four boys and one girl. The four boys are the Princes Vincenz (1950), Michael (1951), Christopher (1956) and Karl (1957). The Princess Charlotte was born in 1953.

ARCHDUKE CHARLES LOUIS:

The Archduke Charles Louis was the next Habsburg to marry. After the Socialists in Austria had re-instated the so-called Habsburg Laws which prohibited a member of the House of Habsburg from returning to Austria without first renunciating his rights, the Archduke Charles Louis left Austria and returned to New York. There he worked for the "Société Générale de Belgique", representing many Belgium based companies and manufacturing concerns in the United States.

In the course of his duties in New York and Washington, he met the daughter of Prince Eugène de Ligne, who was the head of a Belgium noble family that traced its origins back to Prince Fastré de Ligne who in 1311 married the Countess Jeanne de Condé and thereby took possession of Beloeil. His descendant Prince Charles Joseph de Ligne (1735-1814),was a Marshall in the service of the Emperor Joseph II of Austria, and was born in Brussels at a time when Belgium and the Netherlands were part of the Austrian Empire.

Prince Eugène de Ligne was a career diplomat, who had been Commercial Attaché for the Belgium government in Washington in the years after the war, and also had served as Belgium's ambassador in Paris, Madrid and New Delhi. Princess Yolande, the prince's daughter, had been a student in Washington when she met the Archduke Charles Louis, and their resulting relationship soon developed into a meaningful and lasting one. Their engagement took place in the chapel of St. Michael's College in Brussels in 1949, and their wedding followed in the chapel of the princely Château of Beloeil on January 17, 1950.

The bride wore a white wedding gown with a veil of ancient lace embroided with a multitude of delicate eagles and bees, the symbols of Napoleon Bonaparte. The veil was made from lace originally woven for the basinet of Napoleon's son, the King of Rome, whose mother was Archduchess Marie Louise of Austria. The veil had been passed from the Empress Eugénie, wife of Napoleon III, through the Princess Murat, a descendant of Napoleon's sister Caroline Bonaparte, to the family of the Prince de Ligne.

Resplendent on her head and securing the veil was a crown of diamonds. Supporting the trailing veil as she held the arm of her father, the Prince de Ligne, who escorted her to the altar, were six little page boys dressed in green velvet suits with huge white collars. The wedding was a gala affair and saw the presence of the Empress Zita, who had again crossed the Atlantic for the occasion. The Emperor Otto von Habsburg, as well as many other prominent guests from the Gotha of Europe, also attended the wedding.

The festivities and reception took place in the Château of Beloeil, a princely residence that had been in the family of the Prince de Ligne for 638 years. The Château, constructed of stone, embellished with red and pink bricks, sits among four guard towers. Two wings extend, one from either side, making the structure one of Europe's most impressive seigneurial castles. The interior houses a splendid collection of paintings and sculptures, as well as a rich and well-stocked library, and is furnished with period furniture of great beauty and value. The Château is surrounded by a park resplendent with formal gardens, fountains, statues, and rare plants.

Following their weddding in Beloeil, the couple lived in Brussels, New York and Washington while the Archduke was still employed by the Société Générale de Belgique, but then they eventually returned to Belgium and settled in Brussels where the Archduke began a career in banking. The Archduchess Yolande presented her husband with four children, two boys and two girls. The boys are the Archdukes Rudolf (1950) and Carl Christian (1954) and the girls are the Archduchess Alexandra (1952) and Constanza (1957).

ARCHDUKE OTTO:

The Empress Zita's first born child, the Archduke Otto, became Emperor upon the death of his father on April 1, 1922. His sojourn in America was spent lobbying the American Senate and President for the reestablishment of an independent Austria. The fact that it eventually happened, was due in large measure to his activities, and to his brothers who supported his mission in England and the Americas.

When he returned to Europe in 1944, the Head of the House of Habsburg participated in the allied war effort in France and the Austrian Tirol through his support and personal activities with the underground, and also took his crusade for Austria's independence to Portugal, France and England with the same zeal and energy that he had demonstrated in Washington.

Even after war's end he reconciled his family's differences with Hungary's Admiral Horthy who had sought and received exile in Portugal after the Soviets had occupied his homeland. Emperor Otto's objectives and Horty's were now the same in so far as Hungary was concerned, their common enemy was the Kremlin.

Although the Emperor's overriding objective had always been the reestablishment of Austria as an independent country with himself as its head of state, he began to develop, as the political realities of the times became more and more evident, a new objective. He saw the urgency for a United Europe standing as a bulwark against communism, and as the means for creating economic strength for Europe out of the chaos in which it then existed.

Fortunately, others had had the same vision, and the basis for the realization of European prosperity had already been in existence for some time. It was the Pan-European Union that had been created in 1922 by Richard Coudenhove-Kalergi, and its off-shoot, the European Parliament which was established and met for the first time in 1947.

However, in order to participate fully in the activities of these organizations, the Emperor Otto had to do two things. First, he had to unburden himself from the shackles of the Habsburg Laws which prohibited him from entering his homeland -Austria, and second, he had to obtain dual citizenship, adding West German to that of Austrian which all members of the House of Habsburg automatically received. The rationale for these rather drastic courses of action became clear when one considers his objectives.

He had recognized that in order to work towards the idea of a United Europe, he had to break the bond of exile that the Austrian Republic's Habsburg Laws imposed on him. He had to be able to move around his homeland, and therefore on May 31, 1961, he signed the "Verzichtserklaerung" (the renunciation of his rights to the Habsburg throne). From then on, he became citizen Dr. Otto von Habsburg in the eyes of the Austrian Government, and was given permission to again enter Austria. However, as Head of the House of Austria and Grand Master of the Imperial Order of the Golden Fleece, he is still regarded by legitimists as the Emperor.

He also realized that he could never represent Austria in the European Parliament, because Austria, as a politically neutral country, had chosen not to join the Pan-European Union. And he could not represent West Germany, who was a member, because he was not a German national. He therefore, by special arrangement with Bonn, also became a West German citizen, without losing his Austrian citizenship.

He had overcome both the obstacles that had prevented him from achieving his new objective of working for a United Europe. He joined the activities of the Pan-European Union and became its president in 1973. He also became a West German deputy to the European Parliament in 1970, a post which he holds to this day.

Dr. Otto von Habsburg and his family established their residence at Poecking, Bavaria, a little town between Munich and the German-Austrian border. The house he lives in is called the "Villa Austria."

During the Summer of 1950, the eldest son of the Empress Zita visited a refugee camp near Bayreuth, a town that Richard Wagner had made famous and which to this day still hosts a world-renowned annual music festival to his memory. There he met the Princess Regina von Sachsen-Meiningen. She was working at the refugee camp caring for the sick and maimed who had assembled there and needed help.

When the Emperor and the Princess met, their mutual attraction signalled the birth of a love story about which story books can be written. She was tall and blond and beautiful, with sparkling blue eyes, a most charming smile and a regal bearing that gave away her aristocratic past. And like the young man who quickly became enamored with this lovely young woman, she was also an "exile."

Her father, Duke Georg von Sachsen-Meiningen had been made prisoner by Soviet troops in 1945 and taken to Siberia where he died in January 1946. Her eldest brother, Prince Anton Ulrich, met a soldier's death in battle during the first year of the war, and her youngest brother, Prince Frederick Alfred had chosen a religious vocation. Her mother was the Countess Clara von Korff Schmising-Kerssenbrock, and now lives an active life of retirement in the province of Lower Austria in Austria, which she has called "home" since 1967.

The wedding between her only daughter, the Princess Regina and the Emperor Otto took place in the ancient Ducal Chapel of the Cordeliers in Nancy, France. Nancy is the historical home of the Dukes of Lorraine, and because he, like all his ancestors who dated back to Austria's Emperor Franz I, was Duke of Lorraine and Duke of Bar, the Emperor Otto chose Nancy, the capital city of Lorraine, as the site for his wedding to the Princess Regina. Nancy was also an appropriate location for the wedding of a Habsburg-Lorraine since it had provided two very distinguished soldiers who served Habsburg Emperors: Field Marshalls François de Mercy (1597-1645) and Florimond-Claude de Mercy (1666-1734). The latter also served as Emperor Franz I's governor in the Banat (Rumania) and later led an Imperial army against the French in northern Italy where he was killed. He is buried in Parma, and his heart was removed and returned to the little ducal church in Nancy where it lies venerated since 1737.

The wedding of the Emperor Otto with Princess Regina took place on May 10, 1951, in an appropriate setting fitting the occasion. It was a gala affair and was attended by many guests and members of the House of Habsburg-Lorraine. The Empress Zita and the Archduke Rudolf had come from New York, the Archduke Felix from Mexico, and the Archduke Robert from London. France was represented by Prince Louis de Bourbon-Parma, brother of the Empress Zita, and the Duchess Clara von Sachsen-Meiningen, mother of the bride, had come from Germany. There were many other notable and noble guests, some of whom came from Italy and Luxemburg, who filled the little ducal church as well as the City Hall of Nancy where a reception was later held. The religious ceremony was conducted by Monseigneur Lallier, the Bishop of Nancy, in the presence of forty priests who had come from Austria and Hungary for the occasion. In addition, there were also many other admirers and well wishers that came to Nancy on that day, turning the ancient city ablaze with the colours of their native costumes depicting the folklore of many of the lands of the old Imperial Empire. There were Hungarians and Austrians in native dress, and also Czechs and Slovaks and Croates. Among all these played a band of Tirolean musicians, gaily dressed in native mountain costumes with colorful jackets, dark britches and white knee socks. When the newlyweds emerged from the church, the band broke into a nostalgic rendition of Josef Haydn's "Gott Erhalte", which must have made the young Emperor's day.

Upon their return from a short honeymoon trip, the newlyweds settled first in the town of Clairefontaine outside Paris, and then in May of 1954 at Poecking. There they took up residence in an imposing two-storey villa in which they still live today, and started to raise a family.

The Archduchess Regina has presented the Empress Zita with seven grand children, five girls and two boys. The Archduchesses are Andrea (1953), Monika and Michaela (twins, 1954), Gabriela (1956) and Wallburga (1958). The two Archdukes are Charles (1961, hereditor to the throne) and Paul George (1964).

ARCHDUKE FELIX:

The Archduke Felix was next in line at the marriage altar. He had spent most of the war year's as the Emperor Otto's unofficial ambassador in the United States, working behind the scene for Austria'sfreedom and independence. He had made many voyages throughout North and South America, lobbying influential people everywhere in the cause and mission of his brother. Among these many people were influential senators and journalists, and his efforts touched the lives not only of President Roosevelt, but of such people as Senators Taft, Fulbright, Keating and Kennedy, but also of many others such as Sol Bloom, James Roosevelt, John McCormack and Mrs. Clare Booth Luce, to mention only a few.(9)

After the war he moved to Mexico where he worked in an investment company. In 1952 he married the Princess Anna Eugenie, Duchess of Arenberg. The marriage took place at Beaulieu in France on November 19, 1952, after which the couple returned to Mexico. There, the Archduke worked as a director of Siporex of Mexico, a manufacturing concern that produced light metal products under Swedish license. Since 1958, Archduke Felix is also the representative of the Belgium Steel firm "Sybetra", as well as a permanent representative of the Société Générale de Banque in Mexico. In addition, he has business interests in ten other Mexican-based companies as either director or president.(9)

Like his older brother Otto, the Archduke Felix fathered seven children, of which two are twins. The Archduchess Anna Eugenie therefore gave the Empress Zita seven grandchildren, of which four are boys and three are girls. The Archdukes are Charles Philipp (1954), Raimund (1958) and Istvan and Viridis (1961) who are twins.

9/ p. 224-228

The three Archduchesses are Maria del Pilar (1953), Kynga (1955) and Miriam (1960).

ARCHDUKE RUDOLF:

The Archduke Rudolf was the next child of the Empress to marry. As already noted, he had married Countess Xenia Czernichew-Besobrasow in the Church of Our Lady of Carmel in Tuxedo Park, New York, on June 23, 1953. She was the daughter of a White-Russian noble family that had escaped the Russian revolution and fled to Paris in 1918, where the Countess Xenia was born on June 11, 1929. The family then moved to the United States where the young Xenia received most of her education, and where she eventually met the Archduke Rudolf.

Following their marriage, they lived for a while in Tuxedo Park, and then in Brussels where the Archduchess Xenia presented her husband with a daughter, the Archduchess Maria Anna (1954).

The Archduke Rudolf was then offered a job in the Belgium Congo, and it was to Bukavu in the Congo that the Archduke moved with his family at the beginning of September 1954. The Archduke became manager of a coffee plantation on the Island of Idjwi. Life was hard, and the environment difficult, which he described in a letter to Madame Zoe De Koninck shortly after arriving in Africa:

> "We arrived here at the beginning of last month. It all started very badly with Maria Anna catching an Otite (ear infection). One of her lungs became congested, but fortunately we could go immediately to a hospital of Soeurs Blanches who took excellent care of her, and in less than a week everything was all right. The beginnings are quite hard in this country -to get used to the climate, to have to be constantly careful -especially for the baby -of the water, the insects, the mosquitos (there is a lot of malaria around here) ... and many contagious diseases. Xenia has to do everything herself ... It is a lot of hard work, much more than in Europe or in the U.S."

It was the Archduke's ability to accept responsibility under adverse conditions, plus a tremendous sense of humor, that allowed him to survive and flourish in that difficult tropical country in the fifties. An example of this sense of humor can be seen in his reply to a letter from Professor Charles De Koninck in which the professor had sent him a humorous poem about Four Trumpets.

> "I had no idea" the Archduke wrote to Madame De Koninck, "that he(Professor De Koninck) was a poet of such a caliber that reading him, you are emancipated from the vulgar things of this world, and are transported, no, elated, to unknown heights, reachable only by the purest thoughts -as demonstrated by the Four Trumpets. Living now in the heart of black Africa, I will try to compose such unearthly verses. After extensive thought, only the title has occured to me: it will be called "The Four Hippopotamuses", which obviously have nothing to do with the Four Trumpets ... Ordinarily, people believe that Hippos are of reduced intelligence. Lately however, several of them were psycho-analysed by Dr. Hamstrung, who came to the tentative conclusion — at the end of a 627 page long book, entitled "The Neurotic Hippopotamus" — that they were animals of vast intelligence, however unrevealed because of severe complexes."

The Archduke and his family stayed in the Congo for five long years. During this time, the Archduchess Xenia bore him two more children: the Archdukes Carl Peter (1955) and Simeon (1958). In the late Summer of 1958, the Archduke and his family left the Congo and returned to Belgium. They then set up residence in Brussels, where the Archduke, then an expert in coffee beans, became a banker. His third son Johannes (1962) was born again in civilization.

They were to live happily for five more years, until a tragic automobile accident on September 20, 1968, took the life of the Archduchess and severely injured the Archduke. The Archduke's tragedy was however unmercifully compounded, when on June 29, 1975, the young (13 year old) Archduke Johannes was run over by an autobus while riding his bicycle. Both mother and son were laid to eternal rest in the family crypt in the Benedictine Monastery at Muri in the Aargau of Switzerland.

Three years after the death of his first wife, the Archduke Rudolf married the Princess Anna Gabrielle von Wrede, the daughter of Prince von Wrede of Ellingen, Bavaria. The Archduchess Anna

Gabrielle not only brought happiness and family purpose back to the widowed Archduke, but gave his family the maternal love and order that had been missing for three long years. She also gave the Archduke a daughter, the Archduchess Catharina. She was born to her happy parents in Brussels in 1972, the residence of the family to this day.

The Castle at Ellingen, an eighteenth century Baroque creation built by the German architect Franz Keller for the Knight Commander of the Teutonic Order, Carl Heinrich von Hortenstein, between 1708 and 1721, has been the seat of the Princes von Wrede since 1815. The castle contains four impressive wings, one of which is a beautiful Baroque church, surrounding an inner courtyard. It was in this church that the Archduke Rudolf married the Princess Anna Gabrielle on October 15, 1971.

The town of Ellingen is situated some 50 kilometers south of the ancient city of Nuernberg. It owes its monumental air to an ancient order of Germanic knights (Deutschorden) that date back to the twelfth century, and whose Franconian commanders resided in Ellingen from the thirteenth to the nineteenth century.

The Deutschorden began as a Hospitaller community founded in the Holy Land in 1128, but was returned home to Germany after the collapse of the Kingdom of Jerusalem. Back in their homeland, the knights laid the foundations for a patrimonial community which eventually became the cradle of the future states of Prussia. In 1525, a Grand Master of the Order, who was a Hohenzollern, dropped the religious tenets of the Order following the religious revolt of Martin Luther. Those knights, who remained faithful to Catholicism, gravitated to the south to what is now Bavaria. The Franconian commander at Ellingen was one of these.

Disbanded by Napoleon in 1809, the Deutschorden has re-awakened somewhat in the last ten decades, and today functions as a religious-charitable body. It again has branches in most large Roman Catholic Centers like Vienna, where the Deutschordenskirche (the church of the German Order) is very active in benevolent and charitable work.

ARCHDUKE ROBERT:

The Archduke Robert, who was second in line to the Habsburg throne, lived in England during most of the war years. He went there just before the outbreak of World War II in 1939, at the request of his brother, the Emperor Otto, to represent him and the Austrian legistimist interests in London.

In the course of his stay in the United Kingdom, he established and maintained Legitimate Austrian relations with Sir Winston Churchill and Lord Halifax. And as Hitler occupied more and more of Europe, the Archduke Robert was joined in London by a number of other heads of governments in exile. Among these were Hoare Belisha of Hungary, Charles de Gaulle of France, Gaston Pallewski of Poland, and Paul Henri Spaak of Belgium. All of these men were more or less favourably inclined to the Archduke's mission, and considered themselves, whenever they met, members of the "Austrian Club."(9)

In 1943, the Archduke Robert was instrumental in the wording of the so-called "Moscow Declaration" which Sir Winston Churchill took to Moscow, and which, with the help and support of President Roosevelt, was accepted against the vehement opposition of Josef Stalin. The declaration confirmed that since Austria was the first country to fall under Hitler, it must be again given its freedom and independence.(9)

A story is also told of the Archduke Robert's friendship with Jan Masaryk, the son of Tomas Masaryk, the ex-president of Czechoslovakia. It seems that one day during a violent rain storm in London, Jan Masaryk had the occasion to drive the Archduke Robert home. When he had safely delivered the Archduke to his residence and was thanked for his troubles, Jan Masaryk remarked "No trouble at all. This is becoming almost a family tradition. After all my grandfather was chauffeur to the Archduke Franz Ferdinand."(9)

After the war, Archduke Robert moved to Paris and then went to Tirol, but was later banished from Austria by the Second Republic which again reinstated the old Habsburg Laws. He went to France, where in December 1953 he married Princess Margherita of Savoy-Aosta. The Princess, who is the niece of the late King Umberto of

9/ p. 205-207

Italy, was the daughter of the third Duke d'Aosta, Viceroy of Ethiopia, and Princess Anne de France, sister of the Comte de Paris.

The wedding took place in the 400 year old Church of Brou in Bourg-en-Bresse, France, and was attended by the Archdukes Charles Louis and Rudolf, who with their mother, the Empress Zita, had come from the United States for the occasion, and by the Emperor Otto who came from Germany. Also attending were Duke Filiberto of Pistoria and Duke Adelberto of Bergamo who had come from Italy. Standing outside the church and municipal hall, were hundreds of Austrian and Italian well wishers who had come from far and wide to be present at that memorable occasion.

After the wedding, the newlyweds travelled extensively while the Archduke attended to business interests in China, India, and throughout South Asia. He then became involved in various banking assignments, including a directorship in the Swiss Bank Lubersac et Cie. In 1967, when this bank became a private company, the Archduke assumed its presidency.(9)

The Archduke Robert and the Archduchess Margherita have settled in Basel, Switzerland, and they gave the Empress Zita five grandchildren, three boys and two girls. The Archdukes are Lorenz (1955), Gerhard (1957) and Martin (1959), and the two Archduchesses are Maria Beatrix (1954) and Isabella (1963).

ARCHDUCHESS CHARLOTTE:

The last of Empress Zita's children to marry was the Archduchess Charlotte. She had returned to Europe from New York in 1955 on vacation, and met there, in the house of her brother the Emperor Otto, the Duke Georg von Mecklenburg.

The Duke was a widower and had two sons and a daughter. An economist by profession, he had studied in Freiburg in the Breisgau from where he received a Doctorate degree in Social Administration. Freiburg, a Medieval city in what is now Bavaria, was under Austrian rule from 1388 to the time of Napoleon, and still possesses its

---

9/ p. 208

magnificent cathedral which was the Catholic metropolitan church of the German Upper Rhine.(9)

During the war, the Duke von Mecklenburg was arrested by Germany's National Socialists for "political Catholic activities" against the state, and confined to a concentration camp at Sachsenhausen. As the area was later being threatened by advancing Soviet forces, an Austrian guard at the prison allowed the Duke to escape to the western allies. He however lost his estates and all his possessions, and was forced to earn his living by working as a translator.(9)

The Archduchess Charlotte and the Duke Georg von Mecklenburg were married at Poecking on July 25, 1956 and settled in the little town of Hohenzollern-Sigmaringen in Baden-Wuerttemberg. There the Archduchess settled down to the life of a housewife, looking after the Duke and his young son, Karl Gregor, who lived with them.

And then on July 6, 1963 the Duke suddenly died from a heart attack, and the Duchess was once again alone. She relocated herself to Munich where she resumed her previous occupation of social worker, and has also, in more recent years, been of service to Dr. Otto von Habsburg with his work and activities in the Pan-European Union. The Duchess Charlotte lived for 26 more years, and died on July 23, 1989 after a long illness. She was buried in the family crypt at Inzighofen, near Sigmaringen, next to her husband.(9, 30)

ARCHDUCHESS ADELHAID:

The Archduchess Adelhaid, second child of the Empress Zita, never married. Her life was fulfilled by her dedication to the care of others, mostly through social service work. She had studied sociology at the University of Louvain, and later at Fordham University in New York. She had earned a Doctorate in Sociology, and spent some time in teaching this subject during her sojourn in the United States.(30)

She returned to Europe in 1945 and occupied herself by helping the more unfortunate in refugee camps. In the early 1950's, she went to Katanga where she did some work in Journalism. But after an almost fatal encounter with a troop of United Nations soldiers, she returned to Europe. Her health was failing, and the climate and political environment of Katanga proved too hostile for her sensitivities.(30)

Upon returning to Europe, she settled in Poecking, and like her sister the Archduchess Charlotte, spent her time helping her brother, Dr. Otto von Habsburg, in his Pan-European activities.(9)

On October 2, 1971, the Archduchess Adelhaid, then 57 years of age, suddenly died. In accordance with her wishes, the Archduchess was buried at Tulfes, a little village in the Austrian Tirol. Her simple grave lies in the cemetary of a little parish church adorned only by a simple wrought iron cross, and protected by the exterior wall of the church against which it backs.(30)

The village of Tulfes had always shown a deep affection for the House of Habsburg. It was one of the first communities in Austria that gave Emperor Otto an honorary citizenship status, and at a time just before 1939, when Austria's chancellor Kurt Schuschnigg was opposing Hitler's invitation to join Germany. By this act of granting a Habsburg homage, Tulfes demonstrated its wishes and support for a restoration of the monarchy. The village's example was followed by hundreds of other Austrian townships and municipalities at the time, and raised real hopes that Legitimism would again triumph. This of course came to an end on March 12, 1938 when Germany annexed Austria by force.(30)

Tulfes, in those days, also granted honorary citizenship to all other members of the Habsburg family, and as such created a sort of tie between its population and their Habsburgs. It was for this reason, and because Tulfes is a beautiful, peaceful and simple town nestled among the Tirolean Alps, that the Archduchess Adelhaid had stipulated that she wished to be buried there upon her death. Her will was done.(30)

CHAPTER 18

SWITZERLAND

It is fitting that this saga of the Habsburg family in Québec should end in Switzerland, for there it all began almost 1000 years earlier. It was there, in what was then the Duchy of Burgund, at the confluence of the rivers Aare and Reuss in the present day Canton of Aargau in Switzerland, that the "Habichtsburg" from which the family name evolved, was built. It seems appropriate, therefore, that it was in Switzerland that the Empress Zita established her final residence, and that it is in Switzerland that the modern day Habsburgs built a family crypt for their eternal repose. But we are a little ahead in our story in this final chapter of the life of the Habsburgs in Québec. Let us therefore go back to the return of the family to Europe, and pick up the story from there.

Shortly after the Empress Zita had taken up residence in Tuxedo Park, her mother, the Duchess Maria Antonia of Bourbon-Parma and her sister, the Princess Isabelle of Bourbon-Parma, moved back to Europe and lived at the Château de Colmar-Berg in Luxemburg. The Château was the home of the Duchess's son, the Prince Felix of Bourbon-Parma, and his wife, the Grand Duchess of Luxemburg.(30)

When in 1954, the Duchess Maria Antonia became infirm, the Empress Zita decided to leave New York and returned to Europe. Although she had made numberous transatlantic crossings in the years 1949-1954, she decided that her place was with her aging mother, and so she too, together with the Countess Kerssenbrock, took up residence at Colmar-Berg. They stayed there until the death of the Duchess Maria Antonia.(30)

The mother of the Empress Zita died on May 14, 1959 at the age of 97. Being a Princess of Bourbon, she was laid to rest in the old

Bourbon crypt in the little Austrian village of Attnang-Puchheim, just north of the Austrian Salzkammergut in the Province of Upper Austria. There, on the outskirts of the village is the old castle of Puchheim which belonged to and served as a retreat for the Spanish Bourbons after the proclamation of the Spanish Republic in 1931. The crypt, located in the chapel of this old castle, contains the remains of a number of Spanish Carlists, including Prince Alfonso Carlos of Bourbon and Austria-Este, who was pretender to the Spanish throne 1931-1936, and his wife, the Princess Maria de las Nieves, sister to the Duchess Maria Antonia and aunt to the Empress Zita. In addition, the crypt also contains the remains of Prince René of Bourbon-Parma, brother of the Empress Zita, whose widow, Princess Margaret of Denmark, still lives in her Danish homeland.

While living at the Château de Colmar-Berg in Luxemburg, the Empress Zita found herself in close proximity to her family. She obtained much happiness from her grandchildren who then were arriving year by year, and it became her habit to vacation with some of them in the mountains of Switzerland. From 1957 to 1959, she was particularly occupied in "baby sitting" the children of her son the Archduke Robert, and it was during the summer of 1957 and 1958 that the Empress spent many pleasant weeks with them at Davos in the Grisons of Switzerland. There, in Davos, was the charming "Pension St. Josephshaus", a small vacation house run by a congregation of religious sisters, and it quickly became endeared to the heart of the Empress. It was simple and clean, the food plain but appetizing, the air always fresh, and the scenery magnificent.(30)

However, when in a following year, the Empress wanted to return to the Pension, she learnt, to her great disappointment, that the place had been fully booked and there was no place for her. The sisters did however, refer the Empress to the old Franciscan monastery at Zizers.(30)

This monastery, which dates back to the 16th century, was last owned by the Counts of Salis-Zizers. In the 1930's, they donated the monastery to the Bishop of Chur, the Reverend Johannes Vonderach, who turned it into an old age home for retired priests and nuns, and who gave it its present name -the "Johannes Stift." In recent years, the religious home was opened up to aged laymen and laywomen who wished to spend their remaining years in the home's peaceful tranquility and religious atmosphere. Its location in the Grisons of Switzerland with its magnificent surrounding scenery makes it an ideal retreat, and in it, the Empress Zita found both the peace and the religious environment she desired. It allowed her to live close to God and to her family. It also allowed her to look down the valleys to the distant mountains in Austria, her homeland, from which she had been banished for so many years and in which her mother now lay buried. It was to be another 20 years before circumstances would allow her to visit her grave.

It was 1962 when the Empress, together with her sister, the Princess Isabelle of Bourbon-Parma and the Countess Kerssenbrock, arrived at Zizers. There they jointly occupied an apartment on the third floor of the Johannes Stift, and shared the tranquility of their new home, resplendently surrounded with snow-capped mountains and fruit orchards and flowering gardens. Of particular joy to the Empress was the annual blossoming of the fruit trees and their accompaning scent of flower blossoms. It was all truly a "heavenly sight" as she once was heard to remark.(27, 30)

Being in close proximity to most of her family, the Empress Zita could periodically vacation from Zizers by visiting her children. She could visit her son, Dr. Otto von Habsburg who lived in Poecking in Bavaria, and the Archdukes Rudolf and Charles Louis who lived in Brussels. And then there was the Archduke Robert who had also moved to Switzerland and therefore became her "next-door neighbour." Two of her children however, remained beyond her reach. They were the Archduke Felix who was resident in Mexico and for whom distance made periodic visits from his mother impractical, and the Archduchess Elisabeth who lived in Waldstein in Austria, behind the pink curtain (the so called Habsburg Laws) which the Empress could not cross without first renouncing her rights to the throne. This, of course, she would not do, and never did.(30)

However, her children who were spread around Europe, and even her son the Archduke Felix who lived in Mexico, would come to Zizers whenever they could, to visit their mother -sometimes alone,

27/ p. 205

and, at other times, with their entire families. And occasionally, when the situation called for it, they would all come to Zizers together.

One such reunion was the occasion of the Empress's 90th birthday. On that day, May 9, 1982, fifty Imperial offsprings gathered at Zizers to honour the Empress. Of these, seven were first generation children of the Empress with their wives and/or husbands, and thirty-seven were grandchildren or great grandchildren of Her Majesty. For some of the younger children present, it was the first time that they met some of their cousins, and when they later got together at play, they sometimes did not know who their playmate was. The story goes that one of the Archdukes was thus overhead asking one of his young cousins, "And who do you belong to?"(27)

From time to time, the Empress would also go to Solesmes near Le Mans, some 200 kilometers southwest of Paris. There she had three sisters who were nuns at a Benedictine Cloister. Her oldest sister, Adelhaid, had become the Prioress of the Cloister, and her sisters, Franziska and Maria Antonia, had joined her there to serve their God. The Empress would usually spend one month every year at this cloister, partaking in its religious life and enjoying once again the company of her sibblings.(30)

Solesmes is also a centre for Benedictine monks. Their monastery there dates back to the eleventh century, and has become known as a centre for Gregorian chants. Their musical renditions have been often recorded and are considered among the best renditions of such religious music in the Christian world.

In the meantime, life for the Empress went on, and she had found in Zizers, the peace and serenity that her advancing years required. In 1973, her servant, friend and confident, the Countess Kerssenbrock passed away after a grave illness. During the agony of her closest friend, the Empress reversed their roles. She cared for, comforted, and nursed the Countess, until she died on February 10, 1973. Her death was a sad ending to a friendship that had endured for more than 55 years, during which time the Countess had risen from servant to family member. She was held in the highest esteem by the entire family, and to show their respect, devotion and gratitude, they laid her to rest in the new family crypt at Muri. The Countess Kerssen-

27/ p. 205

brock, like the Baroness Fuchs who had so faithfully served the Empress Maria Theresia 200 years before, was allowed to share her last resting place with that of the Habsburgs she so loyally served and loved.(30)

The death of the Countess Kerssenbrock left the Empress and her sister, the Princess Isabelle of Bourbon-Parma, alone at the Johannes Stift. The two ladies, continued for a few months to share the apartment at Zizers, but as the years began to take a heavier and heavier toll on the aging Empress, as well as on her sister (who was only six years younger than Her Majesty), they arrived at the point when they needed help. They were joined at Zizers by the Baroness Maria Plappart, who had long been a friend of the Imperial family. She was a sister of Count Forni who for many years had been not only a loyal friend, but also a constant pillar of strength for the widowed Empress and her family. Life at Zizers thus again became somewhat easier for Her Majesty and the Princess Isabelle.(30)

But then, a few years later, on July 30, 1984 the Princess Isabelle of Bourbon-Parma passed away. She was 86 years old when she died, and as a Princess of Parma, was laid to rest in a crypt under the floor of the church at Wartegg Castle near Rorschach in Switzerland. The castle had belonged to her maternal grandmother since the 1860's, and had given refuge during the troubled years of 1914-1918 to her mother. Together with her mother the Duchess Maria Antonia, the Princess Isabelle had lived out those horrible war years at Wartegg, with her young brothers, the Princes René, Felix, Louis and Gaetano. It was appropriate that she should return "home" upon her death.(30)

The death of the Princess Isabelle of Bourbon-Parma was a great loss to the Empress Zita who now was left with only the much younger Baroness Maria Plappart as a companion in the apartment at Zizers. And so, except for somewhat less frequent excursions, the Empress was still very active. She kept up her correspondence and visited her children in Switzerland, Belgium and eventually even in Austria. Yes, in 1982 the Austrian government under Chancellor Bruno Kreisky, had lifted the pink curtain, so that the Empress, then 90 years of age, could again visit her homeland.(30)

It was on May 16, 1982 that the Empress Zita first crossed again from Switzerland into Austria. The border crossing was at Feldkirch, the same town through which she had passed as she left Austria for exile on March 25, 1919, sixty-three years earlier. The purpose of her trip in May of 1982 was to go to Tulfes in the Austrian Tirol to visit the grave of her daughter, the Archduchess Adelhaid. This accomplished, she returned to Zizers.(27)

Her next trip to Austria was to last a little longer. On August 17, 1982, the Empress visited her daughter, the Princess Elisabeth of Liechtenstein, at her home in Waldstein in the province of Steiermark. She spent three happy weeks with her daughter and her family, and also enjoyed a new-found popularity in her old homeland. She was interviewed, photographed, televised, and treated with much respect and attention by the people of her homeland. And she visited Austria's most famous shrine to the Blessed Virgin, the pilgrim church at Mariazell, where over 8000 pilgrims had gathered to pray with the Empress.

Her Majesty's third visit to Austria occured in October of 1982, when she visited the grave of her mother at Puchheim in the province of Upper Austria.

On November 13, 1982, the Empress undertook her visit to Vienna. It was a most auspicious occasion. The Archbishop of Vienna, the most Reverend Cardinal Koenig, personally celebrated Mass in St. Stephen's Cathedral, to which some 10,000 people came to assist. Those who could not get inside this ancient gothic cathedral, whose origins saw the Crusaders off to the Holy Land, and whose bells tolled the defeat of the Turks at the gates of Vienna in 1529 and again in 1683, stood outside on the St. Stephen's Platz, and listened to the service going on inside on loudspeakers. When the Empress Zita arrived at the main entrance of the church, the elected representative of the first district of Vienna, in which the church stands, welcomed her arrival with the words:

> "Your Majesty, a hearty welcome awaits you in the old Imperial capital",

---

27/ p. 218, 219

And when she walked through the 1,000 year old "Riesen Tor" (the Giant Door) which dates back to the remains of an even older church, the famous Hoch and Deutschmeister Kapelle (a festive military band whose origins date back over 200 years and which reached prominence in the days of the Emperor Franz Josef) played the old imperial anthem, "Gott Erhalte."(27)

And then, sitting in the front row on a hard wooden bench (she had refused more elaborate and comfortable seating arrangements) the Empress, surrounded by many of her grandchildren and great grandchildren heard Mass and received Holy Communion. The Archduke Rudolf and Prince Vincens von Liechtenstein, son of the Empress's daughter Elisabeth, read the epistle for the day, and Cardinal Koenig said the Mass. It was not the last time that the Empress visited Vienna. She returned again at the Feast of the Pentecost in the Spring of 1983 when she attended an outdoor Mass in the presence of 130,000 faithful.(27)

Since then, the Empress had made other visits to her beloved homeland, but mostly to her daughter in Waldstein. She had in the past few years suffered from failing eyesight, and her activities had consequently been somewhat hindered. However, she still got around with the aid of the Baroness Plappart who was her constant companion. Even as late as 1988, the Empress had visited her sons in Belgium, and her daughter in Austria and although her eyesight had diminished considerably, her mind stayed ever active. She constantly followed world affairs and newsworthy activities in the lands of her old empire, and she always showed great interest in the comings and goings of her children, grandchildren, and great grandchildren. However, the winter of 1988-1989 proved very hard on her person, and she confined herself during her remaining months, to her apartments in the Johannes Stift in Zizers.

Death came slowly to this great Lady, and she faced it with resignation and great faith. In the weeks before her death, the Empress called her seven living children to her bedside, and bid them each fairwell. "I shall soon depart from this Earth" she told them as they gazed with tear-filled eyes upon this frail, grand Lady, their mother. She was not only one of the greatest Ladies the House of

27/ p. 219, 221

Habsburg had every produced, but a true modern day "Magna Mater Austriae".

In early March she fell into a coma from which she never recovered. The Archduke Rudolf and the Archduchesses Charlotte and Regina had each in turn taken up vigil at her bedside, but it was the wife of the Emperor Otto, the Archduchess Regina, who Fate placed at her bedside when the Empress took her last breath a few minutes before one A.M. on March 14, 1989. The Empress of Austria and Queen of Hungary had left this world to join her God, and her husband, in Heaven.

And after her death, her remains were laid to rest in the Crypt of the Capuchins in Vienna. She, and possibly her husband who currently lies buried in Funchal on Madeira where he died in 1922, will probably be the last Habsburg to ever inhabit this crypt.

Now, like all living beings, the remaining modern day Habsburgs have also thought about their future -when God calls them from this Earth, where will their remains be laid to rest?

The book "Monumenta Augustae Domus Austriacae", written in 1772 by a scholar and clergyman by the name of von Herrgott-Gerbet, dealt with the last resting places of the Habsburgs until the middle of the 18th century. A subsequent work, published in 1925 and written by Karl Ginhart, describes the Crypt of the Capuchins in Vienna, whose last occupant before the Empress Zita, was the Archduchess Maria Josefa (mother of the Emperor Charles I) who died in 1944. And so, the modern day Habsburgs have chosen other resting places for their earthly remains. One of these is in Muri, a place not in Austria, not in Belgium, and not in France, but in the Canton Aargau in Switzerland, not far from the place from which their ancestors took their name -the old Habichtsburg.

There, in the ancient Benedictine monastery's Loretto chapel, they established since 1971, a family crypt. The site is most appropriate, since the monastery was founded in the year 1027 by one Ita of Lorraine, the wife of Count Radbot of Habsburg.(13)

Completed in the year 1064, at which time only a small part of today's imposing structure existed, the church structure of the monastery has seen much change since then. Severely damaged by fire in the years 1300 and again in 1363, it was destroyed through war in 1386. Always rebuilt and somewhat enlarged after each catastrophe, the church structure achieved its greatest redevelopment when in the 16th and 17th century, the cloister was added, as were an abbey and a convent. The entire structure reflects a Gothic character, laid out in accordance with classical Benedictine tradition.(13)

Further modifications saw the Barockization of the old Gothic appearance of the main church, and the closing of the north wing of the four wing cloister. This resulted in the construction in 1698 of the Loretto Chapel in the north wing of the cloister, and the installation of a crypt under its floor. This "Casa Santa" has since 1971 served as a Habsburg crypt, and in addition to the Countess Kerssenbrock, contains the remains of the Archduchess Xenia, the Archduke Rudolf's first wife, and their son, the Archduke Johannes, as well as the hearts of the Emperor Charles I and the Empress Zita.

CHAPTER 19

THE FUNERAL

Following her death on March 14, 1989, the body of the Empress was taken from the Johannes Stift where she had lived, to the Canton Hospital of Chur. There, in accordance with a custom dating back to the Crusades, the heart of the Empress was removed and her body embalmed. The heart was then sealed in an urn and taken to Muri, where it was placed next to a similar urn containing the heart of her beloved husband, the Emperor Charles I, in the family crypt under the Loretto Chapel of the Benedictine Abbey.

Her body was then placed in a simple wooden coffin encased within a metal one, and exposed in the Chapel of the Abbey. There it reposed for a number of days, allowing family and close friends a private opportunity to say good-bye, and for prayer and reflection.

On the morning of March 27, the remains of Austria's last Empress were transported from Muri, across the Swiss-Austrian border at Feldkirch, to the Viennese suburb of Klosterneuburg. There, her remains were laid "in state" in the great marble hall of the 900 year old Augustinian monastery. Her coffin remained there for two more days, allowing foreign dignitaries and visitors from many lands to come and pay their respect. It was reported that thousands of Hungarians and Italians, as well as many hundreds from other parts of the old empire, joined the mourners who filed past her coffin. Looking down from the ceiling of the great hall, was a large fresco depicting the homage of many lands to the House of Austria.

On the third day, her remains were transported to St. Stephen's Cathedral in the heart of Vienna. There, draped in the purple Habsburgflag of mourning, her coffin was exposed in front of the high altar. On the day before the funeral, tens of thousands of mourners again filed past her coffin and inscribed their names in special condolence books provided for the occasion.

On April 1, a magnificent performance of Mozart's Requiem highlighted the Pontifical Requiem Mass sung by Cardinal Dr. Hans Herman Groer, assisted by Bishops from Chur and Feldkirch, as well as by the Hungarian Primate, and Bishops from Bruenn, Eisenstadt, Katowitz and Augsburg. A letter from the Papal Nunciate, the Archbishop Michele Cecchini, extending the condolences of His Holiness, Pope Jean Paul II, to the family of the Empress, was read by Cardinal Groer.

Attending the Requiem Mass in honour of the Empress were her seven surviving children, their spouses and their children, as well as her grandchildren and 14 of her great-grandchildren. In addition, many government and foreign dignitaries also attended the solemn funeral mass. These included Dr. Kurt Waldheim, Austria's president, as well as Austria's immediate past-president, Dr. Rudolf Kirchschlaeger, and officials from Austria's federal, provincial and municipal governments. Mourners from foreign lands included the Grand Duke Jean of Luxembourg, Prince Franz Josef von Liechtenstein, Prince Albert de Liège of Belgium, Prince Juan de Bourbon (father of the King of Spain), Crown Prince Albert of Monaco, Prince Johannes of Thurn and Taxis, Prince Raad (cousin of King Hussein of Jordan), and Crown Prince Sidi Mohammed of Morocco, and various delegations and ambassadors from many lands. The ambassadors from Turkey, the United States, Belgium, Holland and Canada were accorded special seating in the Cathedral, in deference to the help and support their countries had shown the Empress after the fall of the monarchy in 1918.

During the Mass, the first lesson was read in German by the Archduke Charles, eldest son of Dr. Otto von Habsburg, and the second lesson (the letter of St. Paul to the Romans) was read in Hungarian by Princess Elisabeth von Liechtenstein, youngest daughter of the Empress. At the conclusion of the Requiem, both the Hungarian National Anthem (in Hungarian) and the old Austrian National Anthem, "Gott Erhalte" (in German), were sung as the coffin of the Empress was slowly carried to the rear of the Cathedral.

There, it was placed on the old (1876), black, imperial hearse drawn by six black horses. (For Archdukes of the House of Austria, Spanish protocol required the use of a second hearse, painted red.) The hearse used for the Empress was the same one that had also carried the remains of the Empress Maria Anna (1884), the Crown Prince Rudolf (1889), the Empress Elisabeth (1898), and the Emperor Franz Josef (1916), to their last resting places in the Crypt of the Capuchins.

Accompanied by an honour guard of 1,000 infantry, arranged in various companies and dressed in the uniforms of the old monarchy, the procession slowly made its way from the Cathedral to the Church of Capuchins. Walking behind the hearse were the seven children of the Empress and their families, members of the clergy, including Cardinal Groer, President Waldheim and other members of Austria's government, and many foreign dignitaries. When the procession arrived at its destination, the coffin was carried to the door of the church were an age-old custom was re-enacted.

The door of the church was closed, and inside, standing on guard, was a bearded monk. Outside, in front of the coffin supported by six palbearers, was the master of ceremonies of the procession. With a long staff, he knocked three times on the closed door. "Who wishes to come in", asked the monk from inside the church. "Zita", came the reply, "the Empress of Austria and crowned Queen of Hungary; Queen of Bohemia, Dalmatia, Croatia, Slavonia, Galizia, Lodomeria and Illyria; Queen of Jerusalem; Archduchess of Austria; Grand-duchess of Tuscany and of Cracow; Duchess of Lorraine and Bar, of Salzburg, Steiermark, Corinthia, Krain and Bukovina; Grandprincess of Siebenbuergen; Markcountess of Moravia; Duchess of Upper and Lower Silesia, of Modena, Piacenza and Guastalla, of Auschwitz and Zator, of Teschen, Friuli, Ragusa and Zara; Princess-Countess of Habsburg and the Tyrol, of Kyburg, Gorizia and Gradisca; Princess of Trient and Brixen; Markcountess of Upper and Lower Lausitz and Istria; Countess of Hohenembs, Feldkirch, Bregenz and Sonnenberg; Lady of Triest, Catarro, and of the Windischmark; Grandwoiwodin of Serbia; born Princess of Bourbon, Princess of Portugal and of Parma". "I do not know her", replied the monk from behind the closed door.

The master of ceremonies again knocked three times with his staff, and again the monk asked "Who wishes to come in?" "Zita, Her Majesty the Empress and Queen" answered the master of ceremonies. And again the monk replied "We do not know her."

After the third attempt at entrance signalled again by three knocks with the staff on the door, the monk again asked, "Who wishes to enter?"

This time, the master of ceremonies replied, "Zita, a mortal human and a sinner". At this, the monk threw open the door, and bid a simple "Then come in."

The coffin was then carried into the church, where His Eminence, Cardinal Koenig received the deceased and blessed the coffin with incense and holywater. Surrounded by mourners, her family, and many dignitaries, Cardinal Koenig led the assembled in prayer, while the Vienna Choir Boys sang "O Haupt voll Blut und Wunden" and the monks closed the service with a Salve Regina.

The coffin was then carried on the shoulders of six palbearers from the chapel to the crypt, passing the sarcophagi of the Emperor Charles VI, the Empress Maria Theresia and her husband Emperor Franz, and the Emperor Franz I of Austria, to the crypt chapel underneath the church. Outside the church on the Albertina Platz, a gun crew fired a 21 gun salute, and precisely as the 21st salvo was fired, the coffin was laid to rest on the floor of the Crypt Chapel, next to a statue of the Mother of God. Across the Chapel stood a bust of the Emperor Charles I, who still buried in Funchal on Madeira, is awaiting his return to Vienna and an eternal resting place next to his wife, the Empress Zita.

Cardinal Koenig then prayed for "Our sister, The Empress Zita" and asked Our Lord "To give her eternal peace and to let her rest in peace."

In the Crypt of the Capuchins, the gathered assembly of cardinals and bishops, members of the Imperial family, and special guests, paid Her Majesty their last respects. In a closing gesture, Count Nostiz, one-time secretary to the Imperial family, presented the key to the coffin of the Empress to her eldest son, Dr. Otto von Habsburg, and he in turn, in accordance with tradition, passed it on to the keeper of the crypt.

The Crypt of the Capuchins now harbours the remains of 12 emperors, 17 empresses, and some 115 other members of the House of Habsburg. Its closed doors now symbolize the end of 1,000 years of Austria's history -a history of triumph and glory, of defeat and disillusionment -in short, the end of an era. FIAT VOLUNTAS TUA.

EPILOGUE

CHAPTER 20

PARMA AND QUEBEC

When the Duchess of Bourbon-Parma, Maria Antonia, arrived in Québec in 1940 with her daughter, the Empress of Austria, they were not aware that an emissary from Parma had preceded them by some 80 years. The emissary was a monument in the St. Charles cemetary, parts of which came from Parma, Italy, and parts of which were native to Québec. The parts that came from Parma, had been intended to glorify the Duke of Reichstadt, son of Napoleon Bonaparte and Marie Louise of Austria, a Habsburg princess who became Empress of France and later, the Duchess of Parma.

The Archduchess Marie Louise, eldest daughter of the Emperor Franz I of Austria, married Napoleon Bonaparte in Paris on April 2, 1810. The nuptials were arranged by France's Ambassador in Vienna, Marshall Alexandre Berthier and Austria's Foreign Minister Clemens Wenzel Nepomuk Lothar Count Metternich, in an attempt to ensure a peaceful co-existence between Austria and France after Austria's defeat by Napoleon in 1809. The fact that Napoleon's first marriage with the Empress Josephine did not produce children, motivated the Emperor of France to enter into this union with the eldest daughter of the exalted Austrian Emperor. His hopes were soon fulfilled, for on March 20, 1811 she bore him a nine pound baby boy. He was named Napoleon Francois Joseph Charles, and he was to be known as the "King of Rome", a title that had been recommended to Napoleon by his Senate on February 17, 1810, more than a full year before the birth of his son.(6)

When Napoleon was again defeated and banished to Elba in 1814, the Empress of France returned with her son to Vienna. The Congress of Vienna gave to the Empress of France the Duchy of Parma, and it was to its capital, the ancient City of Parma, that the Empress Marie Louise came on April 20, 1816. Her five year old son however, was kept in Vienna to be converted from a French Prince to an Austrian Archduke. This task was entrusted to a highly placed adviser to the Court, Count Moritz Dietrichstein-Proskau, who also happened to be a good friend of one General Albert Adam Neipperg, who the Austrian Emperor had sent to Parma to run the business of government.(6)

The city of Parma dates back to 183 B.C. when it was a small Roman settlement. It had been the seat of the Estes and Viscontis, and had at one time been owned by the Sforzas, as well as by King Louis XII of France. In 1545 Pope Paul III elevated the city to the status of capital of the Duchy of Parma, and placed there Pier Luigi Farnese as its ruler. The Dukes of Farnese did well, for they ruled the Duchy for over 200 years.(6)

When the Farneses eventually died out, the Duchy came into the hands of the Bourbons who established the dynasty known as the Bourbon-Parma. It was 1748, and under their leadership, Parma became a centre of art, culture, theater and music. It was from Parma that the Austrian Emperor Josef II chose his bride, the Empress Isabelle, and it was to the House of Bourbon-Parma that the young Archduke Charles of Habsburg looked to select his bride, the Princess Zita.(6)

When the Empress Marie Louise came to Parma in 1816 and became the Duchess of Parma, she found there a beautiful palace -the Palazzo Ducale -which Giovanni Boscoli had built for the Farneses in 1564. Enlarged under the Bourbons in the 18th century, the Palazzo subsequently became the centre of culture and influence in the region, and Parma became known as the "Athens of Italy."(6)

When Marie Louise settled in the Palazzo Ducale, the place was surrounded by a beautiful park, adorned with statues, vases and other monuments. There was even an arched temple built on a man-made hill, and a Palazzo del Parco, or garden palace, in which guests could lounge and enjoy a man-made pond filled with golden carp. For more formal occasions, there was the Palazzo Ducale del Colorno, a sort of guest palace for very important visitors. It had four imposing

6/ p. 324-326

corner towers, as well as a throne room, and had been built in the 17th and 18th centuries by the Dukes of Farnese.(6)

By 1816, the saga of the son of Napoleon reached a critical impass. Although Marie Louise, Duchess of Parma, had hoped that her son would one day come to Parma and become its sovereign ruler, the great powers of Europe who had defeated Napoleon, had other plans. They had decided that under no circumstances did they want the son of Napoleon on a throne in Parma, or at any other place for that matter. They also had decided that Parma itself, after the death of Marie Louise, should return to the House of Bourbon, and not to any descendants of Marie Louise.(6)

Because of these restrictions, the Emperor of Austria decided to grant to the son of Napoleon some Bohemian domaines known as Reichstadt, but stipulated that after his death, these too would not fall to any of his successors, but should go to the House of Habsburg-Lorraine. At the same time, he decreed on March 18, 1818 that the son of Napoleon I and Marie Louise, would from that day on be called "The Duke of Reichstadt". The seven year old boy had thus already gone through almost as many titles as he had years. Born the son of Napoleon I, he was a "Prince of France", became "The King of Rome", was known by many Bonaparte legitimists as "Napoleon II", by the Parmese Court as "The Prince of Parma", and now by Imperial decree, "The Duke of Reichstadt."(6)

When Napoleon I Bonaparte died in final exile at St. Helena on May 5, 1821, his widow the Duchess of Parma married General Neipperg, the Austrian Emperor's administrator and business manager of governmental affairs at Parma. The wedding took place in Parma on August 8, 1821 with the full knowledge of the Emperor Franz back in Vienna. It was not an unexpected marriage, for the Duchess had already given the General two children -a daughter, Albertine, in 1817 and a boy, Wilhelm Albrecht, in 1819. Needless to say, these unions were kept very confidential, and the two children grew up as the Countess and the Count Montenuovo, an Italian name that when translated into German, means "Neuberg" (New mountain), a word phonetically very close to "Neipperg."(6)

6/ p. 330-331, 334-335, 355-356

Marie Louise's marriage to the General was a happy one, but ended abruptly on February 22, 1829 when Neipperg suddenly died. She buried him in a specially-made tomb in the Palatina chapel of Santo Ludovico in the Palazzo Ducale.(28)

Her son, the Duke of Reichstadt, by then a young man of 18, was still being kept in Vienna. He had never been permitted to visit Parma, and his mother only saw him when she went to the Imperial Capital, which was about once every two years, or about six times during her life with General Neipperg in Parma. She was therefore deeply concerned when she came to Vienna in the Summer of 1832, and saw her son seriously ill. He had for some time suffered severe bronchial disorders. These were first noticed during the late winter of 1831-32, but because of great optimism and medical treatment administered to the young prince by the attending physician, whose omniscient name was Dr. Malfatti, no words of urgency had been transmitted to his mother in Parma. When the gravity of the situation was finally made known to the Duchess of Parma in June of 1832, she immediately headed for Vienna. When she arrived at the Schoenbrunn Palace and was brought to her son's bedroom -it was the same room that Napoleon had slept in when he had spent 158 days at Schoenbrunn in the Summer of 1809 -she had to hold back her grief as she looked upon her physically degenerated son and took him in her arms. He had developed severe Pneumonia which caused him gruesome side-effects and pain. He began to expectorate pus and his breathing required all his remaining strength. On July 22, 1832 he died. Both the Emperor Franz, and his Foreign Minister Count Metternich, happened to be away from Vienna, and the task of comforting and caring for the dying prince were left to his mother and the Archduchess Sophie who had become the Duke of Reichstadt's closest companion.(6)

As he passed away, he was attended at his bedside by the Archduke Franz Karl, husband of the Archduchess Sophie (mother of the two year old, future Emperor Franz Josef I) his mother the Duchess Marie Louise, and a few of his gentleman attendants.(6)

The Emperor Franz returned immediately to Vienna, and the Duke of Reichstadt was given a grandiose funeral. His coffin, transported

6/ p. 364

on a horse drawn gun carriage, was flanked on all sides by torch-bearers, and brought to the chapel of the Hofburg, the Imperial winter palace. There the deceased son of Napoleon was exposed until July 24, when his remains were moved for internment in the crypt under-neath the Church of the Capuchins not far from the Hofburg. As was tradition, and in accordance with Imperial etiquette, his mother, the Duchess of Parma, did not enter the crypt.(6)

When the Duke of Reichstadt had been laid to rest amongst his deceased Habsburg predecessors, the Baroness Louise Sturmfeder, the Duke of Reichstadt's nurse for many years, remembered a com-ment once made by her unhappy charge: "Entre mon berceau et ma bière est un grand zero" (Between my cradle and my coffin is a big zero).(6)

Meanwhile, back in Parma, life went on. When the Duchess Marie Louise returned from the funeral in Vienna, she was very despondent. She had lost two husbands and a son, and her life now became without purpose. There were political uprisings against her in Parma, insti-gated by the Carbonari whose nationalism ran counter to Habsburg policy. When these uprisings were finally stopped, she settled into a "merry widow" role and spent all her energies improving the life of her Parmesians.

She had built the "Teatro Reggio" and now set about to build a conservatorium. She surrounded herself with renowned musicians and actors, among them Giovanni Bottesini the cellist, Arrigo Boito the lyricist, and Niccolo Paganini the violin virtuoso. Out of a provincial city, she created the musical city of Parma, and provided the environment and facilities that allowed another famous son of Parma to achieve greatness as a cellist and conductor, Arturo Tos-canini.(6)

She built bridges across the rivers Taro and Trebbia, and dams to control them. She also built hospitals, homes for orphans, and schools, and enlarged and modernized the university. And in this way she endeared herself in the hearts of her Parmasians, to whom she soon became known as "la buona duchessa" (the good Duchess).(6)

6/ p. 366-367, 368-369

Marie Louise lived for 15 more years following the death of her son. She married for the last time two years later, the Count Charles René de Bombelles, and died 13 years later on December 17, 1847 at the age of 56. Her remains were transported to Vienna, accompanied by an honour guard of 150 hussars, and laid to rest in the Crypt of the Capuchins next to her son, the Duke of Reichstadt. The Emperor's eldest daughter had come home for the last time.(6)

Some years later, in 1857 Parma was visited by a banker and merchant from Québec. His name was William Venner, and he had come to Italy to buy mineral waters which he imported to Québec. While passing through Parma he came across a monument that was for sale. He purchased it, had it disassembled, and transported it back to Québec.(43)

Back in Québec, William Venner hired the Québec Architect Charles Baillargé to incorporate the pieces of the Parma monument, with local materials from Québec, into a tomb for the Venner family. The finished product that Monsieur Baillargé produced was erected in the St. Charles Cemetary in the Parish of St. Roch for the Venner family in 1862.(43)

The Venner mausoleum is still to be seen in the St. Charles Cemetary to this day. It stands imposingly close to the cemetary's main gate on rue St. Vallier and consists of a foundation, six Corinthian columns supporting an entablature made up of architrave, frieze and cornices, and is topped with a flat roof on which stands a classical funerary urn. The frieze is embellished, inside and out, with crowns of laurel honouring the intended occupant of the monument. Within the structure, which is supported by a foundation of cut stone and brick, is a capping of white Carrara marble supporting a life-size figure of Christ. The statue of Christ replaces an earlier figure of a weeping woman which was imported from Parma, but which no longer exists.(43)

Below the imposing monument is a burial cavern of red brick, 3 meters wide, 4 meters long, and 4 meters high, sufficiently large to hold 30 leaded coffins. The monument commands a plot of ground measuring some 525 square feet, and was erected by Jean-Baptiste Artem Tapin, to whom the Architect had confided the work. Tapin

6/ p. 388

also surrounded the site with an ornate wrought-iron fence that was forged at the foundry of Philip Whitty, who also had provided the iron work for Québec City's Dufferin Terrace. The stone required by Artem Tapin in addition to the pieces imported from Parma, was obtained from the Deschambault quarry near Québec and from Pointe aux Trembles near Montréal, and was cut to size by the stonehewers Ambroise Bélanger and Isidore Morrissette. The work was completed in 1862, and received its first sarcophagus in 1867, the remains of Marie Anne Levallée, the wife of William Venner. Since William Venner's death in 1890, when he was laid to rest beside his wife, the burial crypt below the monument has been filled to capacity with descendants of William Venner, the man with the Parma connection.(43)

The unanswered questions of course concern the original monument in Parma: where was the monument located in Parma, what did it look like, who was it intended for, and who was its architect? There are no papers, no invoices, no bills of sale answering these questions. Contacts in Parma and research in Québec carried out by the author, has so far proven fruitless in providing the answer, and until answers are provided, we can only postulate the following possibilities:

1) The monument had been erected as part of a burial tomb in the Palatine Church of Santo Ludovico, but became obsolete when the Duchess of Parma built a burial crypt in the Church of the Madonna della Steccata.

2) The monument had been erected as part of a burial tomb for the family of Marie Louise, including the King of Rome, but became obsolete when the Duke of Reichstadt and his mother were eventually laid to rest in Vienna.

3) The monument had been erected as a cenotaph by the Duchess of Parma for her son the King of Rome, but became obsolete because of subsequent political circumstances.

4) The monument had been erected as a Cenotaph for ceremonial use and became no longer structurally viable.

5) The monument had been specifically constructed as a cenotaph for one particular use and then dismantled after that occasion.

6) The monument dated from the time before the arrival of the Duchess of Parma and was no longer structurally sound and had to be dismantled.

7) The monument had been used as a decoration in the Ducal Park of the Palazzo Ducale and was no longer structually or politically viable.

8) The monument had never been intended to honour the King of Rome -that it had been built to honour a young woman. This presupposes that a monument for a King would be more belligerous in nature, and would not have had the figure of a woman as its centre piece.

Anyone of the eight above mentioned hypotheses could explain the origin of the Parma monument that William Venner had brought to Québec. The only thing we know for certain is that Count Neipperg was buried in the Palatine Church of Santo Ludovico when he died in 1829, and that a monument made by the sculptor Lorenzo Bertolini marked his tomb. We also know that Count Neipperg's remains as well as the Bertolini monument were later moved to the Church of the Madonna della Steccata, and that the ducal chapel was later discontinued as a church and turned into a warehouse. The Bertolini monument and Count Neipperg's bones are now to be found in a niche to the left of the main portal in the nave of the church.(28)

As already mentioned, the Duchess of Parma, Marie Louise, lies in the Kaisergruft (the Crypt of the Emperors) underneath the Church of the Capuchins in Vienna. After her death on December 24, 1847, the Duchy of Parma reverted to the Bourbons and remained in their hands until the Spring of 1859, when Louise de Bourbon, and her 11 year old son Robert, the future father of the Empress Zita, were driven out of Parma by Italian nationalists. It was the end of Parma as an independent state.

To complete the story, it must be noted that in 1940, during the last war, Adolf Hitler had the sarcophagus of the Duke of Reichstadt moved from Vienna to Paris. It rests there now in Les Invalides, next to his father, Napoleon I Bonaparte.

CHAPTER 21

TWO QUEBEC HOMES

THE VILLA SAINT JOSEPH:

It is one of the enigmas of history that the War of the Austrian succession resulted in the conflict between England and France during which, in 1759, New France was lost to the British crown. The French King, Louis XV, had considered the price to save Québec, which Voltaire had referred to as "quelques arpents de neige" (a few arpents of snow) too high, and preferred to marshal his resources against the Prussians whom he saw as a greater threat to France.

And so it came to pass that the following decades saw not only the beginning of Britain's colonial domination of the two Canadas, but also its economic domination of French Canada. English-speaking merchants, lumber barons, and soldiers settled in and around Québec, and as their fortunes flourished, they bought lands on which to build their homes. Most of the lands east of Québec had comprised the Seigneury of Sillery, parts of which were subdivided and sold in the early 1600's.

One of these subdivisions became the Mission of the Jesuits who had come to New France to evangelize the "savages" and to build schools for the settlers. Their first house was built in 1637 on land surrounding a small bay in the St. Lawrence river which the Indians had called "Kamiskoua-Ouangachit." Two Jesuit fathers who lived and worked there in 1638, Fathers Paul Le Jeune and Jean DeQuen, offered the mission to the patronage of Saint Joseph. The small bay which harboured their mission became known as "l'anse Saint-Joseph."(16)

As the Seigneury was further subdivided, the lands along the river received names that have endured to this day. In addition to Anse Saint Joseph, they included Anse du Foulon, Anse St. Michel, and Pointe à Puiseaux, to name only a few. And little by little, by the end of the XVIII and beginning of the XIX centuries, magnificent villas began to appear on the cliffs overlooking these bays. Many carried English names, such as Spencer Wood, Spencer Grange, Marchmont, Benmore, Kirk Ella, and Kilmarnock. These villas, were originally intended as summer homes for the well to do merchants and high ranking military and government officials from Québec, but they soon became their permanent residences. Spencer Wood, to mention just one, became in 1849 the official residence of the Governor of Lower Canada until it was destroyed by fire in 1860. Prior to 1849, it had belonged to a merchant named Henry Atkinson, who as president of the Horticultural Society of Québec in the 1830's, had built at Spencer Wood, formal Gardens which became famous and which were mentioned in the Encyclopedia of Gardening of London, and in the Gardener's Magazine in 1837.(16)(17)

When he sold Spencer Wood to the Government in 1849, Henry Atkinson kept the northerly part of the land for himself and built on it the house known as "Spencer Grange." It was his new residence, and he lived there until he died. In 1856, his daughter, Harriet Mary, married James Macpherson-Lemoine.

They moved into Spencer Grange in 1860, and lived there until 1912 when James Macpherson-Lemoine died. His daughter, Sophia Ann and her husband Frank Rhodes then lived at Spencer Grange until their death, when the house came into the possession of the Community of Sisters of Ste. Jeanne d'Arc.(16)

The Sisters acquired Spencer Grange in 1934, and, at the suggestion of their founder, renamed the house "Villa Saint Joseph" in honour of the partron saint of workers. Père Marie Clément Staub had founded the Community of Sisters of Ste. Jeanne d'Arc as an Order dedicated to the care of priests, and in accordance with their mission, the good Sisters turned the Villa Saint Joseph into a retire-

16/ p. 64, 69
17/ p. 17

ment home for infirm and old priests. They turned it into a modern day "Bethanie" (today El-Azareyeh), a biblical village near Jerusalem in Judea, where the Saints Marthe and Marie aided and took care of the Apostles.(20)

At the request of the ecclesiastical authorities, the Sisters completely transformed the Villa Saint Joseph. They divided it into two parts; one part being the living quarters for the old priests, and the second part being allocated for use by the Sisters who would be caring for their aged charges. They also installed in the Villa a small chapel in which the Blessed Sacrement could be exposed and Mass could be said.(20)

The Villa Saint Joseph was inaugurated in 1934 by the Auxiliary Bishop of Québec, His Excellency Monseigneur Plante. The inauguration was attended by the Mother General of the Order, and by all the Sisters of the Mother House. The Abbé Irénée Frenette directed the ceremonies which dedicated the Villa to Saint Joseph and requested his patronage.(20)

In 1940 when the Empress Zita of Austria arrived in Québec, the few old priests, who were resident in the Villa were relocated, and the Villa was made available to Her Majesty, her family, and her entourage. They found in it an ideal refuge, totally satisfactory to their needs. The Archduke Rudolf described the Villa in the following words:

> "The Villa was very modern, incredibly well heated. It was completely furnished, and it had a marvelous little chapel which my mother appreciated very much. And we also had a dining room and a large salon. It was all very comfortable. The house also had many rooms, which suited us ideally, since we were so many. Even my grandmother, who came to us from New York, stayed with us."

The house was also sufficiently large to accommodate the Princess Isabelle of Bourbon-Parma, sister of the Empress, the Countess Kerssenbrock, Miss Dobler, the Counts Degenfeld and Eltz when they stayed in Québec, and a small staff of personal servants who had come from Europe to serve the Empress. All in all, the Imperial family found the home very pleasant and comfortable, and were very happy to live in it during their stay in Québec.

When the Empress Zita left Québec for Tuxedo Park, the Villa Saint Joseph reverted to its former use. The Sisters of Ste. Jeanne d'Arc again used the villa as a home for old priests, but after a few years sold it to a Québec City developer who turned the surrounding grounds in a subdivision of single family homes, known as Parc Lemoine. The Villa then fell into private hands and became first a private nursing home, to which purpose it was well suited because of its many rooms and facilities, and eventually into a private home. It stands today, a memory to what it once was, somewhat neglected and isolated. The chapel, once solemn and revered, no longer sanctifies the residence, and a statue of Saint-Joseph welcoming the visitors no longer greets the pilgrim making his way to this once hallowed Habsburg shrine in Québec. Both have been removed, and the house no longer radiates warmth nor welcomes strangers. It has become a derelict, trying to survive on the sea of change, surrounded by houses of another era.

The trees of Spencer Wood too, have given way to progress. The gardens that used to grace the old house, have become paved streets, and the flowers that once adorned the chapel of the villa, now grace the attractive homes that now surround the villa. And the country lane that once led to its main entrance, has become rue Lemoine on which the villa now bears the number 1321.

NO. 25, SAINTE-GENEVIEVE:

Sitting snuggly in Upper Town, Québec City, in the shadow of the Citadel, is the Cirice Têtu House. This house is not only significant because it represents one of the finest examples of neoclassical architecture in Canada, but because it was the home of the De Koninck family for 27 years. The late Professor Charles De Koninck was Dean of the Faculty of Philosophy at Université Laval when the Empress Zita lived in Québec, and the house became almost a second home to the Archdukes and Archduchesses who were studying at Laval and taking supplementary private lessons in Philosophy at No. 25, Sainte-Geneviève.

In the course of these private tutorials, deep and sincere relationships of respect and friendship evolved between teacher and pupils, which have endured to this day. The house soon became affectionatley known as the "Université De Koninck" by the Archdukes. For many years after he had left Québec, the Archduke Rudolf continued his friendship with Professor De Koninck, first from New York when he was living in Tuxedo Park, and then from the Belgium Congo where he lived and worked for a number of years after his marriage to Countess Xenia Czernichew-Besobrasow in 1953.

And whenever the Imperial family came to visit Québec in later years, they always found "room in the inn" at No. 25, Sainte-Geneviève. In a letter to the Professor and Madame De Koninck, thanking them for one such stay, the Archduke Rudolf lovingly referred to his stay at the "Hôtel Elastique" because the De Konincks always had room for him, no matter how many children happened to be at home at the time. And until the sudden death of Professor Charles De Koninck in 1965, the house remained a welcome and hospitable place to stay whenever Imperial family members came to Québec City in the 1950's and 1960's.(36)

The House at No. 25, Sainte-Geneviève Avenue was built in 1852-1854. It was designed by the Québec architect, Charles Baillargé (1826-1906), who happened to be the same architect who later erected the Venner mausoleum in the St. Charles cemetary. He was one of the most prominent architects in Québec in the second half of the 19th century, during which time he built many private residences, of which No. 25, Avenue Sainte-Geneviève, is among the most luxurious. Charles Baillargé was also well known internationally, and was recognized for his contribution to language, mathematics and architecture. He travelled extensively through Europe, Asia, and the Americas, and was awarded 13 medals of honour and 17 diplomas from various institutions and universities.(22)

In building No. 25, Sainte-Geneviève for a Québec merchant by the name of Cirice Têtu who was its first owner, Charles Baillargé followed the general tradition of the discreet Greek Revival of the 1840's which dominated Québec architecture at the time, while at the same time drawing on the Baroque concepts that became popular in the mid-1850's. The result was a house of ostentatious dimensions, with robust details, both inside and out. The facade was of gray Deschambault stone, and the interior boasted a lavish double sized-drawing room on the second floor, with two large crystal chandeliers and two marble mantles in the style of Louis-Quinze. A Baroque staircase winding upwards, allowed access from the rez-de-chaussée to the second floor drawing room and to the third floor bedrooms.(22)

In 1870, Cirice Têtu's fortunes came to an abrupt end, and he sold the house in 1872. The new owner was the Honorable John Sharples, a prosperous timber merchant of the time. He lived there until he died in 1876, after which the house passed to his succession until 1911, when it was sold to Dr. Nicolas Pinault, a prominent Québec physician and surgeon.(22)

Dr. Pinault kept the house for only one year, and in 1912 sold it to two sisters, Henriette Geneviève and Anne Henriette Cramail. They lived there for nine years and in 1921 sold the house to Major-General Joseph P. Landry. He passed it on to the Honorable Alfred Savard, lawyer and King's Consul, who made No. 25, Sainte-Geneviève his home for the next twelve years.(22)

In 1939, the house was leased to Professor Charles De Koninck, who purchased it the following year. The house remained with the De Koninck family until 1966, the year after the professor died. It was then sold to Raymond Rousseau who made it his home for 10 years. In 1976, the house was sold to Mr. and Mrs. Gil Rémillard who lived there for two years. In 1978 the home was acquired by Mr. Antoine Prévost, a prominent Québec painter who lived in it for three years, and then sold it in late 1981 to Messrs Peter Patton and Stefan Saska. These gentlemen however, kept the house for only about a year and a half, and again sold it in April 1983, this time to its present owner, Mr. Pierre Maranda.(36)

Mr. Maranda had made some extensive renovations to No. 25, Sainte-Geneviève. He modernized its furnishings, fittings and facilities and has brought the old house up to 20th century standards. Nevertheless, No. 25, Sainte-Geneviève remains largely unchanged, and the house is still one of the most exquisite and best maintained examples of neoclassical Greek revival architecture in Canada.

CHAPTER 22

FOUR FAMILIES

The many people who gave of themselves to help and comfort the Imperial family during their stay in Québec in the 1940's are too numerous to mention and honour individually. Many of them have already been mentioned in the course of this book, and if there are some that have been missed, it is because they have remained in the background at their own volition. There are nevertheless four families whose contribution to the Imperial family was extraordinarily significant, and whose contribution invites special mention. They are, the family of the Catholic religious community in Québec, and the Families Maître Stanislas Germain, Professor Dr. Charles De Koninck and Professor Dr. Charles Engel.

THE CATHOLIC RELIGIOUS COMMUNITY:

The good graces and christian benevolence of the family comprising the Catholic religious community in Québec during the 1940's was not only helpful, but made possible the Imperial family's stay in Québec. From Cardinal Villeneuve down to the nuns in the convents of Jésus-Marie and Ste. Jeanne d'Arc, hearts were opened and resources were made available to house, cloth, heat and sustain the Empress and her charges. These people loved and honoured Her Majesty in ways that only French Canada could, paying her their utmost respect and treating her with their highest reverence, the likes of which Her Majesty had not experienced since before the collapse of the Austrian-Hungarian Empire in 1918.

From teachers such as the Reverend Père Georges Henri Lévesque to men such as Monseigneur Alphonse Marie Parent and Cardinal Maurice Roy, the Imperial family received the help and support they needed to meet their academic goals and to satisfy their religious convictions. They made Her Majesty feel "at home" in the Catholic environment of Québec, and they provided Her Majesty's children with an educational system modelled after the academic reforms instituted by the Empress Maria Theresia of Austria during the mid-eighteenth century. The reforms, initially instituted at the Theresianium in Vienna, quickly spread through the then existing Austrian empire and were subsequently adopted by most of Catholic Europe. It is of interest to note that the "Theresian" system of education (leading to a Baccalaureat in Arts after 12 years followed by a 3-4 year University degree in Philosophy or Science) was the system followed in Québec up to the time of the Parent Commission's recommendation in 1961, after which Québec joined the rest of Canada and the United States who were using the established"British" system.

Of the many Sisters whose life the Empress Zita had touched in the 1940's, few remain. Nevertheless those who still recall those days at Jésus-Marie and at Ste. Jeanne d'Arc, do so with fondest memories. They thank God, too, that they were permitted to play a small part in the life of this great Lady in Québec.

THE GERMAINS:

One of the first families to interface with the Empress Zita in Québec was the Germains. Maître Stanislas Germain was a partner in the legal firm of "Germain, Pigeon, Thibodeau and Roberge" which was approached in 1940 by Monseigneur Alphonse Marie Parent, then Secretary of the Faculty of Philosophy at Université Laval, to look after the legalities associated with settling the Imperial family. These responsibilities fell on Maître Stanislas Germain, not only because he had long been associated with Université Laval, but also because he knew his way around in the inner circles of government. He was a former associate of the Honourable Ernest Lapointe,

51. The house at Tuxedo Park, New York.

52. The Empress at Tuxedo Park.

53. The castle at Waldstein in Steiermark, Austria.

54. The Village of Zizers in Switzerland.

55. The Johannes Stift in Zizers.

56. The 90th birthday celebration of the Empress at Zizers.

57. The Empress with the Countess Kerssenbrock.

Gott dem Allmächtigen hat es gefallen, am 10. Februar 1973 nach langer und schwerer, mit großer Geduld und in ungeminderter Heiterkeit ertragenen Krankheit, unsere innigstgeliebte Korffi

Therese Gräfin von Korff
gen. Schmising-Kerssenbrock
Sternkreuzordens-Dame

in ihrem 86. Lebensjahr wohlvorbereitet zu sich zu berufen. Sie war durch 55 Jahre die treueste Vertraute unserer ganzen Familie.

Zita Kaiserin von Österreich, Königin von Ungarn etc.

mit ihren Kindern:	ihren Schwiegerkindern:
Otto	Regina
Robert	Margherita
Felix	Anna Eugenie
Carl Ludwig	Yolande
Rudolf	Anna Gabrielle
Charlotte	Heinrich
Elisabeth	

und ihren 33 Enkeln

Die Beisetzung fand am 13. Februar 1973 im engsten Kreis in der Klosterkirche zu Muri, Kanton Aargau, Schweiz, statt.

D 8134 Pöcking
Hindenburgstraße 15

58. Death notice of the Countess Kerssenbrock.

59. The Village of Tulfes in Tirol, Austria.

60. The Benedictine Abbey at Muri in Switzerland.

61. The grave of the Archduchess Adelhaid.

62. The Loretto Chapel in the Abbey at Muri.

IHRE KAISERLICHE U. KÖNIGLICHE HOHEIT
ERZHERZOGIN XENIA VON ÖSTERREICH
GEB. GRÄFIN CZERNICHEW-BESOBRASOW
GEBOREN IN PARIS AM 11. JUNI 1929
VERUNGLÜCKT AM 20. SEPTEMBER 1968

63. Rememberance plaque to the Archduchess Xenia.

64. Wartegg chapel in Switzerland with the tomb of Princess Isabelle.

65. The Bourbon tomb at Puchheim in Austria.

66. The Imperial funeral hearse and coffin of the Empress Zita.

67. Miss Herma Dobler.

68. Count Henry Eltz.

69. Monseigneur Alphonse Marie Parent.

70. Maître Stanislas Germain.

71. Professor Charles De Koninck.

72. Professor Charles Engel.

73. Dr. Otto von Habsburg with his son before a portrait of his father.

who was then a Minister in the Government of Québec, and he was a personal friend of the Honourable Louis Philippe Pigeon, a respected judge in the Supreme Court of Canada. In short, he was a man of influence who had a reputation of being resourceful, capable and energetic. He could get things done and was known as a man who could solve problems.

Stanislas Germain was educated at the Petit Seminaire de Québec and at Université Laval. At the Université, he attended law school, and financed his studies by selling electrical appliances -gadgets that were new to rural Québec in those early years of the 20th century. He came from an old Québec family that traces its roots back to the 17th century, when its forefathers came to New France from Le Mans in the Department of Sarthe in France. His father, Victor Stanislas, was born in the "rang du petit bois de l'ail" of St. Basile in the County of Portneuf, Québec, and became a "Fonctionnaire au Parlement de Québec" (civil servant). He married Georgiana Pettigrew of Québec. They had 12 children, of whom four were boys and eight were girls. Stanislas was their third son, the oldest being Victorin who became a priest, the second being Ernest who became a businessman, and the youngest son, Joseph, became an Optometrist. Between them, Joseph Germain humorously relates, "they looked after their client's souls, made sure they had good eyes to see their way through business, and kept them out of jail in the process."

Stanislas Germain, who was born in Québec in 1904, married Paule Beaulieu of Montréal, and settled down in Québec to raise a family. At this he proved to be also very successful, for they had nine children. In order of their birth, they were Claudette (1933), Odile (1934), Pauline (1936), Twins Paul and Pascale (1939), Marielle (1941) Louis (1942), Elisabeth (1945) and Natalie (1948).

The two youngest Germain children were honoured by the Imperial family in that they became God children to Imperial family members. The Archduchess Elisabeth became Godmother to Elisabeth Germain, and the Archduke Rudolf is Godfather to Natalie Germain, the last child born to Madame Paule and Maître Stanislas Germain.

Upon the death of Maître Germain in 1975, Madame Germain moved to France where she joined two of her daughters in the religious order of lay-nuns, called the "Institut Notre Dame de Vie." The Mother House of this order is located near the small village of Venasque in the county of Venaissin in Southern France, not far from Avignon. Madame Paule Germain spent ten years serving God and mankind at Venasque, and in 1985 transferred to St. Paul d'Abbotsford, Québec. It is there that she worked as a lay-nun in the newly established Québec mother house of the Institute, before retiring and moving back to Quebec City where she now resides.

THE DE KONINCKS:

The De Koninck connection with the Imperial family started in Belgium in 1930. Young Zoe Decruydt (now De Koninck) was studying in Mouscron, a little town in Belgium near the French border, at a school run by an order of religious teaching nuns who also ran a school in Brussels, known as "Notre-Dame de Marie." As it happened, the Archduchess Adelhaid was a pensionaire at that school, and since at examination time, the students from Mouscron used to take their examinations in Brussels, young Zoe Decruydt found herself sitting beside a student who happened to be the Archduchess Adelhaid, the oldest daughter of the Empress Zita. "I never thought then", recalled Madame De Koninck, "that I would one day run into her in Québec."

Madame De Koninck was born in Detroit, Michigan, of immigrant Flemish parents. She lived in Detroit until she was 11 years old, when her family moved back to Belgium. Her father, Alois Decruydt, who was a contractor, wanted his children to have the benefit of a Flemish Catholic education, and returned to Europe. Like many immigrants of the times, he felt more at ease in "the old country", where the language, the religion, and the culture was much more to his liking. Among his many friends in Flanders, the place to which he had returned,was a Louis De Koninck, the father of Charles De Koninck. It was through this connection that Zoe Decruydt met her future husband.

Karel (Charles) De Koninck was born in 1906 at Thouront in West Flanders, Belgium. He studied with the Dominican Fathers in Louvain, and from them obtained a deep religious conviction which would influence him for the rest of his life. For a time he seriously contemplated entering the religious life, but he could not see himself in the isolation that such a vocation required, and decided against it. He nevertheless was deeply influenced by Christian philosophy, and the pursuit of this discipline became his true calling.

He travelled to the United States when still a young man, and studied philosophy at the University of Detroit, where he had received a scholarship and earned a Masters Degree. However the call of his homeland soon saw him return to Belgium. There he entered the Catholic University of Louvain under a private scholarship, obtained his Doctorate in Philosophy, and became a highly respected Christian philosopher. He then married Zoe Decruydt and the two newlyweds settled down in Louvain. The year was 1933.

Meanwhile back in Québec, the Secretary of the newly formed Department of Philosophy at the Université Laval thought that it would be beneficial to Laval to host a visiting professor from Europe in its newly created Department of Philosophy. Its first Dean was Professor Arthur Robert, and he believed that the temporary assistance of a teacher, experienced in this discipline, would get the Department off to a good start. The Abbé Maurice Roy, agreed, and they sent off invitations to Paris and to Louvain, hoping that they would receive two referrals, one of which they would use. But as it happened, only one replied, and he was contacted and hired.

But when the boat from France docked in Québec in the late Summer of 1935, two professors stepped ashore and came to Laval. Both apparently had "accepted" the invitation, but only one had bothered to indicate his acceptance in writing. Thus the University all of a sudden found itself with two visiting Professors of Philosophy, and with typical French "politesse" retained them both. One was Professor Jacques de Monléon from the Institut Catholique de Paris, and the other was Professor Charles De Koninck from the Catholic University of Louvain.

Both professors were put to work and were apparently equally appreciated, for the one year contracts under which they taught during the first year, were soon extended. Professor De Koninck was offered an extension for another two years, which he accepted. But Professor de Monléon preferred to keep his roots in France. He returned to France, but nevertheless came back to Québec every year on individual one-semester assignments until well into the early 1970's.

Professor De Koninck remained in Québec and became a permanent member of the teaching staff at Université Laval. He worked there for 30 years, becoming Dean of the Department of Philosophy from 1939 until 1956, and during the last months of 1964 and until he died on February 13, 1965. On the day of his death, Professor Charles De Koninck was in Rome, having been sent there by Québec's Cardinal Maurice Roy. Just before his death, Professor De Koninck was awarded the title "Dr. Spiritus", meaning "expert in religious philosophy." He was the first layman philosopher ever to be awarded this honour by the Church.

Professor De Koninck was an outstanding Christian philosopher. His fame had spread throughout the Christian world, and he was greatly sought out as a teacher. Many students came to him from all over the world -from Europe, from the United States and even from as far away as South America. He also travelled a lot and was invited to attend many religious seminars, not only in Rome, but in other great Catholic centres in Europe and in the Americas. He was also sought from far and wide as a visiting professor of philosophy, and in 1956 he was invited to Madrid where he lectured for five weeks on his philosophical treatises. He also wrote books on this subject which have been widely published and read.

Professor Charles De Koninck and his wife Zoe had twelve children, seven boys and five girls. They were Thomas (1934), Arthur (1935), Dominique (1936), Godelieve (1938), Marie-Charlotte (1941), Rodolphe (1943), Maria (1945), Joseph-Marie (1947), Jean Marie (1948), Zita (1949), Gabrielle (1950 -stillborn), and Peter (1952). The close tie between the De Konincks and the Imperial family is underlined by Godparent/Godchild relationships. The

Empress Zita was Godmother to Zita De Koninck (Noel de Tilly) and Rodolphe De Koninck is Godson to the Archduke Rudolf and to the Archduchess Elisabeth. In addition, the Archduke Charles Louis is Godfather to Marie-Charlotte De Koninck.

THE ENGELS:(37)

Unlike the Germains and the De Konincks, the Engels are relatively new to Québec. They only came to Québec City after the Empress had already left, but their ties with the Imperial family, particularly with the Archduke Rudolf, merit them an honourable tribute in this book. As a prominent Québécois of Austrian origin, Professor Charles Engel is a staunch admirer of the Imperial family. His support of its cause, and his interest and support of the age-old traditions of the Church of Rome, stem to a large extent from the monarchistic and religious values instilled in him by his family, especially by his father.

Dr. Charles Engel is the son of His Excellency Jean (Hans) Engel, an Austrian industrialist of great prominence, whose work, interests, and affinities caused him to spend much of his life in France. Born in Vienna, in the late eighteen-eighties, Jean Engel lived in the last days of the Austrian monarchy which, in spite of political unrest, were glorious in the intellectual and cultural perspective. Already before the first World War he lived for some years in Paris but returned to his Country to serve during the war for over four years in combat, as an officer of the Austrian-Hungarian army.

After the first World War, Jean Engel married the descendent of an old Prague family, prominent as industrialists and in the medical field (one of Mrs. Engel's ancestors was the physician of Emperor Franz I of Austria), and devoted himself to the development of the economic cooperation between Austria and the other major components of the former Austrian monarchy, with France and Germany. From its beginning he was active in the Pan-European Movement founded by Count Coudenhove-Kallerghi, an organization whose present President is the Archduke Otto.

From a business trip undertaken after the Anschluss to France and Morocco, Jean Engel did not return to occupied Austria, but established himself in Paris, being made, in recognition for his important services to France, by special decree, together with his family, a French citizen.

After the war which he spent in France, he was charged by the French Government, presided by General Charles de Gaulle, with an economic mission in Austria, and could thus provide much needed help to the country of his origin. He then devoted himself to the re-establishment of economic and industrial cooperation between France and Austria.

Mr. Jean Engel's links to the Jesuit Order, the ties he had established during the war with the Papal Nuncio in Vichy, and especially his friendship with one of the most remarkable churchmen of our times, Cardinal Eugène Tisserant, Dean of the Sacred College, as well as his close relationships and friendships with Austrian Church leaders, in particular with Vienna's Archbishop Cardinal König, made it possible for him to work for the Church again on a supra-national basis. Founding member of the Pontifical Marian Academy, he was a prominent member of the organizing committees of the centennial celebrations of the apparitions of the Holy Virgin in Lourdes and of the eight-hundred year celebrations of the Austrian Sanctuary of the Holy Virgin in Mariazell. Taking part in these celebrations were many prominent personalities from the Church of Rome and from the House of Habsburg. These included the Archduke Hubert Salvator, his wife the Archduchess Rosemary, and the Duchess Clara Sachsen-Meiningen. In addition to this link with the Imperial family, Mr. Jean Engel had the privilege to be honoured by the friendship of Prince Xavier of Bourbon Parma, the brother of the Empress Zita.

Jean Engel, who had known Pope Pius XII and who was received quite frequently by Pope John XXIII and Pope Paul VI, was an official delegate of the Equestrian Order of the Holy Sepulchre of Jerusalem at each opening and closing session of the 2nd Vatican Council, and had the honor to accompany Pope Paul VI in his historic pilgrimage to the Holy Land.

Professor Charles Engel was born in 1922 in Vienna, where he grew up and where he received his primary and most of his secondary education. After the National Socialist takeover of his native Austria, he continued his studies in Switzerland and France where he obtained his B.A. degree at the University of Grenoble. He then joined the Swiss Federal Institute of Technology in Zurich where he received an M.Sc. degree in Chemical Engineering and a doctorate in Technical Sciences, as a collaborator of Professor Leopold Ruzicka, a Nobel Prize laureate and native of the Austrian Monarchy. Later he obtained a "doctorat d'Etat" in Physical Sciences at the University of Paris. In 1951 he married Miss Edith Braillard in Lucerne. The end of their honeymoon took them to London, Ontario, where he accepted an associate professorship in medical research in the world-famous department of Dean J.B. Collip, co-discoverer of insulin. Now a renowned chemist and chemical endocrinologist, Professor Engel accepted in 1958 a chair in Organic Chemistry at Université Laval.

The Engels live in Sillery, and have raised four children, two girls: Lucie (1953) and Christiane (1955), both married, and two boys: Francis (1956) -a gynecologist, also married, and Marc (1960). They have four grandchildren.

Among the interests of Professor Charles Engel outside of his profession are his activities in the age-old Equestrian Order of the Holy Sepulchre of Jerusalem. This Order was founded in the year 1098 by Godfrey of Bouillon, Duke of Lower Lorraine, who led the first Crusaders to the Holy Land. The Order, which is still very active, has, as its principal mission, the support of Christianity in the Holy Land, a considerable task since hardly 3% of the peoples living there are Christians.

The Order offers moral, religious and financial support to these Christians by providing them with schools, religious and cultural institutions necessary to sustain their faith among the many other religions prominent in the area; and with dispensaries, hospitals, and schools for the disabled. The Order promotes the cause of ecumenism and peace in a land of such importance to the spirituality of mankind, but which is torn and divided.

The Order of the Knights of the Holy Sepulchre of Jerusalem is directed by a Cardinal Grand Master. It is organized into geographical divisions, each headed by a "Lieutenant", the spiritual guidance of whom is in the hands of a Grand Prior. The present Grand Master is His Eminence Giuseppe Cardinal Caprio who succeeded the late Cardinal Maximilien de Furstenberg of Belgium, whose predecessor had been the Cardinal-Dean Eugène Tisserant.

One of the three Canadian Lieutenancies, centered in Québec City but comprising the majority of Eastern Canada, is headed by His Excellency Professor Charles Engel. The Grand Prior of the Québec Lieutenancy is the Archbishop of Québec and Primate of Canada, His Eminence Cardinal Louis-Albert Vachon. The Québec Lieutenancy has been active in furthering the cause of education in the Holy Land and played an important role in the development of Bethlehem University, founded by His Holiness Pope Paul VI. It collaborated with the Lieutenancies of France and Toronto in building a school in one of the two entirely Christian villages of the Holy Land, and is now building with the Toronto Lieutenancy in a new suburb of Amman, a kindergarden, as a first project for a new and important Christian center.

Through the common concern for the cause of Christianity in the Holy Land, the ties of the Engel family with Prince Xavier of Bourbon of Parma, who had been himself for many years Lieutenant of the Order in France, and with the family of Archduke Hubert Salvator, were surely not without influence on their future relationship with the Imperial family. Indeed, having come to Québec only in 1958, Dr. Engel's personal relationship with the Empress and her son, the Archduke Rudolf, began only after Dr. and Mrs. Engel had been introduced to Her Majesty and to His Imperial Highness by their friends, Me. Stanislas Germain and Madame Charles De Koninck. However, the communion in their religious convictions, their commitment to the same fundamental ideals, and the love for, and devotion to, Austria, soon elevated their relationship to one of mutual respect and understanding, and further deepened the veneration by the Engels of Her Majesty and her family, not only in view of their exalted rank, but also for the greatness of their souls. They treasure the sympathy shown to them by Archduke Rudolf and Archduchess

Anna Gabrielle, and will always remember with deep gratitude the graciousness so often extended to them and to their children by Her Majesty the Empress, up to the very end of her life.

As an Austrian whose roots go back to the time before the light of the last Catholic Empire in Europe was extinguished, Professor Charles Engel today stands as a reminder of that light in the new world. It is fitting that he chose to make his home in Québec, in the same city that gave refuge to Her Majesty, Zita of Habsburg-Lorraine, the last Empress of Austria and Apostolic Queen of Hungary.

APPENDIX A

GENEOLOGICAL CHARTS

LEGEND

(birth)	:	year of birth
(+death)	:	year of death
(birth-death)	:	lifespan
b	:	place of birth
m	:	married
D	:	Duke
K	:	King
Q	:	Queen
RK	:	Roman King
E	:	Roman Emperor
EA	:	Emperor of Austria
*	:	reigning sovereign

A-1

GENEOLOGICAL BACKGROUND OF THE
EMPEROR CHARLES I OF AUSTRIA

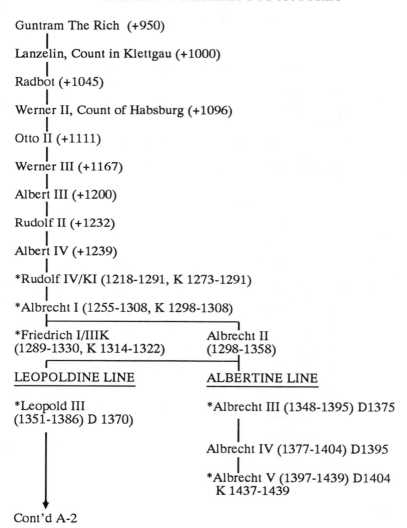

Guntram The Rich (+950)

Lanzelin, Count in Klettgau (+1000)

Radbot (+1045)

Werner II, Count of Habsburg (+1096)

Otto II (+1111)

Werner III (+1167)

Albert III (+1200)

Rudolf II (+1232)

Albert IV (+1239)

*Rudolf IV/KI (1218-1291, K 1273-1291)

*Albrecht I (1255-1308, K 1298-1308)

*Friedrich I/IIIK   Albrecht II
(1289-1330, K 1314-1322)   (1298-1358)

LEOPOLDINE LINE   ALBERTINE LINE

*Leopold III   *Albrecht III (1348-1395) D1375
(1351-1386) D 1370)

           Albrecht IV (1377-1404) D1395

           *Albrecht V (1397-1439) D1404
            K 1437-1439

Cont'd A-2

A-2

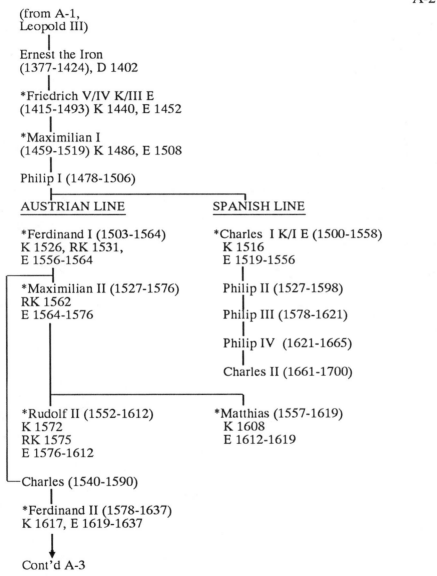

(from A-1,
Leopold III)

Ernest the Iron
(1377-1424), D 1402

*Friedrich V/IV K/III E
(1415-1493) K 1440, E 1452

*Maximilian I
(1459-1519) K 1486, E 1508

Philip I (1478-1506)

AUSTRIAN LINE   SPANISH LINE

*Ferdinand I (1503-1564)   *Charles I K/I E (1500-1558)
K 1526, RK 1531,   K 1516
E 1556-1564   E 1519-1556

*Maximilian II (1527-1576)   Philip II (1527-1598)
RK 1562
E 1564-1576   Philip III (1578-1621)

                                 Philip IV (1621-1665)

                                 Charles II (1661-1700)

*Rudolf II (1552-1612)   *Matthias (1557-1619)
K 1572   K 1608
RK 1575   E 1612-1619
E 1576-1612

Charles (1540-1590)

*Ferdinand II (1578-1637)
K 1617, E 1619-1637

Cont'd A-3

A-3

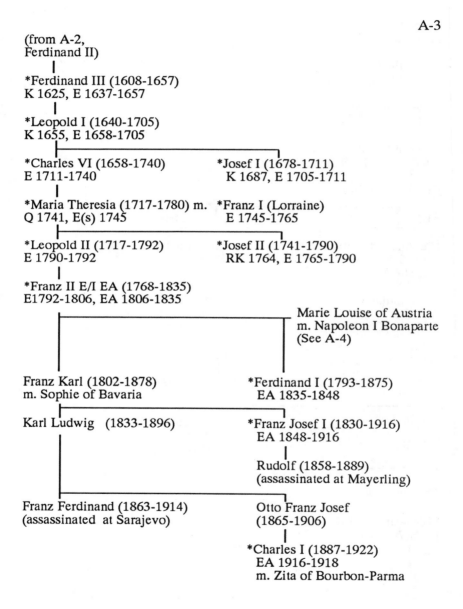

(from A-2,
Ferdinand II)

*Ferdinand III (1608-1657)
K 1625, E 1637-1657

*Leopold I (1640-1705)
K 1655, E 1658-1705

*Charles VI (1658-1740)   *Josef I (1678-1711)
E 1711-1740   K 1687, E 1705-1711

*Maria Theresia (1717-1780) m.   *Franz I (Lorraine)
Q 1741, E(s) 1745   E 1745-1765

*Leopold II (1717-1792)   *Josef II (1741-1790)
E 1790-1792   RK 1764, E 1765-1790

*Franz II E/I EA (1768-1835)
E1792-1806, EA 1806-1835

                                Marie Louise of Austria
                                m. Napoleon I Bonaparte
                                (See A-4)

Franz Karl (1802-1878)   *Ferdinand I (1793-1875)
m. Sophie of Bavaria   EA 1835-1848

Karl Ludwig   (1833-1896)   *Franz Josef I (1830-1916)
                              EA 1848-1916

                              Rudolf (1858-1889)
                              (assassinated at Mayerling)

Franz Ferdinand (1863-1914)   Otto Franz Josef
(assassinated at Sarajevo)   (1865-1906)

                              *Charles I (1887-1922)
                              EA 1916-1918
                              m. Zita of Bourbon-Parma

GENEOLOGICAL BACKGROUND OF THE EMPRESS ZITA

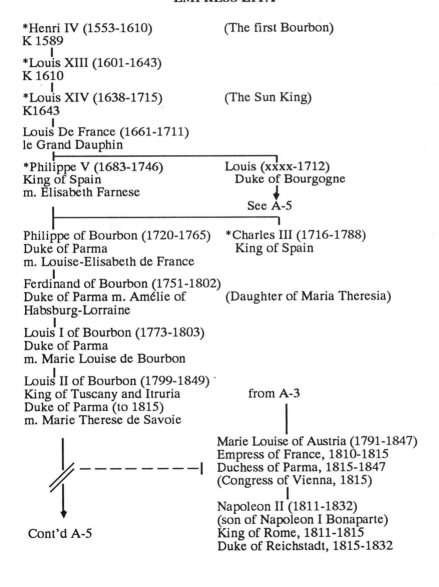

*Henri IV (1553-1610)   (The first Bourbon)
K 1589

*Louis XIII (1601-1643)
K 1610

*Louis XIV (1638-1715)   (The Sun King)
K1643

Louis De France (1661-1711)
le Grand Dauphin

*Philippe V (1683-1746)   Louis (xxxx-1712)
King of Spain   Duke of Bourgogne
m. Elisabeth Farnese

                             See A-5

Philippe of Bourbon (1720-1765)   *Charles III (1716-1788)
Duke of Parma   King of Spain
m. Louise-Elisabeth de France

Ferdinand of Bourbon (1751-1802)
Duke of Parma m. Amélie of   (Daughter of Maria Theresia)
Habsburg-Lorraine

Louis I of Bourbon (1773-1803)
Duke of Parma
m. Marie Louise de Bourbon

Louis II of Bourbon (1799-1849)
King of Tuscany and Itruria
Duke of Parma (to 1815)   from A-3
m. Marie Therese de Savoie

                             Marie Louise of Austria (1791-1847)
                             Empress of France, 1810-1815
                             Duchess of Parma, 1815-1847
                             (Congress of Vienna, 1815)

                             Napoleon II (1811-1832)
Cont'd A-5   (son of Napoleon I Bonaparte)
                             King of Rome, 1811-1815
                             Duke of Reichstadt, 1815-1832

A-5

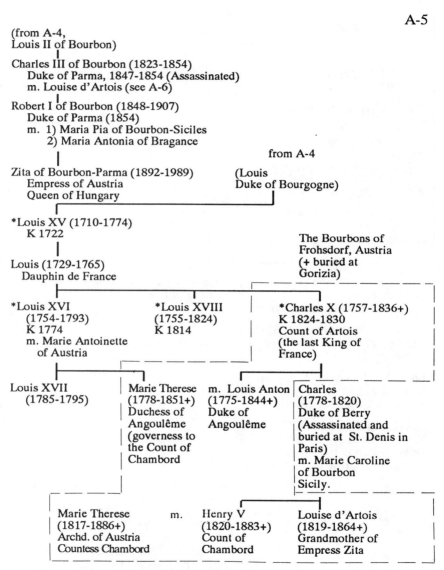

(from A-4,
Louis II of Bourbon)

Charles III of Bourbon (1823-1854)
    Duke of Parma, 1847-1854 (Assassinated)
    m. Louise d'Artois (see A-6)

Robert I of Bourbon (1848-1907)
    Duke of Parma (1854)
    m. 1) Maria Pia of Bourbon-Siciles
       2) Maria Antonia of Bragance

Zita of Bourbon-Parma (1892-1989)   (Louis
    Empress of Austria   Duke of Bourgogne)
    Queen of Hungary

from A-4

*Louis XV (1710-1774)
    K 1722

The Bourbons of
Frohsdorf, Austria
(+ buried at
Gorizia)

Louis (1729-1765)
    Dauphin de France

*Louis XVI   *Louis XVIII   *Charles X (1757-1836+)
    (1754-1793)   (1755-1824)   K 1824-1830
    K 1774   K 1814   Count of Artois
    m. Marie Antoinette   (the last King of
       of Austria   France)

Louis XVII   Marie Therese   m. Louis Anton   Charles
    (1785-1795)   (1778-1851+)   (1775-1844+)   (1778-1820)
                        Duchess of   Duke of   Duke of Berry
                        Angoulême   Angoulême   (Assassinated and
                        (governess to   buried at St. Denis in
                        the Count of   Paris)
                        Chambord   m. Marie Caroline
                                                           of Bourbon
                                                           Sicily.

        Marie Therese   m.   Henry V   Louise d'Artois
            (1817-1886+)   (1820-1883+)   (1819-1864+)
            Archd. of Austria   Count of   Grandmother of
            Countess Chambord   Chambord   Empress Zita

Note: The notation "King of France" indicates here an inherited function, and differs from
    that of King Louis Philippe of Bourbon-Orleans (1775-1850) who was proclaimed King
    by the people in 1830.

A-6

DESCENDENTS OF THE EMPRESS ZITA AND
THE EMPEROR CHARLES I

Charles I (1887-1922)
  m. Zita of Bourbon-Parma (1892-1989)

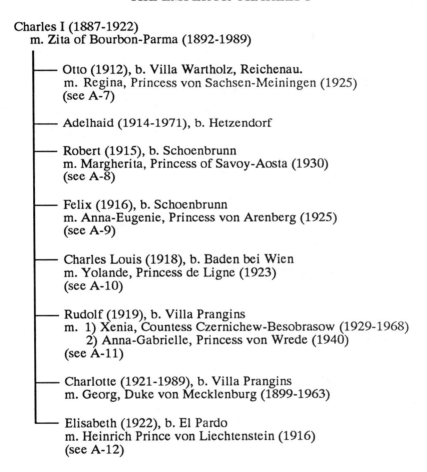

— Otto (1912), b. Villa Wartholz, Reichenau.
  m. Regina, Princess von Sachsen-Meiningen (1925)
  (see A-7)

— Adelhaid (1914-1971), b. Hetzendorf

— Robert (1915), b. Schoenbrunn
  m. Margherita, Princess of Savoy-Aosta (1930)
  (see A-8)

— Felix (1916), b. Schoenbrunn
  m. Anna-Eugenie, Princess von Arenberg (1925)
  (see A-9)

— Charles Louis (1918), b. Baden bei Wien
  m. Yolande, Princess de Ligne (1923)
  (see A-10)

— Rudolf (1919), b. Villa Prangins
  m. 1) Xenia, Countess Czernichew-Besobrasow (1929-1968)
       2) Anna-Gabrielle, Princess von Wrede (1940)
  (see A-11)

— Charlotte (1921-1989), b. Villa Prangins
  m. Georg, Duke von Mecklenburg (1899-1963)

— Elisabeth (1922), b. El Pardo
  m. Heinrich Prince von Liechtenstein (1916)
  (see A-12)

A-7

OTTO (1912)
m. Regina, Princess von Sachsen-Meiningen (1925)

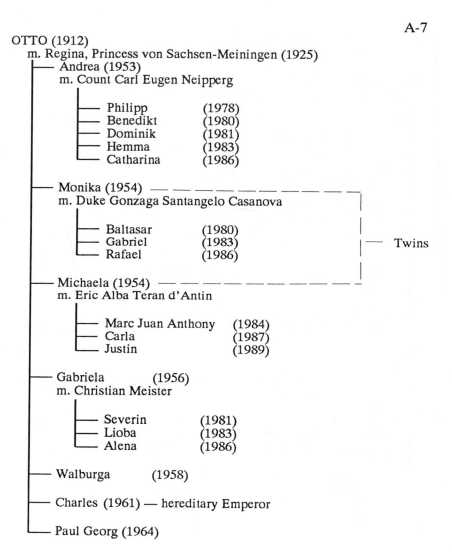

   Andrea (1953)
    m. Count Carl Eugen Neipperg

       Philipp   (1978)
       Benedikt   (1980)
       Dominik   (1981)
       Hemma   (1983)
       Catharina   (1986)

   Monika (1954)
    m. Duke Gonzaga Santangelo Casanova

       Baltasar   (1980)
       Gabriel   (1983)   — Twins
       Rafael   (1986)

   Michaela (1954)
    m. Eric Alba Teran d'Antin

       Marc Juan Anthony (1984)
       Carla   (1987)
       Justin   (1989)

   Gabriela   (1956)
    m. Christian Meister

       Severin   (1981)
       Lioba   (1983)
       Alena   (1986)

   Walburga   (1958)

   Charles (1961) — hereditary Emperor

   Paul Georg (1964)

A-8

ROBERT (1915)
  m. Margherita, Princess of Savoy-Aosta (1930)

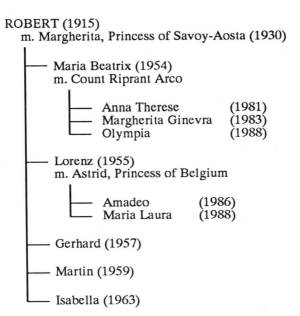

Maria Beatrix (1954)
m. Count Riprant Arco

Anna Therese   (1981)
Margherita Ginevra   (1983)
Olympia   (1988)

Lorenz (1955)
m. Astrid, Princess of Belgium

Amadeo   (1986)
Maria Laura   (1988)

Gerhard (1957)

Martin (1959)

Isabella (1963)

A-9

FELIX (1916)
   m. Anna Eugenie, Princess von Arenberg (1925)

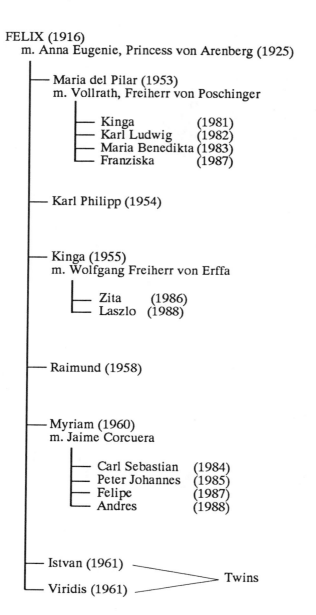

     Maria del Pilar (1953)
     m. Vollrath, Freiherr von Poschinger

          Kinga   (1981)
          Karl Ludwig   (1982)
          Maria Benedikta (1983)
          Franziska   (1987)

     Karl Philipp (1954)

     Kinga (1955)
     m. Wolfgang Freiherr von Erffa

          Zita   (1986)
          Laszlo (1988)

     Raimund (1958)

     Myriam (1960)
     m. Jaime Corcuera

          Carl Sebastian (1984)
          Peter Johannes (1985)
          Felipe   (1987)
          Andres   (1988)

     Istvan (1961)
                          Twins
     Viridis (1961)

A-10

CHARLES LOUIS (1918)
   m. Yolande, Princess de Ligne (1923)

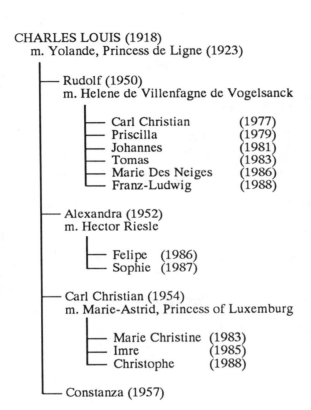

├── Rudolf (1950)
│   m. Helene de Villenfagne de Vogelsanck

│   ├── Carl Christian   (1977)
│   ├── Priscilla   (1979)
│   ├── Johannes   (1981)
│   ├── Tomas   (1983)
│   ├── Marie Des Neiges (1986)
│   └── Franz-Ludwig   (1988)

├── Alexandra (1952)
│   m. Hector Riesle

│   ├── Felipe   (1986)
│   └── Sophie   (1987)

├── Carl Christian (1954)
│   m. Marie-Astrid, Princess of Luxemburg

│   ├── Marie Christine (1983)
│   ├── Imre   (1985)
│   └── Christophe   (1988)

└── Constanza (1957)

A-11

RUDOLF (1919)
   m. 1)   Xenia, Countess Czernichew-Besobrasow (1929-1968)

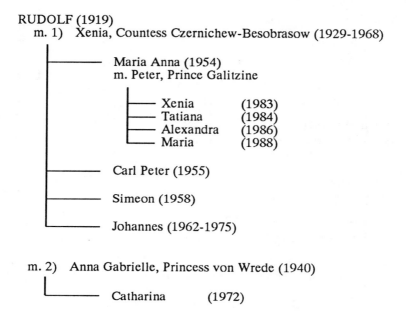

                 Maria Anna (1954)
                 m. Peter, Prince Galitzine

                         Xenia   (1983)
                         Tatiana   (1984)
                         Alexandra (1986)
                         Maria   (1988)

                 Carl Peter (1955)

                 Simeon (1958)

                 Johannes (1962-1975)

   m. 2)   Anna Gabrielle, Princess von Wrede (1940)

                 Catharina   (1972)

A-12

ELISABETH (1922)
  m. Heinrich, Prince von Liechtenstein (1916)

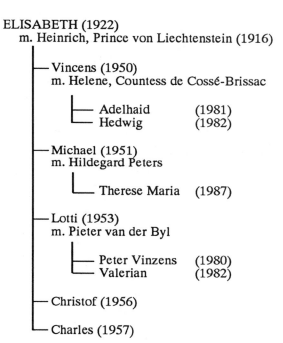

Vincens (1950)
  m. Helene, Countess de Cossé-Brissac

      Adelhaid   (1981)
      Hedwig   (1982)

Michael (1951)
  m. Hildegard Peters

      Therese Maria (1987)

Lotti (1953)
  m. Pieter van der Byl

      Peter Vinzens (1980)
      Valerian   (1982)

Christof (1956)

Charles (1957)

APPENDIX B

LIST OF PUBLISHED SOURCES

References	Published Source and Author
1	DAS HAUS HABSBURG — Adam Wandruszka, Herder, 1980
2	DIE HABSBURGER IN LEBENSBILDERN — Richard Reifenscheid, Styria, 1982
3	THE HABSBURG MONARCHY — A.J.P. Taylor, Penguin, 1948
4	THE HABSBURGS — Edward Krankshaw, Corgi, 1972
5	IMPERIAL TWILIGHT — Bertita Harding, Bobbs-Merrill, 1939
6	MARIE LOUISE — Irmgard Schiel, Deutsche, 1983
7	KAISER KARL, EIN BILD SEINES LEBENS — Leo Smolle, KuK Schulbuecher, 1917
8	KAISER KARL — Erich Feigl, Amalthea, 1984
9	KAISERIN ZITA — Erich Feigl, Amalthea, 1982
10	ZITA — Tamara Griesser-Pecar, Luebbe, 1985
11	KAISER KARL — Heinz Rieder, Callway, 1981
12	DIE KAISERGRUFT — Eberhard Kusin, Bastei, 1973
13	KLOSTER MURI — Schweizerische Kunstfuehrer, 1982
14	FRANZ FERDINAND VON OESTERREICH-ESTE — Gerd Holler, 1982
15	LE PLUS CÉLÈBRE MONUMENT FUNÉRAIRE DE QUÉBEC — Robert Germain, Study Paper
16	LE VIEUX-SILLERY — André Bernier, Gouvernement de Québec, 1982
17	QUE RESTE-T-IL DE SILLERY — Fabienne Deschênes, Presses H.L.N. Sherb, 1984

References Published Source and Author

18   SILLERY (No. 17, 20) — Associations des Anciennes de
            Jésus-Marie
19   DOMI — 1949/50/51 — Collège Classique, le Couvent
            Jésus-Marie
20   LE LYS — Echo de Jeanne d'Arc, Vol. VI, Anne 16, No. 1
21   LES MERCENAIRES ALLEMANDS AU QUÉBEC —
            Jean Pierre Wilhelmy Maison des Mots, 1984
22   25, AVENUE SAINTE-GENEVIÈVE, QUÉBEC —
            Christina Cameron (Academic Paper, 1973)
23   TRAUMSCHLOESSER — Plechl und Trumler, Brands-
            taetter, 1986
24   AUSTRIA — DATES, HISTORY AND CULTURE —
            Walter Kleindel, 1978
25   HAUSBUCH DER OESTERREICHISCHEN GESCHI-
            CHTE — Heinz Siegert, Kreymayr & Scheriau, 1976
26   EXTRACTS FROM NEWSPAPERS, MAGAZINES,
            AND CLIPPINGS — Provided by Madame De Koninck,
            Sillery, Québec
27   ZITA — KAISERIN VON OESTERREICH, KOENIGIN
            VON UNGARN — E.H.P. Cordfunke, Boehlau, 1986
28   ARCHIVES D'ÉTAT PARMA — Dr. Maria Parente,
            Parma, 1987
29   PAN AMERICAN AIRWAYS and the BOEING COM-
            PANY — Letters, 1986

APPENDIX C

LIST OF PERSONS INTERVIEWED

Reference Information Source

30   ARCHDUKE RUDOLF OF AUSTRIA
Sixth child and youngest son of the Empress Zita and Emperor Charles I. Currently residing in Brussels, Belgium.

31   MISS MARGUERITE MACDONALD
Retired teacher, cousin of the Honourable P. François Casgrain, Minister of State in the Government of Canada in 1940. Currently residing in Sillery, Québec.

32   PÈRE GEORGES HENRI LÉVESQUE
Retired Dean of the Faculty of Social Sciences at Université Laval. Teacher of the Archdukes Rudolf and Charles Louis, and of the Archduchess Charlotte, and later also of the Archduchess Elisabeth.

33   Sisters of the Collège Jésus-Marie in Sillery, Québec.
SISTER VERONICA NADEAU, Archivist and Historian
SISTER CHARLOTTE GENEST, Teacher and friend to Miss Herma Dobler, Secretary to the Empress.
SISTER MONIQUE FOURNIER, Teacher at the Convent.

34   SISTER MARGARET MARIE
Historian at the Community of Sisters of Sainte Jeanne d'Arc in Sillery, Québec.

35   MADAME ODILE GERMAIN
Daughter of Maitre Stanislas Germain, Advocat, who was instrumental in settling the legal affairs of the Empress during her sojourn in Québec.

Reference Information Source

36   MADAME ZOE DE KONINCK
     Wife of Professor Charles De Koninck who was Dean of
     the Faculty of Philosophy at Université Laval in the
     1940's.

37   PROFESSOR CHARLES ENGEL
     Professor of Chemistry at Université Laval.

38   MADEMOISELLE MARGUERITE BARRY
     Personal friend of Miss Herma Dobler.

39   COUNTESS JANET ELTZ
     Wife of Count Eltz, friend of the Imperial Family. Cur-
     rently residing in Engelskirchen, West Germany.

40   MR. NANDOR LOEWENHEIM
     Former Consul General of Austria in Montréal, and friend
     of Count Eltz.

41   MADAME CECILIA CAPELLA
     Resident and current owner of the house in Tuxedo
     Park, N.Y. into which the Empress moved after she left
     Québec.

42   MR. RAYMOND DIONNE
     Historian residing in St. Romuald, Québec.

43   MR. ROBERT GERMAIN
     Historian residing in Ste. Foy, Québec.

44   MR. JEAN G. BADOUD
     Vice-chancelier, Chancellerie Communale, Ville de Neu-
     chatel, Switzerland.

45   MADAME PAULINE DUBUC TREMBLAY
     Fellow student with the Archduchess Elisabeth at the
     Université Laval.

APPENDIX D

LIST OF ILLUSTRATIONS
Explanations and Sources

1. THE EMPRESS ZITA (source - E. Feigl, P. 528)

2. THE HABICHTSBURG IN SWITZERLAND
   The castle in the Aargau in Switzerland which gave its name to the Habsburg dynasty. (source - Wandruska, P. 48-2)

3. DUKE ROBERT AND DUCHESS MARIA ANTONIA OF BOURBON-PARMA
   The father and mother of the Empress Zita. (source - Cordfunke, P. 11)

4. THE VILLA PIANORE IN ITALY
   Summer home of the Duke Robert. Birthplace of Princess Zita of Bourbon-Parma. (source - The Archduke Rudolf)

5. THE PALACE AT SCHWARZAU
   Family home of the Bourbon-Parmas where young Zita grew up and where she first met the Archduke Charles Franz Josef. (source - The Archduke Rudolf - Photographer K. Skolik, Vienna)

6. OFFICIAL WEDDING PORTRAIT
   Taken after the wedding of the Archduke Charles and the Princess Zita on October 21, 1911. (source - Smolle, P. 49 - Photographer K. Pietzner, Vienna)

7. KING CHARLES IV AND QUEEN ZITA OF HUNGARY WITH THEIR FIRST BORN, THE CROWN PRINCE OTTO
   On the occasion of the crowning of the Emperor and Empress of Austria as King and Queen of Hungary in Budapest on December 30, 1916. (source - Oesterreich Konservative, May/June 1982, and Smolle, P. 93, Photographer H. Schumann, Vienna)

8. THE LAXENBURG NEAR VIENNA
    The official residence of the Emperor Charles and the Empress Zita in Vienna from 1916-1918. (source - Smolle, P. 104, Photographer Kilopot, G.m.b.H., Vienna)

9. THE HUNTING PALACE AT ECKARTSAU
    Imperial family residence following their flight from Vienna upon the collapse of the Empire on November 11, 1918. (source - Cordfunke, P. 125)

10. THE VILLA PRANGINS IN SWITZERLAND
    First place of exile of the Imperial family after leaving Austria. Birthplace of the Archduke Rudolf and base of operations for the restoration attempts at the Hungarian monarchy. (source - Feigl, P. 480)

11. THE QUINTA DEL MONTE ON MADEIRA
    Final place of exile on Madeira, and the house in which the Emperor Charles died on April 1, 1922. (source - Bertita Harding)

12. THE DECEASED EMPEROR CHARLES I
    (source - The Archduke Rudolf)

13. THE WIDOWED EMPRESS ZITA IN 1923
    Taken at Lequeitio, Spain, showing the children from left to right: Rudolf, Felix, Otto, Elisabeth, Adelhaid, Charlotte, Robert, and Charles Louis. (source - Bertita Harding)

14. THE CHÂTEAU DE HAM IN STEENOCKERZEEL
    Home of the Empress Zita and her family in Brabant, Belgium from 1930 until 1940. (source - Bertita Harding)

15. FLYING THE ATLANTIC
    The Boeing B-314 "Yankee Clipper" in which the Empress crossed the Atlantic from Lisbon to New York in 1940. (source - Pan American Airways)

16. INSIDE THE BOEING CLIPPER
    Cut-away drawing of the Boeing Clipper showing the compartmentalized accommodation. (source - The Boeing Company, Photo No. 9915B)

17. ARRIVING IN QUÉBEC
    The Archduchess Elisabeth, the Empress Zita, the Archduchess Charlotte and the Archduke Rudolf in Québec City in 1940. (source - Madame Zoe De Koninck)

18. THE COLLÈGE JÉSUS-MARIE IN SILLERY
    The convent in Sillery, Québec, where the Empress stayed upon coming to Québec and where the Archduchess Elisabeth completed her university entrance preparation, 1940-1941. (source - Archives, Jesus-Marie)

19. THE ARCHDUCHESS ELISABETH AND THE PRINCESS ELISABETH AT THE COLLÈGE JÉSUS-MARIE
    The Archduchess Elisabeth of Austria and the Princess Elisabeth of Luxemburg as students at the Collège Jésus-Marie. (source - Archives, Jésus-Marie)

20. THE ARCHDUCHESS ELISABETH WITH HER TROOP OF GIRL GUIDES
    The Archduchess Elisabeth (F.R. left) as deputy leader of the 8th Company of Girl Guides of Notre Dame. (source - Madame Odile Germain)

21. THE EMPEROR OTTO VISITING THE ARCHDUCHESSES CHARLOTTE AND ELISABETH AND THE ARCHDUKE CHARLES LOUIS IN QUÉBEC
    (source - Madame Zoe De Koninck)

22. THE ARCHDUKE RUDOLF UPON GRADUATING FROM UNIVERSITÉ LAVAL
    (source - Madame Zoe De Koninck)

23. THE ARCHDUKE CHARLES LOUIS UPON GRADUATING FROM UNIVERSITÉ LAVAL
    (source - Madame Zoe De Koninck)

24. THE IMPERIAL STUDENTS WITH PÈRE GEORGES HENRI LÉVESQUE AT UNIVERSITÉ LAVAL
    The Archduchess Charlotte and the Archdukes Rudolf and Charles Louis with Père G.H. Lévesque, Dean and founder of the Department of Social Sciences at Université Laval. (source - Père G.H. Lévesque)

25. THE VILLA SAINT JOSEPH IN SILLERY
     North view of the house at 1321 Lemoine, home of the
     Empress Zita from 1940 to 1950. (source - Photo taken by
     the author)

26. A FAMILY PORTRAIT IN THE VILLA SAINT JOSEPH
     A family portrait taken in the Villa Saint Joseph's parlour.
     From left to right : The Emperor Oto, the Archduke Rudolf,
     the Empress Zita, the Archduke Charles Louis, and the Ar-
     chduchesses Elisabeth and Charlotte. (source - Madame Zoe
     De Koninck)

27. THE CHAPEL IN THE VILLA SAINT JOSEPH
     Showing a statue of the Christ Child of Prague and a picture
     of the Virgin, both of which were possessions of the Empress
     Zita. (source - Sisters of Ste. Jeanne d'Arc, Sillery)

28. AFTER MASS AT THE VILLA SAINT JOSEPH
     Father O'Donnell, a visiting priest from St. Thomas College
     in St. Paul, Minnesota, after having said Mass in the Villa
     Saint Joseph attended by Princess Isabelle of Bourbon-Par-
     ma, Mlle. Louise De Koninck, the Empress Zita, Madame
     Zoe De Koninck, and the Duchess Maria Antonia of Bour-
     bon-Parma. (source - Madame Zoe De Koninck)

29. THE ARCHDUKE RUDOLF VISITED BY THE ARCHDUKE
     FELIX AND THE EMPEROR OTTO
     The Archduke Rudolf with the Archduke Felix and the Em-
     peror Otto in Québec. (source - Madame Zoe De Koninck)

30. THE EMPEROR OTTO VISITING HIS BROTHERS IN
     QUÉBEC
     The Emperor Otto visiting the Archdukes Rudolf and Charles
     Louis in Québec. (source - Madame Zoe De Koninck)

31. THE TWO ZITAS
     The Empress Zita with her godchild Zita De Koninck (Ma-
     dame Noel de Tilly) in the drawing room at 25, Avenue
     Sainte Geneviève. (source - Madame Zoe De Koninck)

32. THE DE KONINCK RESIDENCE AT 25, AVENUE SAINTE
    GENEVIEVE The Cirice Têtu house at 25, Avenue Sainte
    Geneviève, Québec which was the home of the De Koninck
    family from 1939 to 1966. (source - Photo taken by the
    author)

33. THE ARCHDUKE RUDOLF IN ALBERTA
    The student Archduke Rudolf assisting the wheat harvest in
    Alberta during the summer of 1941. (source - Père G.H.
    Lévesque)

34. HUNTING IN ROBERVAL
    Attending a hunting weekend organized by Père G.H. Léves-
    que at the home of his brother in the Lac St. Jean area in
    Québec. From left to right : Mr. Léonce Lévesque, the bro-
    ther of Père Lévesque, L'Abbé Maurice, Archduke Charles
    Louis, Madame Léonce Lévesque, L'Abbé Ernest, Archdu-
    chess Elisabeth, Archduke Rudolf, Countess Kerssenbrock,
    and Archduchess Charlotte. (source - Père G.H. Lévesque)

35. VISITING THE MUSÉE CHINOIS WITH PÈRE LÉVESQUE
    Visit to a private museum of Chinese artifacts collected by
    Jesuit missionaries in China. Attending the visit with Père
    G.H. Lévesque (in white) are Princess Isabelle of Bourbon-
    Parma, Duchess Maria Antonia of Bourbon-Parma, Empress
    Zita, Archduchess Adelhaid, and various members of the
    Jesuit Order in Québec, including Père Louis Lavoie (stan-
    ding behind Père Lévesque) and Père Bergeron (seated at
    Père Lévesque's left). (source - Père G.H. Lévesque)

36. IN THE FOYER OF THE MUSÉE CHINOIS
    The Empress Zita, Duchess Maria Antonia of Bourbon-Par-
    ma, Archduchess Adelhaid, and Princess Isabelle of Bour-
    bon-Parma. (source - Père G.H. Lévesque)

37. VISITING THE HUNGARIAN SISTERS OF SOCIAL SER-
    VICES IN MONTREAL
    The Empress Zita, the Duchess Maria Antonia of Bourbon-
    Parma, and the Princess Isabelle of Bourbon-Parma, visiting
    the Hungarian Sisters of Social Services at their home at
    3629 rue Ste. Famille in Montréal. (source - Madame Lily de
    Zoltvany)

38. THE EMPRESS ZITA AND FRIEND
     The Empress visiting a friend at the Ursuline convent in
     Québec City. (source - Madame Zoe De Koninck)

39. THE BAPTISM OF NATALIE GERMAIN
     Youngest child of Maitre Stanislas and Madame Paule Ger-
     main. Identified in the portrait are: 1. His Excellency Mon-
     seigneur Maurice Roy, Archbishop of Québec, 2. Duchess
     Maria Antonia of Bourbon-Parma, 3. Princess Isabelle of
     Bourbon-Parma, 4. Archduchess Charlotte, 5. Archduchess
     Elisabeth, 6. Archduke Rudolf, 7. Countess Kerssenbrock, 8.
     Honorable Garon Pratte, Judge of the Court of the King's
     Bench, 9. Madame Garon Pratte, 10. Victor Germain, 11.
     Madame Charles De Koninck, 12. Stanislas Germain, 13.
     Claudette Germain, 14. Abbé Ernest Lemieux, Superior of
     the Grand Seminaire, 15. Abbé Aderville Bureau, 16. Charles
     Boisvert, 17. Monseigneur A.M. Parent, Secretary of the
     Université Laval, 18. Madame Roméo Blanchet, 19. Madame
     Charles Boivert, 20. Madame Jacques de Monleon, 21. Ma-
     dame Pauline D. Brillon, 22. Madame H.T. Maxwell, 23.
     Maria Côté, 24. Liliane Beaulieu, 25. Dr. Roméo Blanchet,
     26. Roger Thibaudeau, 27. Professor Charles De Koninck,
     Dean of Philosophy, 28. Madame Roger Thibaudeau, 29.
     Jeanne Germain, 30. Madame Wilfrid Deziel, 31. Countess
     C. Tisckievitz, 32. Abbé Victorin Germain, 33. Count L.
     Tisckievitz, 34. Charles Larin, 35. Madame L.P. Pigeon, 36.
     Jacques de Monleon, 37. Madame C. Larin, 38. Madame W.
     Desjardins, 39. Madame Paul DesRochers, 40.. Louis-Phi-
     lippe Pigeon, 41. J. Henry Maxwell, 42. Therese Germain,
     43. Paul DesRochers, 44. Ernest Germain, 45. Paul Germain,
     46. Louis Germain, 47. Odile Germain, 48. Marie St. Jac-
     ques, 49. Pauline Germain, 50. Marielle Germain, 51. Pas-
     cale Germain, 52. Natalie Germain. (source - The Archduke
     Rudolf)

40. THE LUXEMBURG FAMILY IN QUÉBEC
     From left to right: Princess Elisabeth; Prince Jean; Princess
     Marie Gabrielle; Princess Alix; Prince Felix of Bourbon-Par-
     ma; The Grand Duchess Charlotte of Luxemburg; Princess
     Marie Adelaide; and Prince Charles. (source - Madame Zoe
     De Koninck)

41. A VISIT FROM PRINCE XAVIER
     On a picnic celebrating the visit to Québec of the Empress
     Zita's brother, Prince Xavier of Bourbon-Parma. From left
     to right: Princess Isabelle of Bourbon-Parma; Princess Ma-
     deleine, the wife of Prince Xavier; the sister of Princess
     Madeleine; the Empress Zita; Duchess Maria Antonia of
     Bourbon-Parma; and Prince Xavier. (source - Madame Zoe
     De Koninck)

42. THE VENNER MAUSOLEUM IN QUÉBEC
     The monument erected by William Venner in the St. Charles
     Cemetary in Québec City in 1861. The monument is derived
     from parts of a monument erected to the Duke of Reichstadt
     in Parma, and from stone quarried in Québec, and assembled
     in accordance with a design by Québec Architect Charles
     Baillargé. (source - Madame Germain Thibodeau-Shee)

43. THE ARCHDUCHESS ELISABETH AND PRINCE HEIN-
     RICH VON LIECHTENSTEIN
     Married at Lignieres, France, on September 12, 1949. (source
     - Madame Zoe De Koninck)

44. THE PRINCESS YOLANDE DE LIGNE AND THE AR-
     CHDUKE CHARLES LOUIS
     Married at Beloeil, Belgium, on January 17, 1950. (source -
     Madame Zoe De Koninck)

45. THE PRINCESS REGINA VON SACHSEN-MEININGEN
     AND THE EMPEROR OTTO
     Married at Nancy, France, on May 10, 1951. (source - Ma-
     dame Zoe De Koninck)

46. THE COUNTESS XENIA CZERNICHEW-BESOBRASOW
     AND THE ARCHDUKE RUDOLF
     Married at Tuxedo Park, New York, on June 23, 1953.
     (source - Madame Zoe De Koninck)
     The Archduchess Xenia died in an automobile accident on
     September 20, 1968.

47. THE PRINCESS MARGHERITA OF SAVOY-AOSTA AND
     THE ARCHDUKE ROBERT
     Married at Bourg-en-Bresse, France, on December 28, 1953.
     (source - Madame Zoe De Koninck)

48. THE ARCHDUCHESS CHARLOTTE AND THE DUKE
    GEORG VON MECKLENBURG
    Married at Poecking, Bavaria, on July 25, 1956. (source -
    Madame Zoe De Koninck)
    The Duke Georg von Mecklenburg died on July 6, 1963.
    The Duchess Charlotte died on July 23, 1989.

49. THE PRINCESS ANNA GABRIELLE VON WREDE AND
    THE ARCHDUKE RUDOLF
    Married at Ellingen, Bavaria, on October 15, 1971. (source -
    The Archduke Rudolf)
    Standing next to the Archduke Rudolf is the Archduke Jo-
    hannes from his previous marriage to the Archduchess Xe-
    nia, and the Archduchess Isabella, daughter of the Archduke
    Robert and the Archduchess Margherita.
    The Archduke Johannes died in a tragic collision between his
    bicycle and an autobus on June 29, 1975.

50. THE WEDDING RECEPTION FOR MISS JANET ANN STE-
    VENSON AND THE COUNT HENRY ELTZ
    Married at Montréal, Québec, on December 17, 1955.
    (source - Countess Janet Eltz)
    The reception was given for the bride and groom by the
    Austrian Consul General in Montreal, Mr. Nandor Loewen-
    heim, in his home in Westmount, Québec. See page 209 for
    names of invited guests.

51. THE HOUSE AT TUXEDO PARK, NEW YORK
    The residence of the Empress Zita after she left Québec and
    before she returned permanently to Europe. The figure stan-
    ding is an actual photograph of Mark Twain, American
    Humorist and Author, who had also lived in this house.
    (source - Madame Cecilia Capella)

52. THE EMPRESS AT TUXEDO PARK
    The Empress Zita, the Archduchess Charlotte, and the Ar-
    chduke Rudolf, in front of their home in Tuxedo Park in
    1953. (source - Feigl, P. 512)

53. **THE CASTLE AT WALDSTEIN IN STEIERMARK,- AUSTRIA**

Home of the Princess Elisabeth and her husband Prince Heinrich von Liechtenstein, at Waldstein in the province of Steiermark, south of Vienna, in Austria. (source - The Archduke Rudolf)

54. **THE VILLAGE OF ZIZERS IN SWITZERLAND**

A small village in the Grisons of Switzerland. (source - The Archduke Rudolf)

55. **THE JOHANNES STIFT IN ZIZERS**

The converted monastery at Zizers which now serves as a retirement home for old priests and nuns and for others seeking a religious environment in their declining years. The Empress Zita maintained a small apartment here until her death in 1989. (source - The Archduke Rudolf.

56. **THE 90TH BIRTHDAY CELEBRATION OF THE EMPRESS AT ZIZERS**

The gathering of the Imperial family at the Johannes Stift in Zizers on the occasion of the Empress Zita's 90th Birthday on May 9, 1982. Front row, left to right: Archduchess Anna Eugenie (Princess von Arenberg), Archduchess Regina (Princess von Sachsen-Meiningen), Archduke Otto, Empress Zita, Archduke Robert, Archduchess Margherita (Princess of Savoy-Aosta), Archduchess Yolande (Princess de Ligne). Second row: Archduke Felix, Archduchess Anna Gabrielle (Princess von Wrede), Archduke Rudolf, Archduchess Charlotte von Mecklengurg, Prince Heinrich von Liechtenstein, Princess Elisabeth von Liechtenstein, Archduke Charles Louis. (source - The Archduke Rudolf)

57. **THE EMPRESS WITH THE COUNTESS KERSSENBROCK**

The Empress Zita with the Countess Therese von Korff Schmising-Kerssenbrock, her confident, companion, and loyal servant for 55 years. (source - Feigl, P. 512)

58. **DEATH NOTICE OF THE COUNTESS KERSSENBROCK**

The official notice announcing the death of the Countess Kerssenbrock on February 10, 1973. (source - Madame Zoe De Koninck)

59. **THE VILLAGE OF TULFES IN TIROL, AUSTRIA**
   The village in the Austrian Tirol where the Archduchess Adelhaid is buried. (source - The Archduke Rudolf)

60. **THE BENEDICTINE ABBEY AT MURI IN SWITZERLAND**
   The Benedictine monastery at Muri in Switzerland, founded in 1027 by Ita of Lorraine, wife of Count Radbot of Habsburg. (source - The Archduke Rudolf)

61. **THE GRAVE OF THE ARCHDUCHESS ADELHAID**
   The grave of the Archduchess Adelhaid in the cemetary of the parish church in Tulfes. (source - The Archduke Rudolf)

62. **THE LORETTO CHAPEL IN THE ABBEY AT MURI**
   The Loretto Chapel of the Benedictine Abbey at Muri, underneath which is the new family crypt of the Habsburgs. (source - The Archduke Rudolf)

63. **REMEMBRANCE PLAQUE TO THE ARCHDUCHESS XENIA**
   Plaque in the Loretto Chapel at Muri commemorating the Archduchess Xenia, first wife of the Archduke Rudolf. She was the first Habsburg to be laid to rest in the new crypt. (source - The Archduke Rudolf)

64. **WARTEGG CHAPEL IN SWITZERLAND WITH THE TOMB OF PRINCESS ISABELLE**
   Last resting place of the Princess Isabelle of Bourbon-Parma, sister of the Empress Zita. (source - The Archduke Rudolf)

65. **THE BOURBON TOMB AT PUCHHEIM IN AUSTRIA**
   Engraved tombstone covering the Bourbon crypt at Attnang-Puchheim in Austria where the Duchess Maria Antonia of Bourbon-Parma lies in peace. (source - The Rev. Friederich M. Roehrich)

66. **THE IMPERIAL FUNERAL HEARSE AND COFFIN OF THE EMPRESS ZITA**
   The funeral hearse used for funerals of Habsburg emperors and empresses since 1876. (source - Erich Feigl)

67. **MISS HERMA DOBLER**
   Personal secretary to the Empress Zita from 1931 to 1950. (source - Miss Marguerite Barry)

68. COUNT HENRY ELTZ
    (source - Countess Janet Eltz)

69. MONSEIGNEUR ALPHONSE MARIE PARENT
    Secretary of the Faculty of Philosophy of Université Laval, and later Vice-Rector at the Université. (source - The Archduke Rudolf)

70. MAITRE STANISLAS GERMAIN
    Member of the legal firm of "Germain, Pigeon, Thibodeau and Roberge" who handled the legalities for the Empress Zita's refuge in Québec. (source - Madame Paule Germain)

71. PROFESSOR CHARLES DE KONINCK
    Dean of the Faculty of Philosophy at Université Laval, and tutor to the Archdukes Rudolf and Charles Louis and to the Archduchess Charlotte. (source - Madame Zoe De Koninck)

72. PROFESSOR CHARLES ENGEL
    Acquaintance of the Empress Zita and of the Archduke Rudolf, and Professor in the Faculty of Chemistry at Université Laval. (source - Madame Charles Engel)

73. DR. OTTO VON HABSBURG WITH HIS SON BEFORE A PORTRAIT OF HIS FATHER
    Dr. Otto von Habsburg with his son the Archduke Charles standing before a portrait of the Emperor Charles I of Austria. (source - Feigl, P. 529)

APPENDIX E

INDEX OF PERSONS

APPENDIX F

INDEX OF PLACES